MUTUS LIBER "*LOQUITUR*"

THE MUTE BOOK "*SPEAKS*"

An Epistemological Reading of **ALTUS'** *Western Yoga Meditation*

With 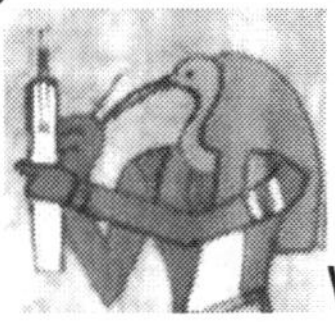 Words

by **ELI LUMINOSUS AEQUALIS** (**P***hilosophus* **J** α**L**χυμευτικός)

सत्यशिव चैतन्य

Sacer Equestris Aureus Or

ISBN-13:978-0615906072
ISBN-10:0615906079 Sacer Equestris Aureus Ordo Inc.
Esoteric Texts division
Charleston, SC, USA

To all the Adepts
who love their neighbors
in the silence of their minds.

CONTENT

ABBREVIATIONS OF WORKS AND AUTHORS

B = *Brāhmaṇa.*
BG = *Bhagavad-Gītā*
EJVS = *Electronic Journal of Vedic Studies*
JAOS = *Journal of the American Oriental Society*
MB = *Mahā Bhārata*
ŚB = *Śatapatha Brāhmaṇa*
U = *Upanishad*
UA = *Aitareya Upanishad*
UAb = *Amritabindu Upanishad*
UB = *Bṛhadāraṇyaka Upanishad*
UC = *Chāndogya Upanishad*
UĪśa = *Īśa Upanishad*
UK = *Kaṭha Upanishad*
UKa = *Kaushītaki-Brāhmaṇa Upanishad*
UKai = *Kaivalya Upanishad*
UKe = *Kena Upanishad*
UM = *Māṇḍūkya Upanishad*
UMaitrī = *Maitrī Upanishad*
UMu = *Muṇḍaka Upanishad*
UNr = *Nṛsiṃhottaratāpanī Upanishad*
UP = *Praśna Upanishad*
UŚ = *Śvetāśvatara Upanishad*
UT = *Taittirīya Upanishad*
UV = *Vajrasūcika Upanishad*
UY = *Yoga Darshana Upanishad*
TB = *Taittirīya Brāhmaṇa*
V = *Veda*
VA = *Atharva Veda*
VṚ = *Ṛg Veda*
VS = *Sāma Veda*
VY = *Yajur Veda*
W = *Monier-Williams, Sir Monier, A Sanskrit-English Dictionary*

SELECTED CONCISE PHILOSOPHICAL TERMINOLOGIES

Apodictic (*adj.* **Apodictical**)**:** clear and necessary self-evident truth.
A-posteriori: that which follows experience.
A-priori: that which precedes experience logically, but not actually.
Art: potentially universal language synthesis of form and idea.
Atmanism: the view that the Supreme Spirit or Self (*ātman*) is the only Reality.
Autoctisi: the self-constructed spark igniting itself.
Autochthonous: Self-generated.
Autogenous: Self-made, Self-born.
Awareness: is the fundamental apodictical presence of the certitude, which underlines and makes possible the consciousness-*of* the world.
Beauty: dawn of knowledge.
Being-for-itself (per-se): the continuous circular reference of a *subject* to its correlated inseparable *object*.
Being-in-itself (in-se): the absolute independent center of the *immanent* circle set apart from the inseparable *subject-object* circular correlation.
Conscience: the only immanent condition that states *existence*.
Consciousness-*of*: is the grasping and apprehension *of* the world in its objective reality.
Creation: the concept of a divine act *pro*ducing everything out of nothing.
***Darśana*:** six philosophical points of views:
- ***Mīmāṃsā́*:** ritual examination;
- ***Nyāyá*:** logical argument;
- ***Sāṃkhya*:** enumeration;
- ***Vaiśeshika*:** distinct nature of substances;
- ***Vedānta*:** end of the *Veda*;
- ***Yoga*:** union.

Discursiveness: the process of a temporal procession ranging over the wide field of juxtaposed events and Experiences; the spreading out of a sequence.
Emanation: the process of emission from a higher source into a lower status, which in turn radiates into another position.
Epoché (ἐποχή)**:** suspending judgment in reference to reality *in-itself*; placing the world between brackets.
Episteme: knowledge, intellectually certain (*adj.* **Epistemic:** capable of knowledge or related to knowledge).
Epistemic loneliness: (see **Solipsism**) the impossibility of the I to know itself as I in-itself or to know another I as I.
Epistemology (*adj.* **Epistemological**)**:** the study of how we know what we know and its validity.
Ethics: search for apodictic moral laws.
Existence: that which is established by *conscience* within the *subject-object* correlation.
For-itself: see Being-for-itself.

Future: projection towards the reduction to consciousness' data.
Gnoseology (*adj.* **Gnoseological**)**:** see Epistemology.
History: weltanschauung's present actualization.
Hypostasis (*pl.* **Hypostases**)**:** principle or substance deriving from another one and at the same time generating an inferior one.
Immanent: that which is inherent or characterizes the circle of the inseparable *subject-object* correlation; the relationship by which the mind, in the epistemic process, reduces the world to an *object for-itself*.
In-itself: see Being-in-itself.
In-se: see Being-in-itself.
Intentionality: experience as stream of consciousness directed toward something.
Intuition: the state of immediate and total com-prehension or in-sight of the objective world without any temporal of spatial juxtaposition.
I-think: the *a-priori* subject constantly united with its object.
Knowledge: the epistemic synthetic correlation of subject and object, which intentions objectivity as otherness.
Liberty: autonomous innate unalloyed permanent state of the self.
Life: satisfying the hunger for representation.
Love: unselfish tension toward the other in-itself
Monism: there is only one reality.
Myth: echo of the Ineffable.
Mythology: a many faceted prism, each side representing a relative omni-comprehensive paradigm of the inner human reality, tracing the generating process of the psycho-cosmological world and denoting a tension *in-itself* that announces and echoes the *Transcendent*.
Mythologem: recurrent fabulous tale repeating itself during different times and places.
Noema (*adj.* **Noematic**)**:** the objective aspect of experience in its modes-of-being-given.
Noesis (*adj.* **Noetic**)**:** the subjective aspect of experience as act-of-perception aiming to grasp the object.
Noumenon (*pl.* **Noumena**, *adj.* **Noumenal**): that which is thought but not known.
Numinous: mysterious; relating to the spirits or gods.
Object: the known as such. The passive one to whom the action indicated by the verb is directed.
Oneiric: pertaining to dreams.
Ontological: the essence or nature of the existent.
Past: consciousness' data.
Per-se: see Being-for-itself.
Philosophy: constantly updated critical holistic rethinking of the World with intentional objectivity and History's mover.
Present: continuum perceptive awareness.
Quantum (*pl.* **Quanta**)**:** elementary particle/s, as a *quantum/a* [Latin: certain amount/s] *of energy* or mass.
Realization: the Apodictical-Certitude that does not necessitate an object, but

intuitively reaches Reality In-Itself beyond any duality.
Religion: dogmatic bondage of a creed, vehicle to the Transcendent.
Science: mathematical intelligibility of nature's blind pro-ject.
Solipsism: (see **Epistemic loneliness**) the loneliness of the 'I' as such.
Subject: the knower as such. The one who does the action indicated by the verb.
Tautology (*adj.* **Tautological**): a repeating circular reasoning.
Transcendent (*n.* **Transcendence**)**:** that which is never experienced or known *in-itself*, but it can be conceived as that which is beyond the subject-object correlation, thus, becoming an *immanent* thought. *Viz.*: God, Goddess, Lord of hosts, Unknown, Fourth state, Non- existent, Death, Future.
Transcendental: the manner in which *objects* are known, as this is possible *a-priori*.
Weltanschauung: World view.

LEGEND OF THE PLATES' SYMBOLS

ALEMBIC: 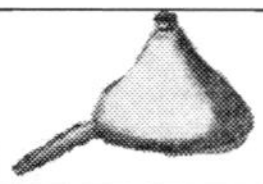 consciousness.

ANGEL:  announcer of the Transcendent.

APOLLO:  mindfulness, the ultimate perceiver, the alchemic gold.

ARMOR:  invincibility.

ATHANOR:  pillar of the world, shaft of consciousness (see caduceus).

ATLAS:  the subject holding the world and relieved by Hercules.

BABE:  Second Unknown self, born from Death/Saturn.

BEAMS OF LIGHT: 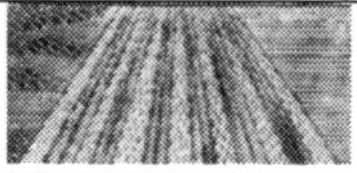 centrality of Pure-Awareness.

BERRIES:  new blossoming.

BOAT:  the crib of rediscovery.

BOULDER: 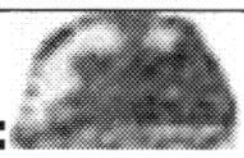 life's milestone.

BOW:  the mystical syllable AUM.

BREATH SUSPENSION: 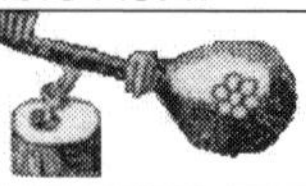  

BREATHING:  inhaling and exhaling;  lungs;  breathing organ.

BUILDING BLOCK:  Transcendent Apodictic-Awareness.

BULL:  fertility and the elemental power of dreams.

CADUCEUS:  pillar of the world, shaft of consciousness (see athanor).

CAGE:  capturing and controlling (see fishing and netting).

CHEVRON: 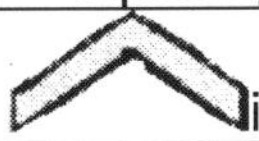 inversion of direction.

CHURCH:  the mother womb.

CIRCLES:  circularities of consciousness.

CIRCULARITY:  the circle of creation as the year or the day.

CITIES:  center of the psyche.

CLOUD: 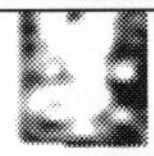 obfuscation of pure consciousness.

COLUMNS:  beginning and conclusion of a stage of life.

CONCENTRATION:  immovable concentration of the mind. 

CUCURBITS:  consciousness.

CUPS:  experience-measuring cups.

DISH:  flowing perceptions; 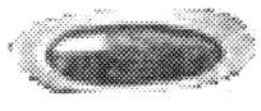 concentrated; 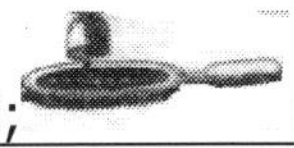 unification of thoughts.

DISTAFF: spins the thread of existence.
DOUBLE HEADED:  looking at the two states of life.
DRAPERIES: 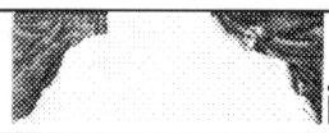internal events (*sub specie interioritatis*).
DREAM: 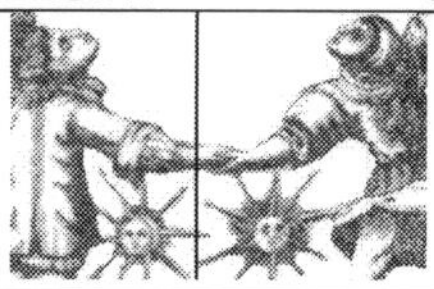 and waking state
DROP: 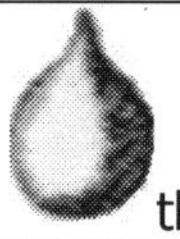 the dew drop of unified realizations. Embryonic unity.
DUCKS:  Sephiroth, the lesser lights from the One Light of Awareness.
DWARF:  the Unknown self.
EAGLE:  the direct perception of intellectual light.
&CC:  progression.
FARM: 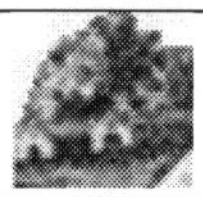 productivity.
FATES SISTERS:  Atropos  Clotho  Lachesis, controllers of destinies.
FIRE: 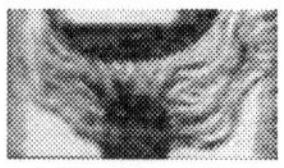 Divine-flame of consciousness and awareness; △ Alchemical symbol. 
FIREPLEACE: where the fire of consciousness *cooks* the *food for thought*.
FISH:  the self traversing all the states of consciousness.
FISHING: objects from the ocean of possibilities (see caging and netting).

FISHING LINE:	 Ariadne's line to trace the way in life's labyrinth.
FLOWERS:	 six days of creation;  the five senses;  bloomed realization.
FUNNEL:	 caduceus' shaft through which travels consciousness.
FOUR:	 the four states of life.
GESTURES:	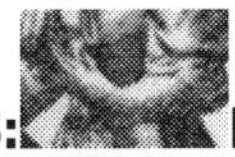 breath  directing  Isis  manifesting  Heaven   silence  unity.
HEART:	 light from the heart.
HERCULES:	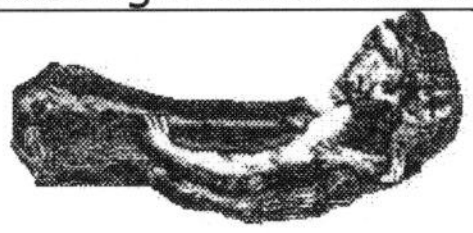 reliever of Atlas' burden.
ISIS:	 pure-objectivity, the *Mother-Word*, which confers sense to the object.
JUPITER:	 Apodictic-Awareness, Transcendence.
KNOT:	 knot of the heart or of being.
LADDER:	 the axis, pillar connecting Heaven and Earth through different life's stages.
LADLE:	 nurturing, tasting and articulation of objects in the mind's experience.
LANDSCAPE:	 life's scenery.

LEAVES:  the physical manifestation of the circles of consciousness.
LION:  the devourer beast.
MAN:  the Subject or the subjective aspect of knowledge.
MIND:  the obstacle.
MEDITATE: Ora.
MERCURY:  the subject-object synthesis in the stillness of pure consciousness.
MOON:  towering = world of duality; secondary  = objectivity.
MORTAR:  crusher of object-thoughts.
MOUNTAIN:  Mount Helicon;
NAKEDNESS:  sleep trance;  paralyzing power, weakness.
NEPTUNE:  controller of the ocean of possibilities.
NETTING:  capturing and controlling world entanglements (see cage and fishing).
NOEMATIC:  objective (moon) aspect of experience in its modes-of-being-given.

NOETIC:  subjective (sun) aspect of experience aiming to grasp the object.

ONE HUNDRED:  a part that forms a whole from the entire.

ONE THOUSAND:  immortality, the return of the Savior and Paradise.

PEACOCK: 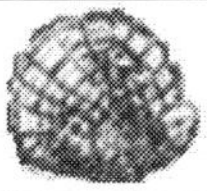 symbolizes the totality of nature and its manifestations.

PESTLE:  crusher of object-thoughts.

PHILOSOPHER'S STONE: 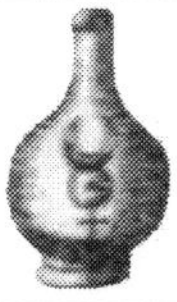 Mercurial Essence of Unity.

PLANETS:  sublimation of subject object.

PRACTICE: ***labora***.

RECTANGULAR FORMATION: 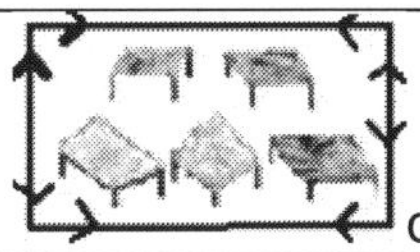 open to all directions.

ROAD:  path of life.

ROBE:  secret concealments.

ROPE:  measuring separation between transcendence and immanence.

ROSE:  awakened state;  sleeping state.

SALT: 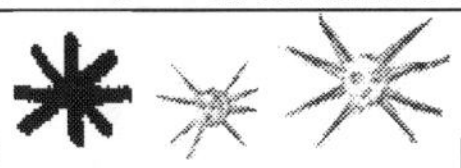 power of transformation, indestructible unification and incorruptibility.

SATURN:  creator and destroyer.

SCALE: 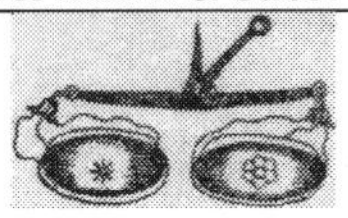 perfect pinpointed balanced concentration.

SHELL:  prosperity, birth, death and rebirth.

SCISSORS:  cut  the thread of existence.

SENSES: 

mind & senses in concentration.

SHEEP:  transformation principle of individuation.

SHEETS: 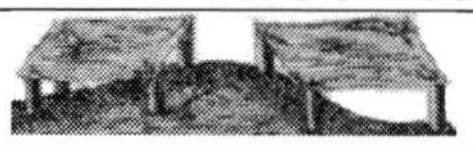 five senses grounded on objectivity.

SCEPTER:  tree of Life, caduceus' central staff without the subject-object serpents.

SIREN:  life's seducer, pitfalls arising from desires and passions.

SIX: VI number of the hexagram ✡, heart-center of consciousness.

SPACE: 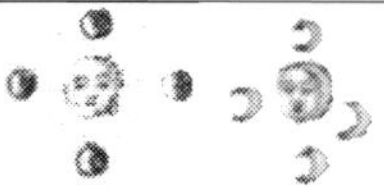 four corners of space.

SKY:  see waters.

STARS:  Sephiroth revealing the Divine;  able to shine unclouded.

STEERING:  directing the boat of consciousness.

SUBJECT-OBJECT:   sun and moon.

SUBLIMATION:  of moon/object  of sun/subject.

SULFUR:   Sun male fiery light of individuation and transformation.

SUN:  towering = Awareness; secondary  = subjectivity.

SWORD:  the alchemical double aspect of strength.

TABLE:  manifestation; 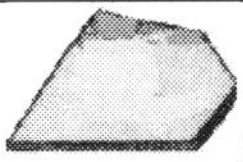 restricted.

TARGET: 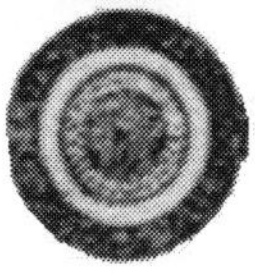 the Supreme Spirit is the target.

TEN: **10** the 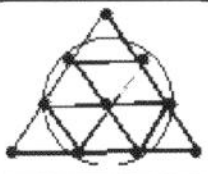 tetractys. Principle of all things and the totality in movement.

TEN THOUSAND: 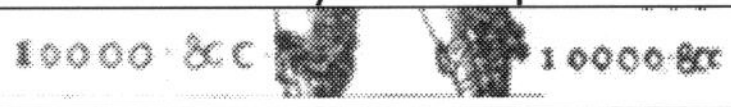

symbolizing completeness, a renovation of the earth.

THORNS: 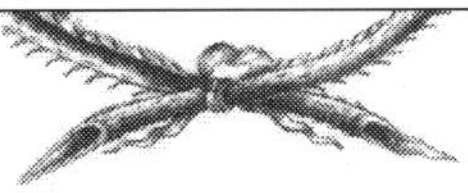 chastity and pains of life.

THREE-PARTED FIN:  the three states of life.

TONGS: 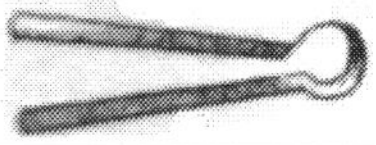 extract the Mercurial Essence, the Philosopher's Stone, the most internal Self.

TOOLS FOR CHEMISTRY:  sifter and  unity sphere.

TOWER:  see athanor.

TOYS:  tennis racquet and ball, life's eternal play,

TRIANGULAR FORMATION: 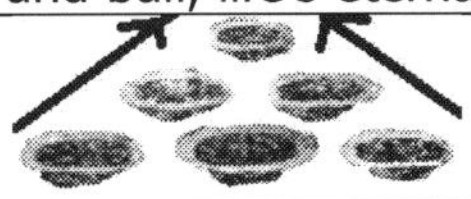 pointing towards...

TRIDENT:  the three states of life united as one by the handle.

TRITON:  the tri-sounding monster of the three stages of life.

TRUMPET:  awakening to a Transcendent reality.

TURKEY: 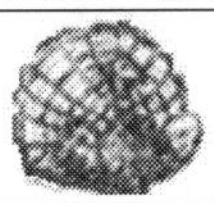 all the blessings that the Earth contains.

TWO: II the principle of dualism.

UNION: 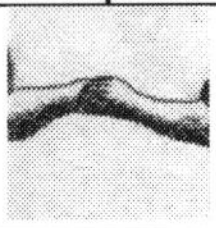 synthesis of subject-object.

VIAL: empty:  consciousness. Full:  consciousness-*of.*
WAKING STATE:  traveling the sea of wakeful experiences. 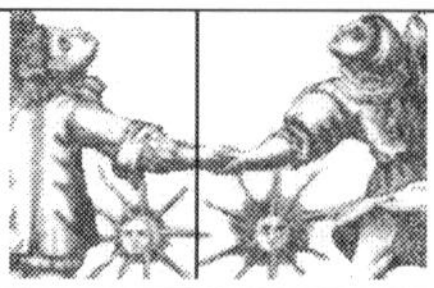
WATERS:  above = Infinite-Transcendence; below = infinite objective possibilities.
WINDOW OF RECEPTIVITY:  waking 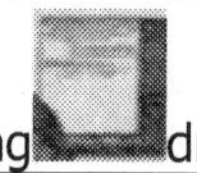 dreaming  sleep  NREM consciousness. Eyes.
WOMAN:  Object; +flowers  Creation-dream; +turkey  Manifestation-sleeping.
WORLD: 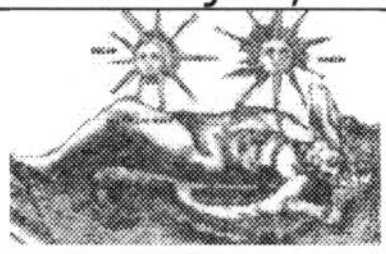 Atlas' burden on Saturn/Hercules.
WORLD OF PASSIONS:  murky swamp where demons lurk.
WREATH:  circle of the circadian rhythm;  glory, victory.
WRINGING: 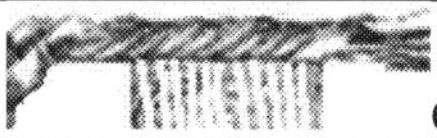 epistemic synthesis of the subject's mind with the senses.
ZERO: 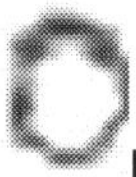 primordial nothingness.

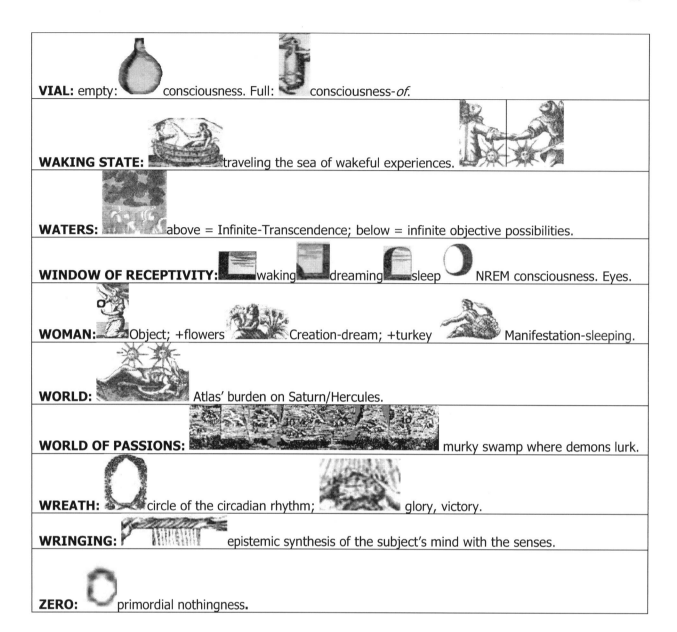

"You came down from your throne
and stood at my cottage door.
was singing all alone in a corner,
and the melody caught your ear.
You came down and stood at my cottage door.
Masters are many in your hall,
and songs are sung there at all hours.
But the simple carol of this novice struck
at your love. One plaintive little strain
mingled with the great music of the
world, and with a flower for a prize you
came down and stopped at my cottage door."

R. Thakur[1]

MUTUS LIBER "LOQUITUR" (The Mute Book *Speaks*)

"O Lord, open thou my lips; and my mouth shall shew forth thy praise,"[2]

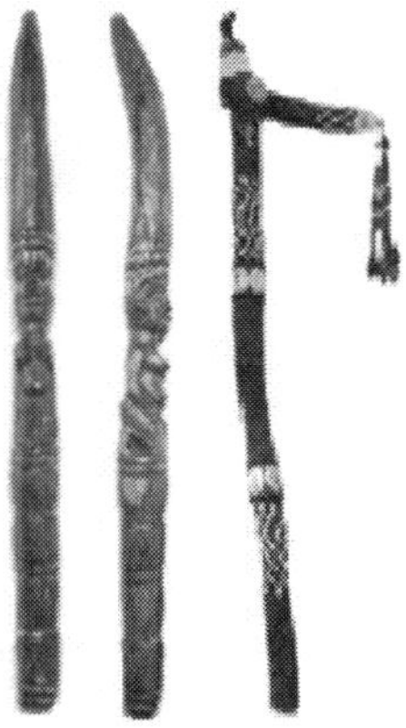

"May Ptaḥ open my mouth... May my mouth be opened, may my mouth be unclosed by Shu with his (ur ḥekau) iron knife, wherewith he opened the mouth of the gods."[3]

~~~

Front and side view of the Santeria divination stick and of the *garabato*, guava-wood-hook with which the Yorùbá Orisha-god Eshu-Eleggua opens the road.
~~~

METHODOLOGICAL FOREWORD

Human Life is hunger for experiences carried out in the mind sustained by psychophysical biochemical reactions.

The *Mutus Liber* is an epistemological treatise. The alchemical laboratory of its author, Altus, is the mind. In it, thoughts are chemical compounds and their processes are reactions producing knowledge. His operation works on the mind. His alchemical transmutation takes place in the mind, by the mind and through the mind in all its stages, conscious, subconscious, unconscious and beyond. Therefore, the key to interpret the plates and to *open the mouth* of the *Mute* Book is gnoseological. The chemical elements, consequently, are only metaphors to describe the epistemic process.

It may be argued that our epistemological approach is purely arbitrary. However, we offer a pragmatic proof test. If our analysis, commentary and interpretation will be capable to explain completely all the *hieroglyphs* and symbols with satisfying coherent and logical explanations without solution of continuity, then it will prove to be correct. Furthermore, if the teaching offered by the book, as we comprehend it, can be successfully put into practice, then it would be sufficient proof that our approach is true and one that Altus himself would have approved.

Contemporary weltanschauungs do not see or go beyond the concrete expressions of their *mineral* surroundings. The world is assumed to be only in its external dogmatically empirical reality. Commercial promotional psychology understands this very well. Therefore, advertisements are very successful in creating and imposing needs that are imposed subliminally on people. They influence consumers to possess superficial and unnecessary goods, which in reality are never freely chosen.

Altus, in his cultural and historical time, intended this book to be mute,

> "*for they* [were] *a very froward generation, children in whom* [was] *no faith.*"[4]

In our current cultural environment, this materialistic perseverance has increased. The book remains misunderstood. In 1882, Carrington Bolton, wrote in his *Chemical Literature*,

> "Perhaps the height of absurdity is reached in the famous *Liber Mutus* [sic.], which consists of a series of fifteen symbolic engravings purposing to disclose the entire Hermetic Philosophy. The utterly unintelligible character of much alchemical literature is occasionally acknowledged by those who otherwise accepted the prevailing popular belief in transmutation."[5]

Today, there is the necessity to *open the mouth*, to *translate* into words the message of this silent *discourse*. Not complying would result in the loss of this great didactic book. Without *translation*, the images of this book would be interpreted only based on their *mineral* suggestion, namely, their denotation. Their allegorical references, which are their real intention, would remain unrelated. However,

> "*The spirit truly* [is] *ready, but the flesh* [is] *weak*"[6]

"Not everyone is ready yet, but many are, and with each person who awakens, the momentum in the collective consciousness grows, and it becomes easier for others."[7]

Throughout world history, apart from great but rare examples of true spiritual awakening, humanity, in search for the Transcendent, managed always to miss it by reducing it to an object of thought. Humans live in a constant dichotomy, namely the separation between mind and body. Growth, development and change seem to be spontaneous and independent from our thinking process. It is almost as if there were two beings in one body.

a) One is the mind, which refers to itself as 'I' and to the body as mine.

b) The other is the body with an unconscious life of its own in which the brain is only one of the organs.

In fact, our mind does not know, among other things, how to regulate the heart rhythm and the flow of blood. However, unconsciously we may do so. As an example, anxiety creates stress, which may lead to hypertension. Nevertheless, the connection between worry and arterial disease is unconscious. Genetic illnesses seem to be unrelated to the mind. We perceive diseases as belonging to a world external to the mind. Nevertheless, paradoxically, it is in our biophysical interiority that sicknesses operate. The mind attempts to close the hiatus through science. Still, even there the body is analyzed as an external object. Feasibly, the unity is in the course of Evolution itself.

There, the unconscious self-regulating processes *strive* to control the body through natural adaptations. Thus, as the marine animal walked on land and the reptile developed wings, perhaps, the future human will be able to mind-control consciously and completely its own body (*cf. Voynich Manuscript*).[8]

Archaic societies had a direct dreaming relationship with the world. The dreamer was the one who guided souls in or out of psychic realms. The psychopomp believed that s/he could move freely between the conscious and unconscious states. The entire spiritual and physical domain was realized to be interconnected without any solution of continuity. In it, the shaman knew the right path and retraced it for lost and ailing souls. Through magnified dreams, the members of primitive life styles were mended and felt reconnected with their ancestral history.

Gradually, ancient societies started losing their dreaming power. A class of priests, who become the interpreters of the gods' will, substituted the shaman. Eventually, divinities became visible in temples. There, the hierophants, the keepers of sacred mysteries, claimed to be able to open the idols' eyes. They took care of the carved deities, made offerings and fed them. However, besides the priestly caste and outside colossal sanctuaries, the other members of those cultures lived in fear of death. They had lost touch with their gods and fell prey of their capricious spree.

Medieval western and middle-eastern societies resolved the tyranny of those gods with the worship of one merciful God. Nevertheless, He was in a remote Heaven and His return was to be that of a Judge with no mercy for the impenitent sinners. The hiatus between the individual offender and the Divinity was profound. The Dominus-Master was one. All the others were unworthy servants. As servants, humans managed to preserve their individual ego, never willing to surrender it to the true spiritual realm.

> "*He that loveth his life shall lose it; and he that hateth his life in this world shall keep it unto life eternal.*"[9]

In fact, the Ego does not hate its own life, nor gives up its identity or its thinking process. Plato rhetorically asks if the ego-*slave* in the Cave,[10] having realized the truth,

> "would care for such honors and glories, or envy the possessors of them? Would he not say with Homer:[11] - *Better to be the poor servant of a poor master, and to endure anything, rather than think as they* [the slaves] *do and live after their manner?*"

To Plato's question, we answer, -Yes, the slave wants to retain his submissiveness rather than give up his distinct ego-identity. To say *I am God's servant* is a way to preserve the mind as an individual separated from the Divine. The lord-servant relation implies a duality. It is to that duality that the ego does not want to renounce. It is its own self-image that the ego is in love with. A true lover, on the other hand, at the time of love-climax does not realize any separation from the loved one. Indeed, the onset of distinction destroys the moment of shivering-unity. When the apex is over the duality resumes and the true unification is lost.

The ego would rather die than give up his/her thoughts. However, this death has a different meaning from the Biblical injunction. To commit suicide or to die for freedom on the barricades of a revolution is an affirmation of individuality rather than a *spiritual hate* for life. Thus,

> "*thou shalt not bow down thyself to them, nor serve them: for I the LORD thy God am a jealous God.*"[12]

In modern societies, the ego blossomed to an unusual extent. Individuals became the makers of their own fortune. Like new Babel towers, majestic houses of worship have been built. They glorified the separation of the individual from the God they intended to worship with those structures. In reality, they exalted the egotist-gray-eminence not the glory of the Spiritual Power on Earth. Contemporary societies, lost in the search for economic prosperity, have dropped all connection with the Spiritual World. Actually, the word *spiritual* itself becomes meaningless. At best, it can be labeled as *myth*, a synonym for *lie*.

From the beginning, the *Mutus Liber* was misunderstood. *Chemical* minds were unable to grasp the sense of those silent images beyond actual mineral substances. In fact, as early as August 16, 1677, also the *Journal des Savans* misses the point and conceitedly attempts to

> "give soul and words to the many mute figures... to decipher some of them... [Thus,] in the middle of the second plate we see... two human figures... with the character of gold and of silver... The author wants to show that we must put these two noble metals in the philosophers' egg to ferment and open them with salt."[13]

Likewise, most of the book's commentaries turn out to be a mere useless description of the images. Today, lost in those hieroglyphs, the superficial bibliophile considers it, at best, an oddity worth only as collection item.

On the contrary, we intend to make those *hieroglyphs* somehow accessible to the contemporary reader who

"*hath ears to hear*."[14]

Since the book is a hermetic treatise, we will be analyzing every design in all its details. We are convinced that every part of it, including those that may be regarded only as *decorative*, are not so. The book aims to portray that which is secret and ineffable. Therefore, every aspect of it is intentionally metaphorical of higher Truths and contains precise meanings and purposes in all its images.

The effort of the present commentary and explanations is an attempt to *translate* in philosophical terms the images of the *Mutus Liber*, as they reveal themselves to us. This work wants to be a sequel to two recently published books, *Beyond Immortality* and *Awareness*.[15] We want to suggest another way for the realization of Awareness, namely, the one described by this ancient alchemical text.

During our commentary, we will make frequent references to sacred texts from different traditions. Particularly, we will make many frequent references to the *Bible*, since Altus himself quotes it. Specific attention will be given also to the sacred tradition of India and its revealed texts like the *Veda* and *Upanishad*. In fact, those sources, like no other, offer very detailed explanations of esoteric teachings. In particular, we will quote *verbatim* from different *Upanishads* as they may help to clarify our hermeneutical commentary of the plates.

The *Upanishads*, traditionally 108 books, were composed starting around the IX Century B.C. They constitute the *Veda*'s-end (*Ved-ānta*), namely, the completion of the teachings of the much older *Veda*, composed starting from around the II Millennia B.C. All those texts were regarded as having been heard (*śruti*) through a direct divine revelation deriving from introspective enlightenment reached through the meditative practice of Yoga, namely the *yoking* of the individual self to the Supreme Self.

Finally, these frequent parallels with non-Western religious texts, do not intend to prove historical contacts or exchanges between Altus and those other cultures. The comparisons are valid only as analogies springing from common human ground engaged in the same search for the Transcendent. We do not suggest that one myth may have influenced the *Mutus Liber*. We believe that different mythical visions sprung autonomously and independently. However, each mythical symbol reveals the same psycho-cosmological paradigm common to all humans. We refer here to a psycho-cosmological universal configuration of the human epistemic conditions, which we may call

> "Elementary Ideas."[16]

In fact, they are

> "part of everyone's ancient, universal biological heritage"[17] and
> "the mental characteristics of man are the same all over the world … in all cultures."[18]

Jung declared,

> "If anyone unacquainted with the psychology of the unconscious wants to get a working knowledge of these matters, I would recommend a study of Christian mysticism and Indian Philosophy, where he will find the clearest elaboration of the antinomies of the unconscious."[19]

Finally, in our conclusion we will offer practical directions on how to apply and put into practice this Alchemical Art.

M·M·XIII,

Eli Luminosus Aequalis (PJ a L χυμευτικός)

सत्यशिवचैतन्य

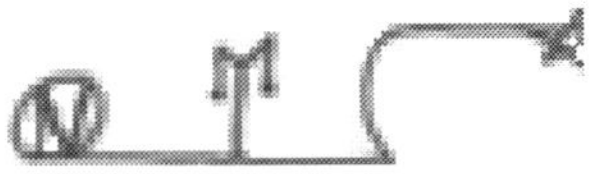

PREFACE

<u>*HISTORY OF THE MUTUS LIBER*</u>

The *Mutus Liber* depicts, on fifteen engraved plates,[20] the stages and the process to attain the Alchemical Philosopher's Stone, namely the Apodictical-Awareness, the building block of the World. The <u>first edition</u> was in 1677. The Plates in our publication are from Manget's 1702-<u>second edition</u>, as published in the 1914 Dr. Marc Haven's edition by Paul Derain.[21] The <u>third edition</u> was in 1725(?).[22]

The slight variances between editions are purely graphic and are not so different as to affect or change our interpretation. In fact, their symbols and metaphors remain the same within all publications.[23]

The *Mute Book* declares to be a hieroglyphic synthesis of

"*the entire Hermetic Philosophy*."[24]

The work is dedicated to the sons of that art and is consecrated to Hermes-Mercury Trismegistus, the three times great god.

The author of this book hides behind the pseudonym of Altus (Latin for *High-Great*). Some have identified him with Jacob (Latin *Iacobus*) Saulat, Soulat or Sulat lord of Marez,[25] a family originally from Cambrai, Normandy, France,[26] whose family cress is a yellow *fourchy* cross on red field with three white shells on black *bend*. It has been pointed out[27] that the name *Altus* is an anagram of Sulat.

On November 23, 1676, the Sun King, Louis XIV, in his "*Concession*," stated that

> "Our good friend Jacob Saulat, Lord of Marez, made it known to Us that <u>has fallen into his hands</u> a Book of high Hermetic Chemistry, entitled: *Mutus Liber... by the author whose name is Altus...* THEREFORE... We have permitted and granted him, as do permit and grant... the publication of the aforesaid Book."[28]

Since the king states that Saulat was the owner of the book, which *fell in his hands*, then, who was the author?

At the Marsh Library of Dublin, in one of the earliest copies of the *Mutus Liber*, owned by the XVII century renowned physician Elias Bouherau, we find hand-written words:

"*Author Isaac* [Latin *Isaacus*] *Baulot*."

He was a prominent pharmacist[29] born in 1619 at La Rochelle, France. Moreover, in this town, in 1677, Altus printed the first edition of the *Mutus Liber*, the Alchemic treatise without words.

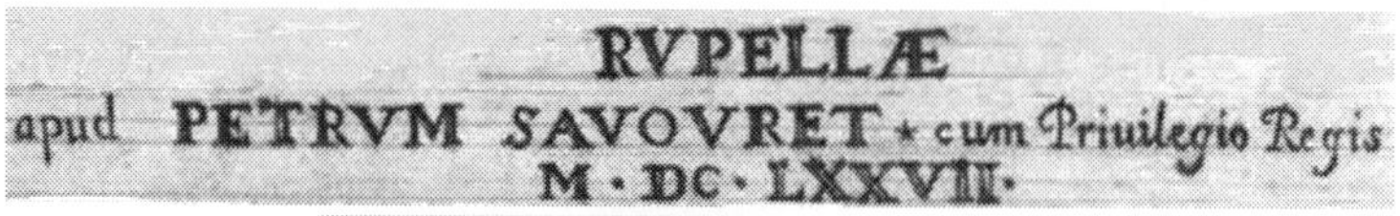
RVPELLÆ
apud PETRVM SAVOVRET * cum Priuilegio Regis
M · DC · LXXVII ·

RUPELLAE [printed[30]] *in LA ROCHELLE*[31]
apud PETRUM SAVOURET * cum Privilegio Regis
at PETER SAVOURET [publisher] ** by Concession of the King*
M·DC·LXXVII· *One Thousand.Six Hundred.Seventy Seven.*

At the end of the religion civil wars that had afflicted France, King Henry IV granted, with the Edict of Nantes in 1598, significant freedom to the Protestant Calvinist Huguenots. Among others rights, he allowed those Protestants to have a free and safe stronghold in La Rochelle. In that ideological Huguenot environment, with Cathar and Gnostic influences,[32] the *Mutus Liber* found support for its Hermetic structure.

Nevertheless, in 1685, eight years after the first publication of the *Mute Book*, the Sun King revoked his grandfather's Edict. Following this revocation and consequent persecutions of the Huguenots, Isaac Baulot, fled France for Holland, together with other Protestants, including Savouret, his publisher.[33]

We do not know of any relation between *Isaacus* Baulot, who met with the philosopher John Locke (1632-1704),[34] and *Iacobus* Saulat, mentioned by the king. However, both Latin names are each other's anagram. Furthermore, Biblically there is a direct relation. Isaac is the father of Jacob and this one, as we will see, appears in the first vignette of our book.

Additionally, Arcère, in his *History of the city of La Rochelle*, states, without giving any further proof,

> "I think the real author was Tollé, physician of La Rochelle, great chemist; Altus, the name used, suits him adequately."[35]

Since *tollé* is French for *protest*, could it be a reference to the author's *Protestant* denomination? Nevertheless,

> "It is a mistake to attribute it to Tollè."[36]

Concluding, even if the *Mutus Liber* was the collaborative effort of many authors, in any case, Altus' intention was to keep the anonymity and to be known only by his pseudonym. This means that the work, as with the sacred Indian texts, was and is intended as patrimony of Humanity. However, the Book has a pedagogical intent. In fact, it is dedicated

"*also to the sons of the spiritual art*"[37]

to whom it instructs:

"*Aware carry-on.*"[38]

The instruction of the book is that of the Art of Final Liberation. Like Yoga, it teaches how to subdue the ego and pursue the Alchemic Transmutation of the individual I into the Supreme Universal Self. The achievement of the identity with that Self is purely an epistemic process. It is the Traditional Way to change our cognitive identification with the world of duality into the realization of the fundamental Apodictical Transcendent Unity. As such, in ultimate analysis, we can state that *Alchemy* <u>is</u> *Yoga* and the contemporary westernized word misunderstands both. In fact, it considers, at best, alchemy a proto-chemistry and yoga a health related workout.

HERMES TRISMEGISTUS[39] AUM

In the Indian tradition, the *hero* Naciketa, the Unknown Sef-in-Itself,[40] states,

> "*I am That Supreme Swan Spirit dwelling in the light clear waters.* [I am] *the beneficent dwelling in the intermediate region, the sacrificer sitting on the wheel-shaped-altar-of-knowledge.* [I am] *the guest residing in the house, dwelling in the human being, sitting in the circle.* [I am] *the truth dwelling in the order of truth, born in truth's order.* [I am] *the wide dwelling in the air, born in water, the soul produced from the friction of Stones* [and] *born in the earth's-milky-rays-of-knowledge.*"[41]

He is the one who covers all worlds with three steps. He is the fifth descent (*avatāra*) of Vishṇu, the Dwarf (*vāmana*) who was able to conquer the three worlds covering them with three steps.[42] The *Taittirīya-Saṃhitā* relates a similar story, in which Indra conquers the world anew for the gods with three strides.[43] The three worlds conquered or covered are the waking, dreaming and dreamless ones.

Naciketa, Vāmana and Indra are three Indian names for the same divine being that manifested his greatness three times. In the West, he was Hermes Tris-megistus, Mercury Thrice-great.[44] He was known since antiquity. Ancient Greek authors mention him. According to the X century Byzantine encyclopedia *Suda,*

> "He was called Trismegistus on account of his praise of the trinity, saying there is one divine nature in the trinity."[45]

In 1460, under the auspices of Cosimo de' Medici (1389-1464) *Signore* of Florence and patron of the arts, friar Leonardo Alberti de Candia brought from Greece to Pistoia, II century AD Egyptian and Greek gnostic texts known as *Corpus Hermeticum.*[46] The texts were translated by the Neoplatonic philosopher Marsilio Ficino (1433-1499) influencing Renaissance thinkers like Giovanni Pico della Mirandola (1463-1494), Giordano Bruno (1548-1600), Tommaso Campanella (1568–1639), just to mention a few. It influenced also scientists like Isaac Newton (1642–1727).

During the Renaissance, the newly discovered texts received a pantheist Neoplatonic and syncretic interpretation. It was believed that the *Corpus Hermeticum* presented a first, pristine and ancient theology (*prisca theologia*) and that Hermes Trismegistus foreshadowed Christianity.[47] A short text known as *The Emerald Tablet* states that Hermes mastered the three parts of the entire universe.

Throughout the XIV and XVII century, Renaissance had developed a humanistic view in all spheres of arts, businesses, politics, religion and sciences. Humans were conceived as the center of the World and the makers of their own destinies. They could know Nature and that knowledge could gives them the power to control the World. Hermeticism was one of the means to achieve that authority.

MYTHOLOGICAL ASPECTS

<u>*Tabula smaragdina*</u>

An alchemic text, *The Book of the Secret of Secrets and the Manifestation of Lights* (*Kitab Sirr al-Asrar*),[48] first appeared in the X century Arabic literature. This Hermetic and Alchemic text was translated into Latin as *Secretum Secretorum*, the *Secrets' Secret* and mythically named <u>*Tabula smaragdina*</u>, *The Emerald Table*.[49] It declares,

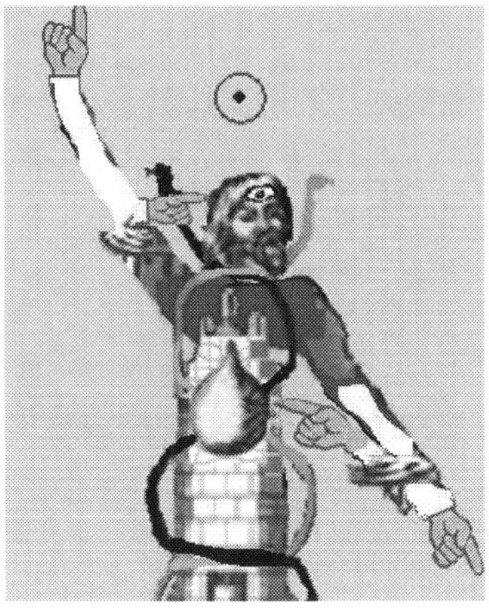

"*That which is below, is just as that which is above. And that which is above, is just as that which is below, to accomplish the miracles of the One Thing... It ascends from earth to heaven, and again descends on earth, and receives the power of the superiors and of the inferiors. Thus, you will have the glory of the entire world. Therefore, may all obscurity depart from you... In this manner, the world was created. Therefore, I am called Hermes Trismegistus, having the three parts of the Philosophy of the entire world. That, which I have said regarding the Sun's operation, is complete.*"[50]

The same concept is expressed symbolically by the hexagram, the Star of David or, as the King of Israel called it,

"*the shield of thy salvation.*"[51]

The triangle pointing above (△) represent the Transcendent world. This triangle pointing below (▽) represents the immanent world. Their joining is the male-female love union. There and Then, Here and Now, both are the same. When interlocked, they meet in the heart. The Indian tradition echoes it in the *Bṛhadāraṇyaka Upanishad* affirming that

> "*s/he who sees this World as different, separated and distinct* [from oneself] *goes from death to death.*"[52]

Metaphor

It is in the innermost recesses of our epistemic and psychological internal heart that we find the key to realize the Transcendent message. In fact, Jesus says,

> ***"WOE UNTO YOU, WHO INTERPRET THE LAW*** [literally]***,***
> ***FOR YE HAVE TAKEN AWAY THE KEY OF KNOWLEDGE:***
> ***YE ENTERED NOT IN YOURSELVES,***
> ***AND YE HINDERED THEM THAT WERE ENTERING IN."***[53]

The *Mutus Liber* is a *Silent Book*, it is Mythos (μῦθος), an eloquent tale. As Joseph Campbell, the great scholar of mythology, once told Bill Moyers, myth's

> "reference is to something that transcends all thinking... the ultimate mystery of being is beyond all categories of thought. As Kant said, the thing in itself is no thing. It transcends thingness, it goes past anything that could be thought... Myth is that field of reference to what is absolutely transcendent... The ultimate word in our English language for that which is transcendent is God. But then you have a concept."[54]

Like polyhedrons, each facet of the multi-aspects of Myths is a particular symbol alluding to a true dimension. Each side becomes a metaphor, namely a thought or a form that takes (*pherō* φέρω) beyond (*meta* μετά) its own appearance. Like when we address someone with the word *honey*. We do not mean the sweet bee-product. We mean something, which conveys

> "*a sweetness to the heart*
> *that cannot be grasped if not felt.*"[55]

Since the heart has no *taste buds*, if we remain stuck in the literal denoting-prose of *honey* as a bee-product we lose its connoting-poetic metaphorical reference.

To the argument that translating the word *mutus* of this book as *muteness* is a

> "philosophical misnomer, [since, images and] all the signs adopted by human industry to manifest thought are words."[56]

We reply, yes, it is still communication, but, nevertheless, a silent one, viz. mute.

> "The equivalent to external noise is the inner noise of thinking. The equivalent of external silence is inner stillness,"

states Tolle.[57]

We sustain that this book's wordlessness has a specific intent. It is always communication, but one of a different scope. If we say,

"Rose is a rose is a rose is a rose,"[58]

we mean the mental evocation of the object produced by the sound of the word rose. It is the wordy <u>concept</u> of that object equal to itself as <u>that concept</u>. That evocation is very distant from the rose itself as

"the *force* that through the green fuse drives the flower."[59]

Altus himself calls his book, *Livre Muĕt,*

"Mute Book, yet all the Nations of the world... can read it and understand it... The Sages say also that it is the most beautiful Book that was ever printed on the topic, having in it things that were never said by anyone. One does not need to be a true <u>*Son of the Art*</u> to understand it immediately."[60]

Altus guides us to give up all *wordy-conceptual* structures that drive away from the intuitive essence. His *muteness* is an initiatory technique into thoughtlessness, where thought distracts from the foundation from which thought itself arises. It is reversing of the dream world to go beyond it. This reversion of our waking thinking process paves the road for the realization of the Ineffable. It is as if he were asking to think with images rather than words. Try to reach the point where an image is worth a thousand words.

Our thoughts are in words, which intention the objects. However, they are not objects independent from our ideas of them. Campbell tells us

"a Zen story about a sermon of the Buddha in which he simply lifted a flower. There was only one man [Mahākāśyapa] who gave him a sign with his eyes that he understood what was said."[61]

Moses, educated at the sacred royal court by the

"*Pharaoh*'s *daughter, and became her son,*"[62]

understood very well the Egyptian culture and the *meṭut neter* (), namely the hieroglyphic sacred

"*words of the god* [Thoth]."[63]

Hieroglyphs, along with Cursive-hieroglyphs and Hieratic, the priestly sacred cursive, were meant to express that which is inexpressible.[64]

How can one convey the concept of color or sound to a person who was born blind and/or deaf? In that case, whatever would be understood would never be really colorful or resounding. From the Egyptian high priests, Moses learned the importance of supporting his sacred writings with metaphorical figurations. Hence, Jesus spoke in parables when referring to the transcendent. Indeed, he emphasizes,

"*Give not that which is holy unto the dogs, neither cast ye your pearls before swine, lest they trample them under their feet, and turn again and rend you.*"[65]

Therefore, which one is the best way to communicate the ineffable? The best way is silence.

"*An image* [was] *before mine eyes,* [there was] *silence.*"[66]

The great Indian sage Ramana Maharshi[67] inspired his disciples and imparted his teaching in silence. Later he wrote,

"*Deep meditation is eternal speech. Silence is ever-speaking; it is the perennial flow of language… 'Mouna'* [silence] *is 'Īsvara-svarūpa'* [God's-Form]. *Hence the text: 'The Truth of Supreme Brahman* [Expansion] *proclaimed through Silent Eloquence'.*"[68]

"Silence in music communicates in a similar manner to silence in speaking."[69]

A Neapolitan song describes this soundless-sound as "*Singing Silence.*"[70] Myths are metaphors, stories and songs that *chant* of an *unutterable silence* beyond their fabulous tales.

"*O ye who have sound intellects*
observe the doctrine that hides itself
under the veil of puzzling verses."[71]

<u>Symbols</u>

The word symbol, Greek *sým-bolov* (σύμ-βολον), means "together (*sŭn* σῠν) thrown away (*bállō* βάλλω)." Thus, it is something that unites while recognizing an absence. It was customary, among Oscan Italic populations, to bury their dead together with a vessel shaped with the silhouette of a bull's face. The bull represented life. However, since life was gone, the vessel was ritually broken and the grief-stricken survivors used to keep a piece of that bowl.[72] That preserved piece was a token, precisely, a symbol between them and the dead person. Like the one-half of a friendship-coin. Then, the symbol becomes an outward sign-object held by one friend while the other half is in the hands of a second friend who is elsewhere, as if Transcendent. Nevertheless, that fragment proves to the first friend the genuineness of the second friend's bond. Therefore, the symbols of our plates, while representing physical graphic objects, allude, concomitantly, to a transcendent reality alluded or realized by the Author himself.

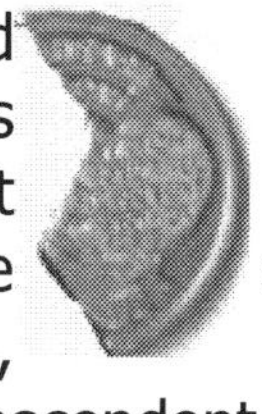

The gods of Mythology

The Psalm declares,

> "*Ye are gods* (אלהים *'elohiym*); *and all of you are children of the most High*"[73]

and Jesus said,

> "*Is it not written in your Law, 'I have said you are gods* (θεοί *theoi*)'? *If he called them gods, unto whom the word of God came, and the scripture cannot be broken,*"[74]

therefore,

> "*the kingdom of God is within you*"[75]

and Paul reiterates,

> "*ye are the temple of God, and the Spirit of God dwelleth in you.*"[76]

The gods, in the Indian tradition, are called *deva, shining* (√*div*) *beings.*[77] They are paradigms, archetypes or templates shaping the human faculties and psyche. They are organs and faculties of the senses (*indriya*), in fact,

> "*All the faculties of the senses become one in their corresponding deities, deeds and the intellectual self all in the Supreme Imperishable One.*"[78]
>
> "*Verily, the gods are the five channels of perception of this heart.*"[79]
>
> "*O Agni,*[80] *Divine-flame, bring here the gods.*"[81]

The epistemic god Agni-fire assimilates the food of knowledge as a '*Digestive-fire.*'

> "*He eats food in all worlds, in all beings, in all Self.*"[82]
>
> "*And in you are all the gods.*"[83]

Regarding the gods, Giordano Bruno states,

> "These are not formally gods, but are named *divine*."[84]

In fact, he reiterates, they are the dynamic psychological forces of the universal human being.

> "The *divinity* dwells in us by means of the reformed intellect and will."[85]

They are the templates that enable us to know the world. They are all the senses with their psychological moods and states, which, from immemorial time shaped, shape and will shape our lives. Heaven and Hell, with all the gods (*deva*) and all the demons (*asura* √*as* = to exist), inhabit our mind and take over our personality. Artistic productions can represent personality changes and/or moods. Therefore, when the gods take over they whip around humans, like Odysseus[86] in the ocean of life.

NIGERIAN *ORISHAS* AND THE SANTERIA "*SEVEN AFRICAN POWERS.*"

The Nigerian Yoruba religion and the Latin American Santeria state that the mind or the head is

"the '*seat*' of the saint[s]"[87]

i.e. the *Ori-sha* gods. In fact, *ori* is the mind, the head and *sha* is the consciousness of the gods.[88]

Likewise, we can understand Hermes Trismegistus to be a paradigm of the Human mind. He, in fact, is great three times or on three levels:

1) When awake, he is great in the waking-state.
2) When dreaming, he is great in the dream-state.
3) When asleep, he is great in the oneiric-state-with-no-dreams.

PHILOSOPHICAL ASPECTS

Certitude and faith

Are dreams real? Before we answer this question, we must define what reality is. Usually, by real we mean that which persists on its own accord, the *thing* in-itself, namely, that which is independent from the experiencer. We mean an object that does not necessitate to be known in order to be. Obviously, this *something* when it is outside our knowledge remains unknown. Consequently, its predicate of *real* cannot be given without becoming a dogma, a thought or a noumenon.

Truthfully, <u>real</u> is only that which <u>ultimately</u> is self-evident or apodictical. Now, when we ask if dreams are real, we mean,

–Do they persist independently from the dreamer?– The answer is,

–Once the dreamer is gone, the dream goes away too.–Then, we could ask,

–Is the underlining psychoanalytic message of the dream real?– The answer is still,

–The message is real only as long as there is a messenger.– But, if we ask,

–Was the experience of the dream real?–The answer can only be,

–Yes.–

The experience itself is proof to itself <u>as</u> experience. That is Certain, Indubitable and Self-Evident Reality. Indeed, <u>any and all</u> experiences are founded on that Certitude, even before we think or have consciousness-*of* them. If again, the question arises,

–That which has been experienced has a reality in-itself independent from the perceiver feeling it?– Then, the only reality would be the certainty of that question as a question.

Enlightenment is Certainty-in-Certitude. Certain-Awareness is that which we are. Certainty is the beginning and the beginning is Certainty. Certitude is the foundation. Certitude is the *Alpha*, the beginning, and the *Ωmega*, the end, of everything. Certainty is never an object of thought. The words we are here writing on Certainty are not the Certainty that founds them. Certainty is Transcendence. Certainty is the Silence of Unconscious States in which and of which nothing can be said. It may be realized as Mindfulness or Consciousness. Nevertheless, when we become conscious-*of*-the-world, then we identify with it forgetting its true origin. Every experience is informed by unshakable certainty. <u>Certitude is the Eternal-Now</u>. By certainty, we do not mean consciousness-*of* something. We mean *faith* as different from dogmatic-belief. We may believe in a World preexisting or outliving us, but we have only *faith* (πίστις *pistis*), namely, certitude in this-experience, as experience and nothing more, right here and right now.

Epistemology

Epistemology, or gnoseology,[89] is the science that researches *how do we know what we know*. It is the analysis of the process of knowledge. Namely, how is it possible that the *I-subject*$_{(s)}$, having an *object*$_{(o)}$ placed before *itself*$_{(s)}$, has a mental *internal-unifying-synthesis*$_{(s+o=u)}$ by which the I$_{(s)}$ <u>*comprehends*</u>$_{(u)}$ *for-itself*$_{(s)}$ the object$_{(o)}$ which is placed before *me*$_{(so)}$? In addition, what is the *difference*$_{(\neq)}$ between the object$_{(o)}$ *comprehended*$_{(u)}$ by me$_{(so)}$ and the *thing-in-itself*$_{(x)}$ when it is *not-*

comprehended$_{(\neq u)}$ by me$_{(so)}$ and/or is only *for-myself*$_{(s)}$? If I$_{(s)}$ were to comprehend$_{(u)}$ that difference$_{(\neq)}$ or the thing-in-itself$_{(x)}$, that thing$_{(x)}$ would become *for-myself*$_{(s)}$ unified$_{(u)}$ in me$_{(so)}$ and, therefore, it would not be the difference$_{(\neq)}$ or the thing-in-itself$_{(x)}$ separated from the I$_{(s)}$ which the I$_{(s)}$ is seeking and referring to it$_{(x)}$. Simply put, can you *see something* without *seeing* it? You may think of it, but that is not seeing it.

$$s+o = so = u \neq x$$ [90]

"*God created man*$_{[so]}$*... male*$_{[s]}$ *and female*$_{[o]}$ *created he them*$_{[u]}$." [91]

We, the subject and the object, as man and woman, inhabit this immanent-

Garden of duality. *Immanent*, from Latin, *im-(in)-manēre* (to in-stay, to re-main intrinsic) is that which *re*mains *in*trinsic between the knower/subject$_{(s+)}$ and the known/object$_{(o-)}$ dichotomy, as the inseparable positive(+)/negative(-) polarities of a dynamo. In the *midst of the Garden*, in its *immanence*, grows the metaphorical epistemic *Tree of Knowledge*,

"*the tree which* [is] *in the midst of the garden.*" [92]

Eating from it means to become conscious-*of* duality.

"*And the eyes of them both were opened, and they knew that they* [were] *naked.*" [93]

Knowledge ushers into this immanent field-of-time: past and future, day and night, life and death, male and female, subject and object. Whatever lies beyond that duality cannot be known. That Unknown is named Transcendent. It goes beyond the subject-object correlation. Like a man and a woman in carnal embrace

"*are no more twain, but one flesh*" [94]

and they are oblivious of themselves and of the external world. Namely, we cannot know the subject-in-itself or the object-in-itself. We cannot know from where our life comes or where it goes. Our life, our true origin is hidden by

"*a flaming sword which turned every way, to keep the way of the tree of life.*" [95]

This sword twister is the vorticose whirlpool of the I-subject$_{(s)}$ uniting$_{(u)}$ with the object$_{(o)}$. It is like the serpent Ouroboros[96] biting its own objective$_{(o)}$ tail. Standing on this circumference, we cannot realize the center that creates that circularity itself.

The Aristotelian Malady

We live in the field of time plagued by what we may call the *Aristotelian malady*. Today it is called Empiricism. What this suggests is that the Intellectual Community has reduced the Socratic *idea* to an image, imprinted by the *external* physical world. What that *external* signifies is not clear. Perhaps, it derives from the spatial tiered location in which the Aristotelian empirical observation had placed the four elements.[97] From his pragmatic analysis, it is easy to deduce that the Earth becomes the center of the Universe itself and woe on the apostates who claim the contrary. Therefore, the object, as such, is the real power which imprints its shape on the mind generating the idea of its external true reality. The thinking being, from its part, is only an accident in the eternal-physical-matter of the world. Spirituality and religions follow suit. The role of the mind is to computerize and organize, according to its intrinsic laws, the world of information. Even saint Thomas Aquinas converted to this perspective, until he realized that it was all straw good only to be burned.[98]

The Prophetic Spiritual Materialism

There are those who label themselves religious. They follow a particular religion and, because they claim to believe in God, they declare themselves spiritualists. At the same time, they may be geographically seeking for a fabled Garden. They may count the years since the First Twenty-Four Hours Day, as if Time itself subjected the Creator to its own flow. They may climb Mount Ararat in a search for an Ark. They worship on a stone in Lumbinī, believed to have been a delivery seat 2,576 years ago, or in a manger, believed to have been occupied 2,013 years ago in Bethlehem, or in a desert Cave. They historicize conceptually and materialize objectively the source of their religious fervor. The spatial-temporal monster deceived them all. Religious dogmas are believed to be in-themselves objectively factual in the space-time realm.

The spiritual materialists believe that if we were to travel back in time, some 3,500 years, we would witness the parting the Red Sea, or 1,980 years ago, we would be present at a crucifixion. These are some of

> "the various ways in which people involve themselves with spiritual materialism, the many forms of self-deception into which aspirants my fall."[99]

It is interesting to notice that when those same people encounter an actual enlightened spirit who identifies with Pure-Awareness, they immediately put him/her to death.[100] That, because they believe in an idolatrous objective reality placed in an external world materialistically conceived as being completely outside the '*I*' and into which the ego finds its satisfying citizenship.

> "It is important to see that the main point of any spiritual practice is to step out of the bureaucracy of the ego. This means stepping out of the ego's constant desire for a higher, more spiritual, more transcendental version of knowledge, religion virtue, judgment, comfort or whatever it is that the particular ego is seeking. One must step out of spiritual materialism. If we do not step out of spiritual materialism, if we in fact practice it, then we may eventually find ourselves possessed of a huge collection of spiritual paths... Our vast collections of knowledge and experience are just part of ego's display, part of the grandiose quality of the ego. We display them to the world and, in so doing, reassure ourselves that we exist, safe and secure, as *spiritual* people.
>
> But we have simply created a shop, an antique shop...

The attainment of enlightenment is called *vajra-like* because it does not stand for any nonsense; it just cuts right through all our games. In the story of the Buddha's life we hear of the temptations of Mara [Death], which are extremely subtle. The first temptation is fear of physical destruction. The last is the seduction by the daughters of Mara. This seduction, the seduction of spiritual materialism, is extremely powerful because it is the seduction of thinking that *I* have achieved something. If we think we have achieved something, that we have *made it*, then we have been seduced by Mara's daughters, the seduction of spiritual materialism."[101]

Temptation, then, is considering the sensible and/or thought experienced-objects as being-there independent from the Certitude of their experience.
Therefore,

"*Many shall come in my name, saying, I am Christ; and shall deceive many.*[102]
For there shall arise false Christs...
Wherefore if they shall say unto you, Behold, he is in the desert; go not forth: behold, [he is] *in the secret chambers; believe* [it] *not.*"[103]
"*For false Christs and false prophets shall rise, and shall shew signs and wonders, to seduce, if it were possible, even the elect.*"[104]

In addition, attributing special objective qualities to sacred texts is equal to relegate them in the realm of material objects. Conceptualizing and objectifying sacred text reduces them to the rank of idols or amulets. The *Amritabindu Upanishad*, one of the sacred texts of India declares,

"*After studying the sacred texts, the wise one in search of realization, should get rid of them as one who sifts rice discards the husk.*"[105]

In fact, as we will see in Plate 15, once we become Aware (*Oculatus*), we should depart (*abis*), indeed, even from this Mute Book. Similarly, Meister Eckhart says,

"*When the Kingdom appears to the soul and it is recognized, there is no further need for preaching or instruction.*"[106]

And Ramana Maharshi states,

"*The sage who is the embodiment of the truths mentioned in the scriptures has no use for them.*"[107]

Both, the *god* of the theists and the *world-in-itself* of the atheists are only thoughts, noumenon, as such they can never be known.[108] Both, theists and atheist do not know what they *think*.[109] By definition, we cannot describe the Transcendent. Nothing can be said about God, not even existence. If we do describe Him, Her, It, God would be reduced within the mind limits. Therefore, the best recourse is *muteness*, silence.

When we seek for the Transcendent in the immanent empirical world we become *Spiritual Materialists*, namely we conceptualize that which is ineffable. We become mental idolaters. We want to reduce the metaphor in one specific form, namely into a concrete empirical tangible one. If we strive for that which is real in-itself$_{(x)}$, beyond the subject-object correlation, then we must let go of both. We cannot expect the subject to be there while the object is gone or vice-versa. The timeless and spaceless mythical Garden of Eden is the absence of the subject-object correlation. It is where Apodictical-Awareness needs no thought. Where there is no tribulation or unsatisfaction because there is no *hungry-desire* for the *fruit of knowledge*. There, *Certainty* does not require a thought to be *certain of being Certain*.

> "*Immediately after the tribulation of those days shall the sun be darkened, and the moon shall not give her light, and the* [objective] *stars shall fall from heaven, and the* [subjective] *powers of the heavens shall be shaken:*
> *And then shall appear the sign of* [True Awareness] *the Son of man in heaven: and then shall all the tribes of the earth mourn, and they shall* [be aware and] *see the Son of man coming in the clouds of heaven* [Awareness] *with power and great glory*...
> *For where two or three are gathered together in my name, there am I* [Awareness] *in the midst of them*...
> *Behold the fowls of the air: for they sow not, neither do they reap, nor gather into barns; yet your heavenly Father feedeth them. Are ye not much better than they?*
> *Which of you by taking thought can add one cubit unto his stature?*
> *And why take ye thought for raiment? Consider the lilies of the field, how they grow; they toil not, neither do they spin:*
> *And yet I say unto you, That even Solomon in all his glory was not arrayed like one of these.*
> *Wherefore, if God so clothe the grass of the field, which to day is, and to morrow is cast into the oven, shall he not much more clothe you, O ye of little faith?*
> *Therefore take no thought, saying, What shall we eat? or, What shall we drink? or, Wherewithal shall we be clothed?*
> *(For after all these things do the Gentiles seek:) for your heavenly Father knoweth that ye have need of all these things.*
> *But seek ye first the kingdom of God, and his righteousness; and all these things shall be added unto you.*
> *Take therefore no thought for the morrow: for the morrow shall take thought for the things of itself. Sufficient unto the day is the evil thereof.*"[110]

When the rush of Pure Apodictical-Awareness irrupts and Consciousness identifies with It, the personal individual mind cannot forget it. It is by being awake and identifying with that Certitude that one reaches Heaven. That Certitude is the Philosopher's Stone of the Alchemic Gold. That Certitude does not need any demonstration because it is Apodictical, It is Self-Demonstrating. Certitude is the Philosopher's Stone that transforms the heavy lead object into the Gold of existence, in Awareness.

"*Watch ye therefore: for ye know not when the master of the house cometh...*
Lest coming suddenly he find you sleeping."[111]

Until the angelic trumpets of Awareness wake you. As depicted in the first plate.

"*And the seven angels which had the seven trumpets prepared themselves to sound.*"[112]

Therefore, be awake

"*Pay attention and pray* [*i.e.* meditate] *that ye enter not into the temptation-of-object-experimentation: the spirit indeed* [is] *willing, but the flesh* [is] *weak.*[113]
"*always pray* [*i.e.* meditate]*, and not to be utterly spiritless.*"[114]

With the return of the individual consciousness-*of* Awareness, the mind conceptualizes also that Certainty. The mind *eats* the *fruit* of conceptual knowledge and, like Gilgamesh in the fog of sleep,[115] becomes unaware of Awareness. We become conscious-*of* that awareness, which, then, becomes an object like that of any other experience. Nevertheless, the certitude of awareness leaves an unforgettable mark, which may turn into fanatical fundamentalism when referred to the religion of the experiencer. Therefore, a prophetic frenzy may take over the neo-spiritual-materialists. At that juncture, there can be a dangerous unbalance of the mind, which, torn between average psychological behavior and deep Mystical-Sanctity, may resolves in the psychosis of maenadic[116] behavior or into demonic possession.

Consciousness-of and Awareness

Let us look around. During the waking and/or dreaming stages of our experience, we see the world as external and/or internal. In both cases, the world is like our *hunting ground*, which provides *food* for our thoughts. Our subject or our consciousness becomes the *hunter* in this *field* in which the objects, concrete and/or abstract, are the preys. Therefore, before anything can be stated, the CONSCIOUSNESS-*OF*-this-objective-world is the first-born. Try, if you can, to state anything of which you are not conscious-*of*. Even if you can, that very moment you become conscious-*of* it. However, there is another important element at the foundation of consciousness, namely CERTITUDE, which we will call AWARENESS. No one, even when stating a made up lie, is not *certain* of that statement as a statement. Awareness, therefore, is the base on which consciousness rests its own heal. That Certitude is the Self of the 'I' or of the Ego. It is the fire, which burns the Biblical bush without consuming it. In fact, from the burning bush, the Transcendent Awareness declares to Moses,

"*I AM THAT I AM.*"[117]

> "*I have come as light* [of Awareness] *into the world, so that everybody who is* *<u>certain</u>* *in me may not remain in darkness.*"[118]

With a different metaphor, we find this concept in the account of Esau and Jacob, portrayed sleeping in the first plate. We should briefly describe the mythological and paradigmatic aspects of those twin brothers.

<u>The Mythological Races</u>

Mythologies are sets of metaphors attempting to describe the ineffable Transcendent. When those metaphors are accepted dogmatically as objective realities in-themselves, then they become *lies*, given that they are not the Transcendent they refer too. Eventually, those descriptions will determine the cultural structures of the populations in which each mythology was born. Accordingly, they will regulate morals, laws, pedagogy and world-views. Each culture, then, will enter in conflict with the other cultures, which hold their different set of metaphors as absolute truths.

Tentatively, we can classify humanity based on mythology. Each culture, then, will distinguish different *Mythological Races*, having nothing to do with biological differences. In fact, people from different ethnic backgrounds may belong to the same *Myth's Race*. As an example, monotheists will never accept animists. The two are separated by irreconcilable differences that set them apart. Eventually, the differences will be so fundamental that may change the physical appearance of their adherents affecting also their biological structure. As an example, consider the lasting impact that centuries of prohibitions, restrictions and obligations in dietary (*e.g.* cannibalism) and/or sexual (*e.g.* inbreeding) behavior may have on genetic structure.

It must be clear that all thinking beings belong to a *Myth Race*. For one, everyone dreams. Dreams are metaphorical references to a world believed, while dreaming, to be real in-itself. Each sleeper dreams according to his/her mythological original background. We bring in the oneiric world the waking experience while the oneiric myths affect the waking state. Science itself postulates a transcendent world. In fact, the scientist considers the universe and its laws real in-itself, which will outlive him or her, but of this, s/he does not nor can have any *scientific* proof.

Furthermore, it is a pertinent question to ask,

– Is the world out there independent from our consciousness?–

The surprise generated by new astronomical discoveries seems to confirm it. However, surprise implies Awareness, but even dreams may contain surprises. Furthermore, planetary history, attested by novel geological findings, appears to endorse the objective persistence of events in time independent from consciousness. So, we can ask,

– Did those occurrences still take place even when consciousness did not register them?–

Nonetheless, while we sleep, even dreams appear to have a sequential structure.

If space and time have a reality in themselves, independent from the consciousness of them, they must have an obtuse and obscure core working on all levels and independent from the consciousness of it. They would have internal forces driving their universal structure. Nevertheless, discussing of it still implies some sort of consciousness. Furthermore, that random universal dynamo generates predictable occurrences. Then again, no physical prediction is possible without consciousness predicting it. Yes, evolution is a random process without an intelligent design, but it is, nevertheless, intelligible.

Quantum physicist J. A. Wheeler was quoted saying, that in the Universe,

"We're all hypnotized into thinking there's something out there."[119]

Therefore, he stated, that the Universe is

"a self-excided circuit."[120]

To illustrate the point, he drew a 'U' for Universe. The right arm represents the Big Bang, which generates the perceiver who puts that singularity into effect by perceiving it.

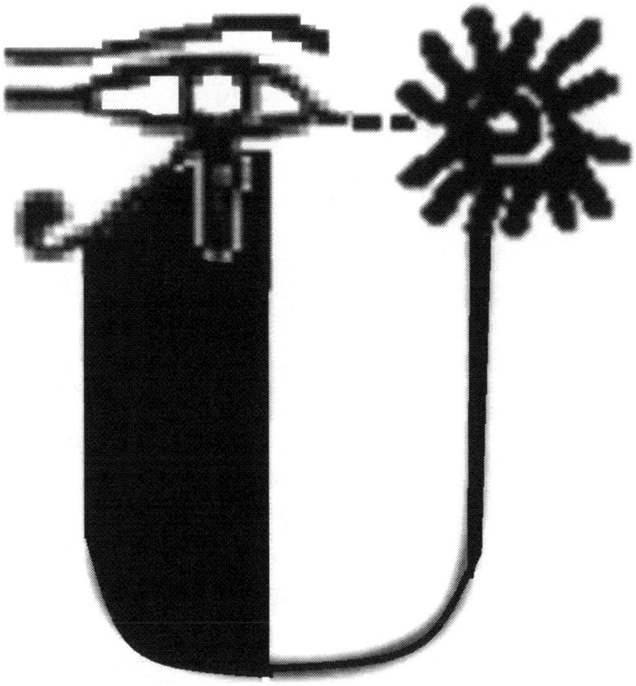

THE BIBLICAL TRADITION

Isaac, Jacob and Esau

The first plate of our book quotes *Biblical* passages regarding Jacob. Our hermeneutical study of those citations does not intend to be the last or the only possible interpretation of the text. Like any mythological traditions, also the figures of Isaac, Jacob and Esau have many facets. However, the graphic setting, offered by Altus in the *Mutus Liber*, supports the following reading of his *Biblical* citations.

The *Bible* tells us that Isaac, Abraham's son, at the age of forty married Rebekah.[121] From her, he got two twin sons. While she was still expectant,

> "*the LORD said unto her, Two races* (גוי *gowy*)[122] [are] *in thy womb, and two manner of races* (לאם *lĕom*)[123] *shall be separated* (פרד *parad*)[124] *from thy bowels; and* [one] *people shall be stronger* (אמץ *'amats*)[125] *than* [the other] *people; and the elder shall serve* (עבד *` abad*)[126] *the younger.*"[127]

Julius Evola, the esoteric Italian traditionalist, states that

> "In reality there are more than many cases of persons, who are exactly of the same physical race, of the same stock, at times even – as brothers or fathers and sons – of the same blood in the most real sense who, nevertheless, cannot understand each other. A frontier separates their souls, their way of feeling and seeing is different and, despite that, the common physical race and the common blood can do nothing. There is a possibility of comprehension, and therefore of true solidarity, of deep unity, only where a common <u>*race of the soul*</u> exists."[128]

Therefore, the fruits of Rebekah's womb belong to two separate *Soul's Races* (גוי *gowy* - לאם *lĕom*). On one side, the *Stronger Spiritual Race* is *'amats* (אמץ), namely, brave, bold, secure, assuring, alert and superior. On the other, the *Subject Telluric Race* is *` abad* (עבד), namely, meant to serve and to be subject to the first one.

At the twins' birth,

> "*the first* [twin] *came out red, all over like an hairy garment; and they called his name Esau*...[129]
> [Also he was] *a hairy man*...[130] *called Edom* [the Red one]."[131]

Esau, *`Esav* (עֵשָׂו) in Hebrew, means he who does, he who works, he who makes or he who produces.[132] Therefore, he is by name, action and appearance fiery, bustling and red while interacting with this world.

> "*And after that came his brother out, and his hand took hold on Esau's heel;*[133] *and his name was called Jacob*...[134] *a smooth man*"[135]

In Hebrew, his name *Ya`aqob* (יַעֲקֹב) means: "heel holder, supplanter, circumvent."[136] Therefore, as a heel holder, he is also the foundation on which the foot rests. In other words, he is the podium on which one stands. As a supplanter, Jacob is the one who will take over by circumventing the usual ways of things.

What is the metaphorical meaning of these biblical persons? We have three figures, Isaac, the father, with Esau and Jacob, his sons. These are the *two manners of people*, the two paradigmatic aspects of the human being.

1) "*Isaac loved Esau, because he* [was] *the mouth of* [his] *hunt.*"[137]

Isaac is *every man*, the enjoyer and consumer of this perception seized by the *mouth*, his consciousness-*of* this world. He, on his deathbed, yearning for another morsel of this world's experience, which he loves so much, begs his Consciousness/Esau,

> "*Go out to the field, and take me* [some] *hunt;*
> *And make me sense a savoury meat, such as I love,*
> *and bring* [it] *to me, that I may eat; that my soul may*
> *bless thee before I die.*"[138]

2) "*Esau was a cunning*[139] *hunter, a man of the* [world's] *field.*"[140]

Esau is a metaphor for the first born of the epistemic process. He is the *hunting*-consciousness-*of*-and-*in*-the-*game*-world. He is the one who seizes the objects and perceives them. He is the one who knows by experience, the one who discriminates and distinguishes. He is the red fire of consciousness, which *cooks* the *food for thought.*[141]

3) "*Jacob* [was] *a plain*[142] *man, dwelling in tents.*"[143]

Jacob is the paradigm of the perfect, complete and pure Aware-Certitude, abiding in the innermost tabernacle of every human being. He is the support of consciousness, without which consciousness itself cannot be.

Consciousness/Esau is self-interested absorption in its own epistemic meal. He

> "*came from the field* [of the objective world]*...*
> *And Esau said to Jacob, Feed me* [food for thought]*,*[144]
> *I pray thee, with that same red* [pottage]*; for I* [am]
> *faint* [without which I would be thoughtless]*: therefore*
> *was his name called Edom* [the *red-hot* one].[145]
> *And Jacob said, Sell me* [recognize me] *this day thy*
> *birthright* [that I am your Only-True-Certain-support]*.*
> *And Esau said, Behold, I* [am] *at the point of death:*
> *and what profit shall this birthright do to me?*
> *And he sold* [recognized] *his birthright unto Jacob...*
> *Thus Esau despised* [his] *birthright.*"[146]

Esau is the totality of all the senses with which consciousness operates. Metaphorically, he is giving up his leadership recognizing Certitude as the foundation of his consciousness. Some passages from the *Chāndogya Upanishad* may clarify this allegory.

> "*Once, the vital spirits of the senses disputed who was superior among them. Speech departed ... and when it came*

back, he asked 'Thus, how have you been able to live without me?' [It answered] *'Like dumb, but living with vital breath* [viz. life's foundation]*.' The eye departed ... and when it came back, he asked 'Thus, how have you been able to live without me?'* [It answered] *'Like blind, but living with vital breath.' The ear departed ... and when it came back, he asked 'Thus, how have you been able to live without me?'* [It answered] *'Like deaf, but living with vital breath.' The mind departed ... and when it came back, he asked 'Thus, how have you been able to live without me?'* [It answered] *'Like an infant, but living with vital breath.' Then when that vital breath was about to depart ... the other senses were uprooted. They all came to him and said 'You are the best among us.'"*[147]

Therefore, *Vital-Breath*, Awareness, Life's Foundation

"is ... the essence of the limbs,"[148]

[is] *"intention, made of mind, tending conceptually towards truth, with the vital breath as body, the light as form, and space as essence, He is the source of every action, of every desire, of every scent, and of every flavor. Encompassing all this, but indifferent, without conferring meaning or sense to the objects."*[149]

"Verily, that Supreme Transcendent Spirit is this Self. It is composed of knowledge, mind, vital breath, sight, hearing, earth, water, wind, space, light, darkness, desire, detachment, anger, tranquility, justice, injustice, and everything else, thus it is composed of this and that. One transforms itself according to his actions and behaviors. Who does good becomes good, who does evil becomes evil. One becomes virtuous by virtuous action and evil-by-evil action. Furthermore, verily, some say that a person is composed of desire indeed. As his desire is, so becomes his will, then, as his will is, so he enacts his deed, finally, he achieves whatever deed he enacts."[150]

This is the metaphoric sense of Esau's abdication to his right of primogeniture. Therefore, Genesis describes how Isaac, before dying, wanted to bless his consciousness/Esau producer of his beloved experience.[151] Isaac, whose

"eyes were dim, so that he could not see, he called Esau his eldest son, and said unto him.../ go out to the field, and take me some venison.../ And make me savoury meat, such as I love, and bring it to me, that I may eat; that my soul may bless thee before I die...|

[And] *Rebekah* [the ensnarer] *spake unto Jacob her son... / Go now to the flock, and fetch me from thence two good kids of the goats; and I will make them savoury meat for thy father, such as he loveth:/ And thou shalt bring* [it] *to thy father, that he may eat, and that he may bless thee before his death. / And Jacob said to Rebekah his mother, Behold, Esau my brother* [is] *a hairy man, and I* [am] *a smooth man:/ My father peradventure will feel me, and I shall seem to him as a deceiver* [which I am not]; *and I shall bring a curse upon me, and not a blessing./ And he went, and fetched, and brought* [them] *to his mother: and his mother made savoury meat, such as his father loved./ And Rebekah took goodly raiment of her eldest son Esau, which* [were] *with her in the house, and put them upon Jacob her younger son:/ And she put the skins of the kids of the goats upon his hands, and upon the smooth of his neck:/ And she gave the savoury meat and the bread, which she had prepared, into the hand of her son Jacob./*

And he came unto his father, and said, My father: and he said, Here [am] *I; who* [art] *thou, my son?/ and Jacob said unto his father, I* [am the real Awareness of] *Esau* [consciousness] *thy firstborn; I have done according as thou badest me: arise, I pray thee, sit and eat of my venison, that thy soul may bless me./ And Isaac said unto his son, How* [is it] *that thou hast found* [it] *so quickly, my son? And he said, Because the LORD thy God brought* [it] *to me.* [Consciousness is in the field of space and time, while Awareness is spaceless and timeless]*/ And Isaac said unto Jacob, Come near, I pray thee, that I may feel thee, my son, whether thou* [be] *my very son Esau or not.* [Isaac had only consciousness-*of* the world but never focused on the Apodictic-Certitude]*./ And Jacob went near unto Isaac his father; and he felt him, and said, The voice* [is] *Jacob's voice, but the hands* [are] *the hands of Esau./ And he discerned him not, because his hands were hairy, as his brother Esau's hands: so he blessed him./ And he said,* [Art] *thou my very son Esau? And he said, I* [am his Awareness]*./ And he said, Bring* [it] *near to me, and I will eat of my son's venison, that my soul may bless thee. And he brought* [it] *near to him, and he did eat: and he brought him wine, and he drank./ And his father Isaac said unto him, Come near now, and kiss me, my son./ And he came near, and kissed him: and he smelled the smell of his raiment, and blessed him, and said, See, the smell of my son* [is] *as the smell of a field which the LORD hath blessed."*[152]

Isaac had never realized the profundity of Jacob. He was familiar only with Esau. Consciousness and Awareness are difficult to distinguish. Consciousness interacts with the object and recognizes it *with-knowledge.*[153] Awareness is the foundation of knowledge. It is its essential Truth. It is <u>Certainty</u>. It is *quickness of spirit*.

As an example, at the sight of a venomous snake, we move away from its path. Upon recognizing that it was a rope mistaken for a serpent, we return on our steps.

Consciousness is e-motional interpretation of experience. Instead, Awareness in-itself is always Non-Judgmental-Certitude sustaining, now the self, now the path, now the snake, now the mistaken view and now the rope.

Jesus says,

"*My kingdom is not* [the consciousness-] *of this world*."[154]

Consciousness is *Lucifer*,[155] the light-bearer of the Aware-Sun *reflecting* and bouncing off from the experienced data. Awareness is the Light of Certitude. It is the Mathematical-Scientific enlightening of the World.

Then, as Desirous (*Uśan*), in the *Kaṭha Upanishad*,

"*recognized* [his son Naciketa] *as he* [who had been] *let loose by* [Mṛtyu/Death],"[156]

similarly, Isaac, having realized Jacob, as the Certainty of Awareness, proclaimed,

"*Let people serve thee, and nations bow down to thee: be lord over thy brethren, and let thy mother's sons bow down to thee: cursed* [be] *every one that curseth thee, and blessed* [be] *he that blesseth thee*."[157]

In fact, Ramana Maharshi says,

"*When we quest with our mind 'Who am I?' and reach the Heart, 'I'* [viz. Esau] *topples down and immediately another entity will reveal itself proclaiming 'I-I'. Even though it also emerges saying 'I', it does not connote the ego, but the One Perfect Existence*,"[158] viz. Jacob.

However,

"*it came to pass, as soon as Isaac had made an end of blessing Jacob, and Jacob was yet scarce gone out from the presence of Isaac his father, that Esau his brother came in from his hunting*."[159]

Therefore, on the onset of death, Isaac realizes Certitude/Jacob. This is not a deceit; it is the restoration of the truthful order of things as willed by God.[160] It is the realization that objectiveness presents itself founded on Apodictical Truth. Beyond the fussiness of objectivity, there is the smoothness of epistemic Certainty. To realize this, it is necessary to *circumvent* (Jacob יַעֲקֹב *Ya`aqob*) the identification with the objective world and realize or bless the Truth on which objectivity is founded. Therefore, Truth is conquered by force,

"*the kingdom of heaven suffereth violence, and the violent take it by force*."[161]

"*And Jacob... wrestled a man with him until the breaking of the day./ And ... he prevailed/*
And he said, Thy name shall be called no more Jacob, but Israel: for as a prince hast thou power with God and with men, and hast prevailed."

When Jacob wakes up into Awareness, he is Israel and *God prevails* (יִשְׂרָאֵל *Yisra'el*).[162]

THE HERMETIC TRADITION

Corpus Hermeticum

During the Renascence, ancient sacred texts, believed to be divinely inspired and known as *The Corpus Hermeticum*,[163] influenced the religious and philosophical perspectives of the Western World. Those texts captivated the minds of great scientists, like Isaac Newton,[164] or illustrious philosophers, like Giordano Bruno.[165] Those writings were attributed to the mythic *Herme*s Trismegistus, hence, the term *Herme*tic Philosophy. Eventually, Hermeticism housed a syncretic view that, at times, incorporated also Neoplatonic and Gnostic elements alongside the ancient wisdom of Orphic-Pythagorean, Eleusinian, Egyptian and Chaldean mysteries. These teaching were understood as leading the adepts, called *Sons of the Art*,[166] to Transcendence Itself. Alchemy was the Art of transmuting heavy-lead-individual-ego into Pure-Gold-Universal-Self.

True Alchemists, like true Yogis, through an internal psychological transmutation, realize their divine reality in them. On the lower plane, namely on the immanent level, some practitioners literally seek to transmute physical metals, namely lead, into gold. The foggy field-time, where the subject-object dichotomy obfuscates the Ultimate-Reality in Itself, does not allow them to *see* beyond physicality. Alchemy, from the Egyptian *Kami-t* ( ),[167] means *black* ( ) *land* ( ), namely Egypt. The Greek *Chēmia* (Χημία) has the same meaning and *chēmē* (χήμη) means *liquid blend*. Arabic added the article *al-* (ال). Thus, *al-kīmīā* (الكيمياء) means the *Egyptian art*.

Hermetic is the adjective from the name Hermes. He is the divine messenger who goes between the gods and the mortals. He is the god of wisdom who built civilization. In Egypt he was known as *Thoth* and was worshipped in the temple of Khmun (Hermo-polis = Hermes'-city) in the form of an Ibis bird[168] (sometimes depicted also as a baboon) and he was titled "*Thrice great*" ( ).

In India, he was the planet Mercury called *Budha* or *Hemna*. From this last name derives the Greek *Hermēs* (Ἑρμῆς). The additional *Trismegistos* (Τρισμέγιστος) means the threefold majestic one. Iris is his winged female counterpart.[169]

In Etruria, he was known as *Turms*.[170] In Rome *Mercury* was "*Ter maximus*,"[171] Three-times supreme. He was identified also with the Biblical Enoch[172] and the Koranic Idris.[173] Tradition has it that he wrote innumerable books. Antiquity regarded him as the first teacher of Alchemy and the spiritual guide of Pythagoras in Babylon. Moreover, the Middle Ages considered him a precursor of Christianity.[174] His symbol is the caduceus, a wand surmounted by a winged ball and flanked by two snakes, as in the Indian *pingalā-sushumnā-iḍā*.

<u>*The Caduceus*</u>

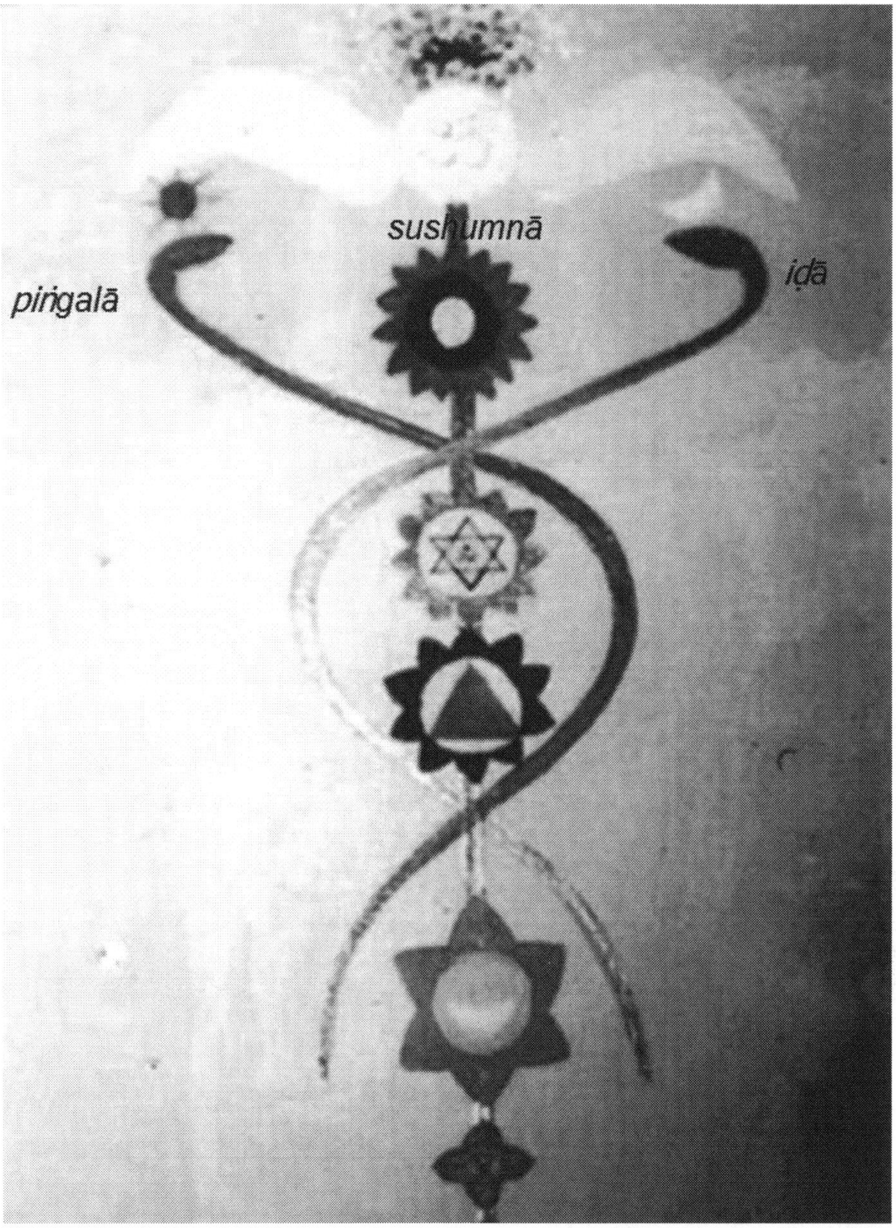

The caduceus is a well-known world symbol. In the contemporary western tradition, it is a medical  emblem. An ancient Roman bronze caduceus from Brindisi, believed to be the staff of Mercury, is on  display  in the *Museo Archeologico* of Naples (Italy).[175] Today, the Greek Orthodox bishops carry the *Paterissa*, 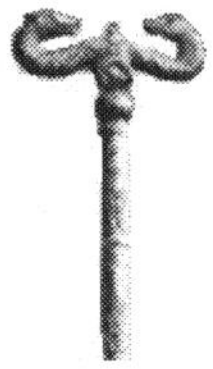 a pastoral staff with the same snake symbol.

In Ancient India, Hermes/Mercury had many other names. He was named *Vid*, Knower, *Rasa*, Flavorful-fluid-nectar, and *Jña*, Wise-Teacher. Therefore, he was the Knowledgeable-*Wise-Teacher* of Alchemy, namely *Rasa-jña-tā* in Sanskrit.[176]

"There is a saying in the Tibetan scriptures: 'Knowledge must be burned, hammered and beaten like pure gold. Then one can wear it as an ornament.' So when you receive spiritual instruction from the hands of another, you do not take it uncritically, but you burn it, you hammer it, you beat it, until the bright, dignified color of gold appears. Then you craft it into an ornament, whatever design you like, and you put it on. Therefore, dharma is applicable to every age, to every person; it has a living quality. It is not enough to imitate your master or guru; you are not trying to become a replica of your teacher. The teachings are an individual personal experience, right down to the present holder of the doctrine."[177]

Alchemy

Alchemy is enlightenment. It transmutes the subject-object correlation into Pure-Awareness.

Alchemy is the inner-realization of the transmutation of the subject-object correlation, as consciousness-*of*-the-world, into its fundamental but ineffable Transcendent-Apodictical-Awareness.

Alchemy has nothing to with chemical reactions of physical elements. However, as a positive offspring, it generated the first rudimental experimentation of chemistry, as we know it today. In fact, the greed for gold and the materialistic-literal-interpretation of its mythological-symbolism produced a plethora of experimentation that impressed also European royalty. Among them, the Holy Roman Emperor Rudolf II

(1576–1612) of Prague was so impressed that in his castle he dedicated an entire wing, known as the *Powder Tower* (*Prašná věž-Mihulka*), only for alchemical experimentations.[178]

In India Mercury was also called *ūrdhvá-pātana*, namely "*the act of causing* (mercury) *to rise*"[179] along the staff. Moreover, it is from that country that we learn the true meaning of the caduceus. Metaphorically, the Indian tradition states that the breath-flow resembles the epistemic process. *Ex-haling* corresponds to the movement towards the object (*i.e.* as in reaching out for the food) and *in-haling* its return into the subject (*i.e.* as in eating the food). These two directions are called channels (*nāḍi*) or snake-like *breaths*. They are the right <<solar direction (*piṅgalā*) that, from the subject, goes to the object and the left lunar direction (*iḍā*) that, from the object, goes back to the subject.[180] Then, the *iḍā-nāḍi* and *piṅgalā-nāḍi* become the two sides of the subject/sun-object/moon circularity, the one Ouroboros, the serpent biting its own tail. These are the two flowing forces of life, like two serpents intertwined, as in a DNA double

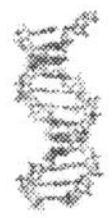

helix,[181] around the Self, the central Tree of Life of the Hermetic caduceus staff. A reminiscent rendering of this tree, with a five-headed Hydra snake coiled around it, is in one of the two swimming pools of the Great Gymnasium of Herculaneum.[182]

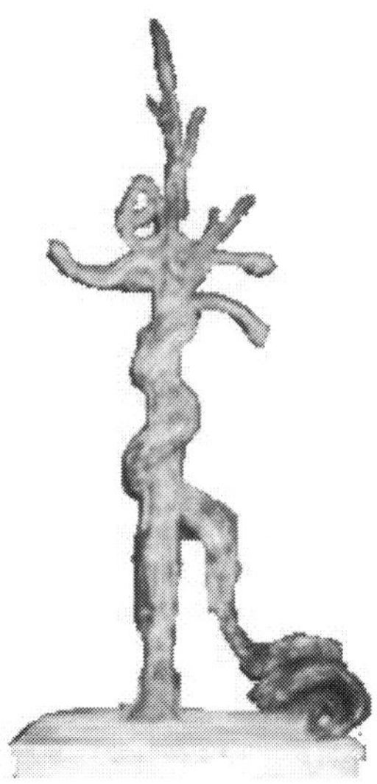

These two serpents or breath wind-flows find unify in the heart-center. Metaphorically, there is the pillar of the world (*axis-mundi*), the *sushumnā*,[183] the good (*su*) artery of the body intentioning the world. The Egyptian tradition portrays it as the *Djed* pillar or Osiris' spine on which stands Rā, the Egyptian god creator, as a hawk wearing on the head the sun disk with the snake *khut*. The sacred Indian texts say that through the spine passage travels *kuṇḍalinī*,[184] the coiled-snake power (*śakti*), symbolically placed at the base of the spine, to reach the suture on the head's crown *brahma-randhra* from which the soul escapes at the time of death. The Egyptian tradition portrays the snake *khut* as the Power encircling Pharaoh Ramses VI's forehead.[185] The Hermetic and the Alchemic traditions portray it as the athanor furnace for chemical digestion.[186] Metaphorically, the athanor represents the human body with the 'I' being the fire. The Indian god Agni (Fire) is regarded as the *Divine-flame* common to all humans, figuratively named Digestive-fire (*Agni vaiśvānara*), equating experience to the physiological process of digestion.

> "*Agni, the Divine-flame is the individual soul, the Leader and the Digestive-fire within a person, who is this one by whom this food is cooked and then eaten.*"[187]

Along the psychophysical intentioning channel of the *sushumnā,* we find vorticose (*cakra*) forces that shape and direct our lives. Each one of these forces is placed, in ascending order, according to the complexity of its evolutionary level. However, these forces, like whirlpools, swallow up the individual who identifies with each one of them. Therefore, these are not anatomical structures, but they are real states of mind that truly affect the surrounding objective world. These vortexes are represented in abstract graphic renderings (*maṇḍala*), which symbolically help to *in*tuit the nature of those particular biopsychic states.>>[188] Like the seven branches of the Jewish candelabrum *Menorah*, there are seven of these biopsychic states.

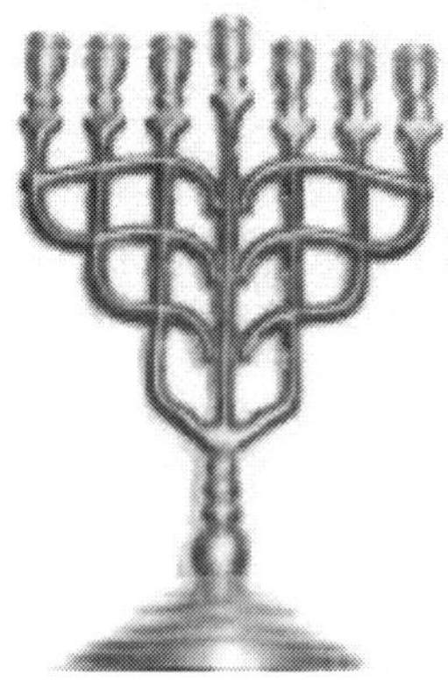

We must clarify that these states or vortices are circles (*cakra*) in the sense that they existentially engulf us. They completely take over our mind, will and effort, to the point that we consider nothing to be more important. Who, among living beings, is out of life? Hospitals are full of people trying to preserve life. Who, among animals, is immune from the urge of sex? Marriage is the institution regulating that drive. Who, among humans, does not struggle to have some form of power? Working places are bustling with laborers producing assets.

Life, *love* and *wealth* are the first three undeniable foundations of our human condition. These are the first three whirlpools along the epistemic intentionality called caduceus. These are not metaphors. They are real existential conditions. By understanding their nature, it becomes easy for us to recognize the true meaning of words like *cakra, centers*, *fires*, *levels*, *vortexes* or *wheels* when placed in conjunction and along the caduceus axis of intentioning existence.

In an ascending order these vortices are:

1) LIFE's VORTEX (*cf.* Skinner), evolving in the Central Nervous System.
2) LIBIDO's VORTEX (*cf.* Freud), generated by sexual drive.
3) POWER's VORTEX (*cf.* Adler, Alfred), in the constant struggle of society.
4) HEART's VORTEX (*cf.* Jung) (the physical organ is only metaphorical), the stage of intuition, which sublimates the previous three vortexes into:
5) PURIFICATION's VORTEX (*cf.* Gandhi), in which the will seeks its own true spiritual interiority.
6) LOVE's VORTEX (*cf.* Dante), the perception center of knowledge where Libido sublimates into pure Transcendent spiritual love.
7) ECSTASY's SEAT (*cf.* Saint Teresa of Avila), in which life's *lead* alchemically transmutes and sublimates into the Pure-*Gold* of Apodictical-Awareness.[189] That is the seat where God

> "*rested on the seventh day from all his work which he had made.*"[190]

Still, we must overcome also the concept of the seventh level (*cf.* Ramana Maharshi). We must give room to Altus' Silence. There,

> "*the mind gets resolved in the object of meditation without harbouring the ideas 'I am such and such; I am doing this and this'...* [in] *this subtle state ... even the thought 'I-I' disappears.*"[191]

THE HEART SUBLIMATING THE VORTEXES ON THE CADUCEUS' STAFF

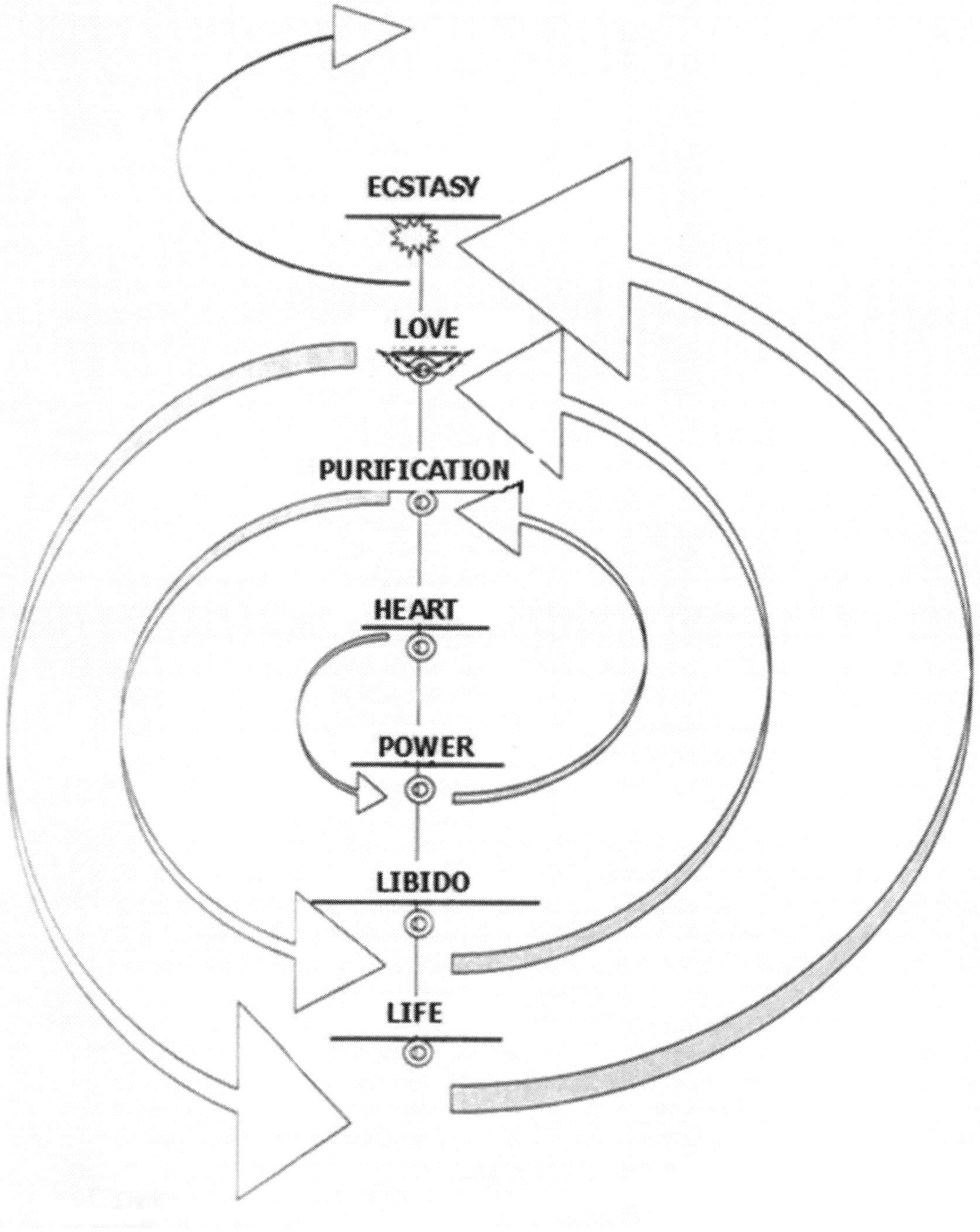

PART I

THE SOUL'S MAP

PLATE 1: "THE AWAKENING"

The book starts with two trumpets awakening the sleeping one and leading the way along the stairway to Heaven. One trumpet awakens from sleep the other from the dream.

TITLE

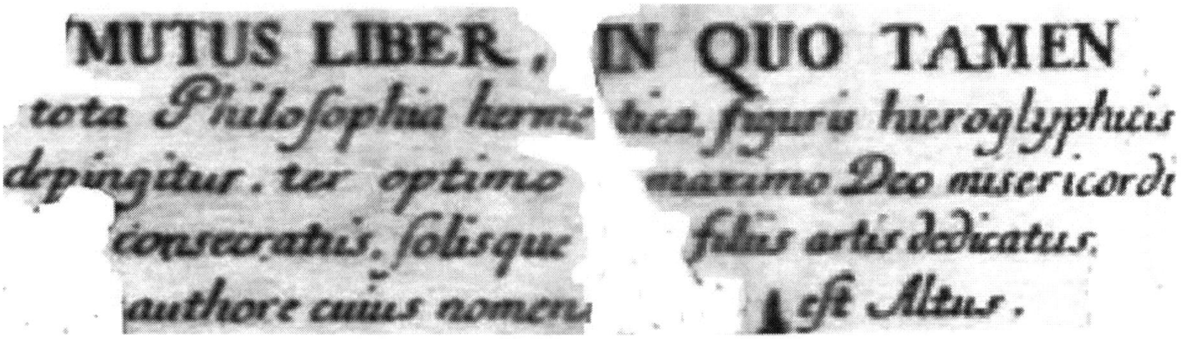
MUTUS LIBER, IN QUO TAMEN
tota Philosophia hermetica, figuris hieroglyphicis
depingitur. ter optimo maximo Deo misericordi
consecratus, solisque filiis artis dedicatus,
authore cuius nomen est Altus.

MUTUS LIBER, IN QUO TAMEN
THE MUTE BOOK, IN WHICH HOWEVER

tota philosophia hermetica, figuris hieroglyphicis

the entire hermetic philosophy, in hieroglyphic figures

depingitur, ter optimo maximo Deo misericordi

is depicted, to the three times best supreme merciful God

consecratus, solisque filiis artis dedicatus,

consecrated, and to the only sons of the [*solar*][192] *art dedicated,*
authore cuius nomen est Altus.
by the author whose name is Altus (Tall-High).

AWAKENING

It must have been the evolutionary example of a primordial *snow monkey*[193] mother to push her youngster to overcome the natural adversity for water and jump into a local Japanese hot spring in order to alleviate the freezing winter. Altus, our author, is doing a similar thing. He is sounding his trumpets to plunge us in a different realm. As with Jacob in this vignette, he is urging us to circumvent, the customary ways of the dream world and to leap into spiritual wakefulness.

The first picture of the *Mutus Liber* sets the tone for the entire book. There is no doubt that the tableau represents the waking-sleeping daily stages of life. by Two roses represent both stages. The one facing  represents the openness of the waking state to this realm. The other rose  turned towards the  ground represents the internal closure into the dream state.

The rose, in general, symbolizes the blood and the sacred Heart of Christ. That flower represents the

"dew of heaven from above."[194]

It is the bud budof regeneration, redemption, resurrection, rebirth and immortality of the soul. The rose is the *flower of the sages* (*flos sapientium*). It corresponds to the Mystical Rose, the Virgin Mary. Its thorns connote pain and chastity. As the oriental lotus is the flower symbolizing the disclosure at the sun of enlightenment, similarly, the rose bud opens up becoming the *Philosopher's Rose* of the alchemic treatises.[195]

The winged beings are awake. The man, Jacob, is asleep. He is dreaming of a ladder with different step or levels. From the ground level of the land of immanence, there is an aspiring ascension towards Transcendence. In the waking, dreaming and sleeping world of duality, placed under the protection of the moon, the bugles' sound of celestial messengers awaken into the Transcendent realm of

"the love that moves the sun and the other stars."[196]

Therefore, the hieroglyphic symbology and mythological metaphors ensue. In fact, that is the only *language* capable to allude to the Ineffable.

To confirm this interpretation, we have mirror-written citations of *Biblical* passages from the *Pentateuch* or the *Torah*. They set the tone of the vignette and of the entire book as well.

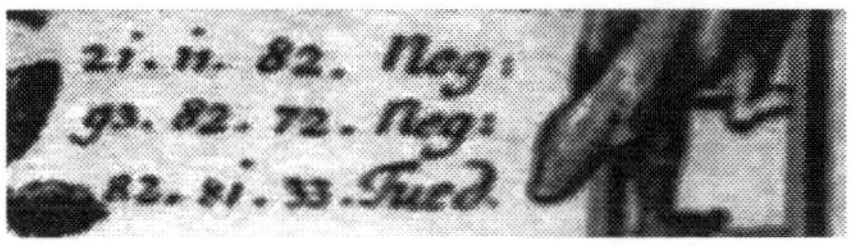

2i. i1. 82. Neg: <> Gen$_{[esis]}$ 28:11.12
93. 82. 72. Neg: <> Gen$_{[esis]}$ 27:28.39
82. 8i. 33. Tued. <> Deut$_{[eronomy]}$ 33:18.28

Genesis 28:11

וַיִּפְגַּע בַּמָּקוֹם וַיָּלֶן שָׁם כִּי־בָא הַשֶּׁמֶשׁ וַיִּקַּח מֵאַבְנֵי הַמָּקוֹם וַיָּשֶׂם מְרַאֲשֹׁתָיו וַיִּשְׁכַּב בַּמָּקוֹם הַהוּא׃

And he [Jacob][197] ***lighted upon a certain place, and tarried there all night, because the sun*** [of Awareness] ***was set; and he took of the stones*** [consciousness-] ***of that place, and put*** [them for] ***his pillows, and lay down in that place to sleep.***

The man depicted in the engraving is the Biblical Jacob. He is a paradigmatic figure representing every-human. Jacob, before he became *Israel*, namely God's power, stopped here, in this consciousness-*of* the material condition grounded into the mineral state of the world under the moon.

Genesis 28:12

וַיַּחֲלֹם וְהִנֵּה סֻלָּם מֻצָּב אַרְצָה וְרֹאשׁוֹ מַגִּיעַ הַשָּׁמָיְמָה וְהִנֵּה מַלְאֲכֵי אֱלֹהִים עֹלִים וְיֹרְדִים בּוֹ׃

And he dreamed,[198] and behold a ladder set up on the earth, and the top[199] of it reached to heaven: and behold the angels of God ascending and descending on it.

In Jacob's dream

"*The Transcendent-Awareness*[200] *stood above it,* and said.../
Thy seed shall be as the dust of the earth, and ... all the families of the earth be blessed./
And, behold, I [am] *with thee.../*
And Jacob awaked out of his sleep, and he said, 'surely the Lord is in this place [of objectivity]*; and I knew*[201] [it] *not'./*
And he... said ... this [objective world is]*... the house of God, and this* [is] *the gate of heaven* [Awareness]*./*
And Jacob rose up early in the morning, and took the stone [object] *that he had put* [for] *his pillows, and set it up* [for] *a pillar .../*
And this stone... shall be God's house [where Awareness abides]."[202]

As described by the *Biblical* passage, similarly in the illustration, it is night. Moon and stars are shining. Jacob stopped his daily wakeful wandering and rested, sleeping

on the earthly stone. He dreamt of a ladder stretching from the immanent to the Transcendent. The ladder is Hermes' caduceus,[203] it is a metaphor for the Central Force of Life. On it, the two messengers (מַלְאָךְ *mal'ak*) from Awareness or theophanic angels (ἄγγελοι *aggeloi*) are the two epistemic polarities, *i.e.* subject/object, moving up and down on that stairway. They

sublimate or materialize each step vivifying it. Three parts divide the visible portions of the ladder. The first stretch of steps is below the angels. There, the messenger moves on the wakefulness of existence.

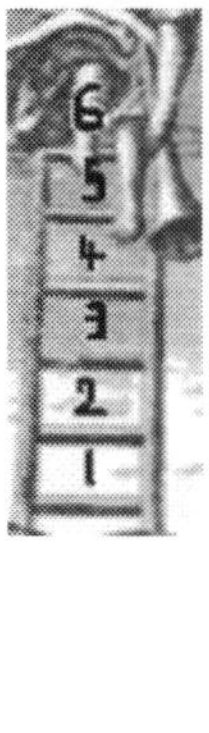

Subsequently, it steps into desirous-dreams. After, it enters into dreamless-sleep. The messengers go up and down our daily existence. The lower angel is life, the higher one is death. The second stretch of the visible ladder is between the two angels. It is life's Axis with six different states of mind. Namely, they are, 1st) Vitality, 2nd)

Libido, 3rd) Power, 4th) Heart-Centrality, 5th) Purification and 6th) Love.

This ladder is different from the stairway of the world; it leads nowhere, only to a discarded bus stop,[204]

"because it makes the crooked way seem straight."[205]

The third stretch of this Plate's visible ladder is composed only of one-step and it is above all angels. It is the seventh step into Ecstatic Heaven transcending all angels. In that Heaven, there are ten stars. In the Jewish Hermetic *Kabbalah,*[206] they correspond to the ten Sephiroth of the tree of life. They are emanations of the Will, Awareness and Consciousness through which the Transcendent reveals Itself.

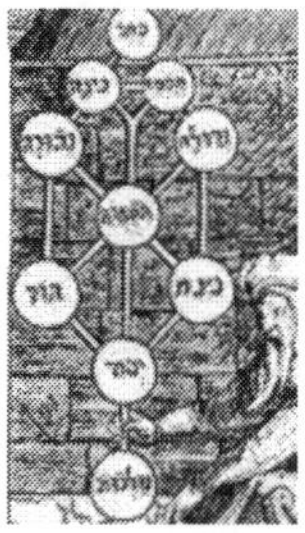

As the power of in-breath, the caduceus is a circular-thunderbolt stretching upwards from the clear water of Pure Awareness.[207]

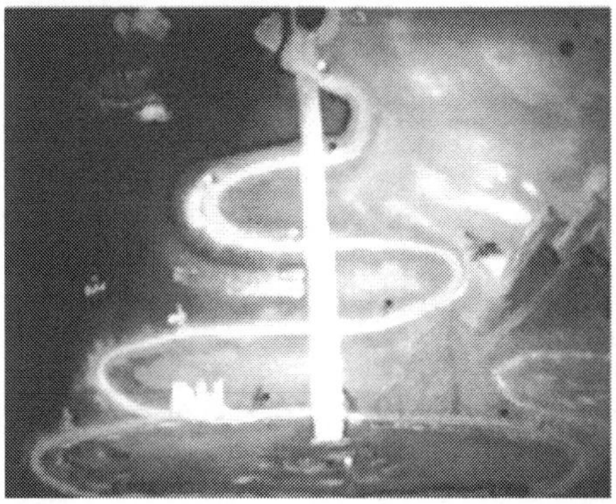

The graphic and the text of Plate 1 portray the *"circadian rhythms."*[208] Namely, the rhythmic cycle that influences all organisms. The sleep-cycle is affected by the continuous

"returning again and again to its origin."[209]

In fact, wakefulness is followed and preceded by sleep. Sleep enters into dreams trailed by deep sleep with no dreams. This, in turn, goes back to dreams and again into wakefulness. In Plate 1, this *circadian rhythm* is portrayed as a flowery rose wreath with thorns, symbols for the pains of life.

Furthermore, the wreath has smaller branches with two  leaves, indicating both wakefulness/dream stages, and three  leaves, to include dreamless sleep. The knot  of being or of the heart[210] ties and keeps the continuous circularity of the garland together. Untying it, as the Buddha does,[211] means to reach liberation. The garland resembles the cosmic Indian circle of fire  into which Śiva-Naṭa-rāja, the Auspicious Cosmic-Dance-King, tramples over the dwarf of ignorance Apa-smāra, namely, the one who is without-remembrance of Apodictical Awareness.

The *Māṇḍūkya Upanishad*[212] (circa 700 BC) described in detail the oneiric cycles.[213] Thousands of years before, the *Vedas* reported that those cycles had been discovered by ancient Indian sages while

"*searching in the heart with introspection.*"[214]

The text identified three different stages of life, namely, wake, dream and sleep without dreams. They correspond also to body, mind and spirit. Furthermore, they are birth, life and death. Finally, they are past, present and future. These three treads are symbolically represented by the trident of Neptune or the *triśula*  of the Indian god Śiva. Those three stages are all unified in a fourth stage represented as a dewdrop.[215]  The Indian tradition calls it *bindu*,[216] the drop of water, of oil or the *zero-dot* (*bindu*), which is the essence of everything. If we want to ascribe any number to the Transcendent, we should say that it is *zero* (*śūnyatā*),[217] the great Indian cypher intuition. In the *Upanishad*, each of the four stages of life is indicated by a letter-sound, thus, AUM (sound ॐ *OM*) surmounted by the fourth one (◡̇), a silent point called *bindu* •.

• The fourth *mute* state is the silence from which we come. It is the dewdrop encompassing all the following three stages. 

▽△

M sound is the deep sleep dreamless third state. Oneiric researches call it the stage of NREM (Non Rapid Eyes Movements). 

▽△

U sound is the dream second state. Oneiric researches call it the stage of REM (Rapid Eyes Movements). 

▽△

A sound is the waking state. 

▽△

• The fourth *mute* state is the silence to which we go. It is the dewdrop encompassing all the preceding three. 

> "The states of dreaming and of waking consciousness appear not to be fundamentally different from one another. We can experience a kind of *inward turning* of our thoughts and mental images during waking periods that resembles dreaming."[218]

The state of dreamless sleep is un-known to the waking and dream state. However, it is like a pure intuition without objectivity emanating from the other two states. This emanation never loses its wholeness. It is as if

> *"One, not asleep, casts a look upon the sleeping senses."*[219]

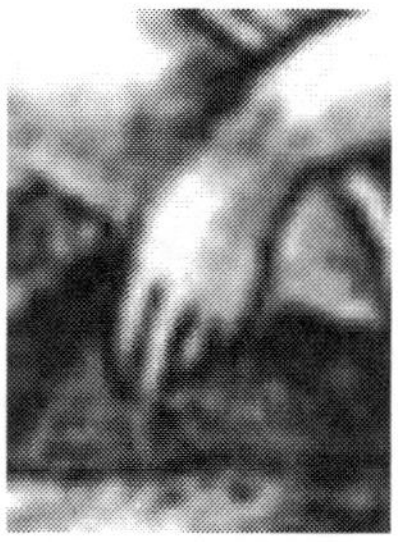

True awakening really takes place when Awareness is present on all four levels. In the drawing, only Jacob's left hand is visible. It is hanging down towards the Earth and it is showing only three fingers. He is indicating that to climb heaven's ladder one must start from the bottom.

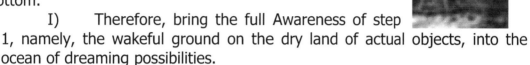

I) Therefore, bring the full Awareness of step 1, namely, the wakeful ground on the dry land of actual objects, into the ocean of dreaming possibilities.

II) Again, bring the full Awareness of step 2, now in the watery dream state of all possible objects, into the stillness of dreamless sleep.

III) Likewise, step, with the full Awareness of step 3, now in the objectless realm, on to the mute silence of the fourth state.

IV) This is the beginning and the end of all those states. In our Plate, the angel is about to move on step 4 with the right foot. Note that it is from this step that he blows his wake-up bugle.

On the fourth level is where Isaac realized Jacob to be the Certainty of Awareness,

> *"as the smell of a field which the LORD hath blessed."*[220]

Genesis 27:28

וַיִּתֶּן־לְךָ הָאֱלֹהִים מִטַּל הַשָּׁמַיִם וּמִשְׁמַנֵּי הָאָרֶץ וְרֹב דָּגָן וְתִירֹשׁ׃

Therefore God give thee [Jacob][221] ***of the dew*** [the regenerative rose] ***of heaven*** [Transcendent Awareness]***, and the fatness of the earth, and plenty of corn and wine*** [all-encompassing Awareness]**.**

Continuing in our *Bible* reading, consciousness/Esau

> *"also had made savoury meat, and brought it unto his father, and said unto his father, Let my father arise, and eat of his son's hunt, that thy soul may bless me./*
> *And Isaac his father said unto him, Who* [art] *thou? And he said, I* [am] *thy son, thy firstborn Esau./*
> *And Isaac trembled very exceedingly, and said, Who? where* [is] *he that hath taken venison, and brought* [it to] *me, and I have eaten of all before thou camest, and have blessed him? yea,* [and] *he shall be blessed."*[222]

Awareness/Jacob has been blessed and recognized as the foundation of the entire world, including Esau/consciousness-*of* the objects.

> *"And Isaac answered and said unto Esau, Behold, I have made him* [*i.e.* Awareness] *thy lord, and all his brethren have I given to him for servants; and with*

corn and wine have I sustained him: and what shall I do now unto thee, my son?/
And Esau said unto his father, Hast thou but one blessing, my father? bless me, [even] *me also, O my father."*[223]

Genesis 27:39

וַיַּעַן יִצְחָק אָבִיו וַיֹּאמֶר אֵלָיו הִנֵּה מִשְׁמַנֵּי הָאָרֶץ יִהְיֶה מוֹשָׁבֶךָ וּמִטַּל הַשָּׁמַיִם מֵעָל׃
And Isaac his father answered and said unto him, Behold, thy dwelling shall be the fatness of the earth, and of the dew of heaven from above;

Therefore, Esau/consciousness-*of* becomes the *hunter* of the subject-object immanent realm, namely the *fatness of the earth*, which is sustained by *the dew* of heavenly Awareness.

Deuteronomy 33:18

וְלִזְבוּלֻן אָמַר שְׂמַח זְבוּלֻן בְּצֵאתֶךָ וְיִשָּׂשכָר בְּאֹהָלֶיךָ׃
And of Zebulun he [Moses] ***said, Rejoice, Zebulun, in thy going out; and, Issachar, in thy tents.***

In fact, Moses, blessing

"*the children of Israel before his death*"[224]

confirms that Zebulun,[225] an exalted son of Jacob, rejoices in pursuing the *external* objectivity of the world, while, Issachar,[226] the reworded one, remains in the tent[227] of the internal tabernacle. There,

"*the eternal God* [is thy] *refuge.*"[228]

Deuteronomy 33:28

וַיִּשְׁכֹּן יִשְׂרָאֵל בֶּטַח בָּדָד עֵין יַעֲקֹב אֶל־אֶרֶץ דָּגָן וְתִירוֹשׁ אַף־שָׁמָיו יַעַרְפוּ טָל׃
Israel then shall dwell in safety alone: the fountain of Jacob [shall be] ***upon a land of corn and wine; also his heavens shall drop down dew.***

This last Biblical verse, quoted by Altus, confirms our hermeneutical clarification. In fact, Israel, the one in whom *Transcendent-Awareness-prevails*, shall be *alone* (בדד *badad*), separated in a trusted security (בֶּטַח *betach*),[229] distinct from the consciousness-*of*-the-object. Awareness, therefore, is Jacob's fountain. The word *fountain* (עין *`ayin*) means mental-and-spiritual-faculty which *irrigates* the land (אֶרֶץ *'erets*) of objectivity with an abundance of food for thought (*i.e.* corn = דגן *dagan*)[230] and possession (*i.e.* wine = תירוש *tiyrowsh*).[231] The Heavenly *fountain* is the roof (טל *tal*)[232] from which comes down the vivifying moisture, the dew (טל *tal*) of the Transcendent.

"*Happy* [art] *thou, O Israel: who* [is] *like unto thee, O people saved by the LORD, the shield of thy help, and who* [is] *the sword of thy excellency! and thine enemies shall be found liars unto thee; and thou shalt tread upon their high places.*"[233]

"*The very purpose of Self-inquiry* <u>*is to focus the entire mind*</u> *at its Source. It is not, therefore, a case of one 'I' searching for another 'I.' Much less is Self-inquiry an empty formula, for it involves an intense activity of the entire mind to keep it steadily poised in pure Self-awareness...* [God] *is always the first person, the 'I,' ever standing before you. Because you give precedence to worldly things, God appears to have reached to the background. If you give up all else and seek Him alone, He alone will remain as the 'I,' the Self."*[234]

In the *Upanishad*, the immortal hero Naciketa urges Death-Mṛtyu,

"Arise! Awake! Having obtained the boons, learn! The sages declare that the path, [as] *a sharp edge of a razor,* [is] *of difficult access* [and] *difficult to cross."*[235]

<<Hesiod[236] had stated that Death-Thanatos was the twin of Sleep-Hypnos, both sons of Nyx-Night and Erebos-Darkness. Therefore, Naciketa urges Death to awaken, to arise from the descending process of creation and to proceed awake through the four steps>>[237] of life.

"Know thyself,"[238]

declares the oracle of Delphi, because

"an unexamined life is not worth living... however, it is not easy to convince you,"[239]

explains Socrates.

"Awake, o sleeper, and arise from the dead, and Christ shall give you light."[240]

"All I can do [admits Tolle] is remind you of what you have forgotten."[241]

"O intelligence, remember the deed, remember o intentional-will, remember the magic, remember."[242]

<<Thus, at the time of death, as the world fades-away, by remembering that deed, we realize that it was the *consciousness-of* which produced the *objective-world-as-it-is-for-us*. This understanding will focus only on consciousness itself, on the Apodictical-Certitude-of-Awareness-in-Itself, beyond the world of representations. Then, we will remember the golden age (*kṛta*), the fourth (*kṛta*) stage of AUM, the silence from which all derives and in which all merges.>>[243]

"The decisive test is to go beyond the Field of Death, [declares Scaligero] to recognize the deadly power of the oblivion of the original sound: because that sound is the memory that guards the meaning of the deed and its orientation. Who remembers the sound, overcomes the apparent death of the soul: overcomes the danger to believe as true this death... Man would not have lost immortality, if he had renounced knowledge."[244]

PLATE 2: "THE EPISTEMIC PATH" (FIRST ASCENSION)

The Way that leads to the realization of Awareness or to the Realization of Enlightenment

THE EPISTEMIC PROCESS

A bright Sun towers above the second plate. What is the meaning of that star in this picture? As the sun makes everything visible, similarly, Awareness dispels the clouds of ignorance. Everything that exists depends on it. Even when we think of something being apart from our awareness, nevertheless that thought finds its foundation on Awareness.

> *"In the beginning was the Fundamental-Evidence,*[245] *and the Evidence was with God, and the Evidence was God... All things were made by him; and without him was not any thing made that was made."*[246]

The Sun in this plate is a metaphor of Awareness. Under It, on the right, appears to be a suggestion of the physical sun.[247]

The *Bṛhadāraṇyaka Upanishad* reports a revealing conversation between sage Yājñavalkya and Janaka, King of Videha.

> *"The supreme ruler politely asked him. -O Yājñavalkya, which one is the real light of a person?-*
>
> *He answered, -Truthfully, one has the light of the sun, o Supreme Ruler. Indeed, due to the sun, one has light and one stays, moves, performs work and then returns.-*
>
> *The king replied, -You are so right, o Yājñavalkya. However, o Yājñavalkya, when the sun has set, which one is the real light of a person?-*
>
> *He answered, -The moon, verily, is one's light. Indeed, due to the moon, one has light and one stays, moves, performs work and then returns.-*
>
> *The king replied, -You are so right, o Yājñavalkya. However, o Yājñavalkya, when the sun has set and the moon has set, which one is the real light of a person?-*
>
> *He answered, -Fire, verily, is one's light. Indeed, due to fire, one has light and one stays, moves, performs work and then returns.-*
>
> *The king replied, -You are so right, o Yājñavalkya. However, o Yājñavalkya, when the sun has set and the moon has set and fire is extinguished, which one is the real light of a person?-*
>
> *He answered, -The word-idea, verily, is one's light. Indeed, due to the word-idea, one has light and one stays, moves, performs work and then returns. For that reason, o Supreme Ruler, also if one's hand is not seen, when the word-idea is uttered, still one may intend it.-*
>
> *The king replied, -You are so right, o Yājñavalkya. However, o Yājñavalkya, when the sun has set, and the moon has set,*

the fire is extinguished and the word-idea has quieted down, which one is the real light of a person?-

He answered, -The Self is one's light. Indeed, due to the Self, this one has the light of intelligence, exists, and perceives, acts and returns.-

Then,' the king asked, -Which one is the Self?-

Yājñavalkya replied, -This person, who is composed of knowledge among the vital senses, is the light within the heart. Being serenely centered in itself, It penetrates both worlds [of wakefulness and dream] *as if It were thinking and moving back and forth. Upon entering the dream state, It goes beyond this dimension and the forms of death... It sleeps dreaming by his own light by his own brightness. In this state, the person becomes self-illuminated... Being Supreme Brahman-Awareness one goes to Brahman-Awareness... When all desires, which are fastened in one's heart, are shed, then, the mortal becomes immortal. In this manner one reaches the Supreme* [Aware] *Spirit.-"*[248]

In the New Testament Jesus is Self-Awareness-in-Itself, he is

"*the light of life*"[249] that "*shineth in darkness, and the darkness comprehended it not... That was the true Light, which lighteth every man that cometh into the world.*"[250]

Again, the Sun, at the top of our tablet, is a metaphor for Awareness and is not a representation of the star of our solar system. In fact, the central part of the plate portrays  another sun on the head of a man  and a moon on a woman's forehead. Both represent the subject and the object. Again, both are depicted in the lower part of the tablet. They represent the two polarities of the process of knowledge.

The draperies  over the two heads remind us that all the events depicted in these plates are allegories of internal (*sub specie interioritatis*) paradigms. They are the hidden internal psychological realities of the external appearance (*sub specie exterioritatis*) of things.

S O

noesi *noema*

On one side there is the **S**ubject, the knower represented as a kneeling man. The praying posture expresses its ***noetic*** aspect, namely ***the subjective property of experience as an act-of-perception aiming to grasp the object***.

On the other side, a woman on her knees symbolizes the object, namely that which is known. The hands and arms' positions symbolize its ***noematic*** aspect, namely ***the objective property of experience in its modes-of-being-given to the subject***.

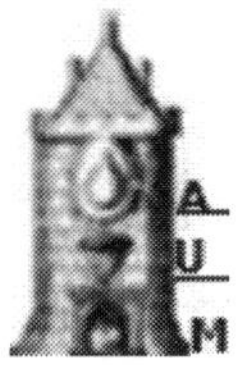

Between the two polarities, the athanor, the channel (*sushumnā*) of the furnace, or the ladder symbolizes the human psyche uniting the **S**ubject and the **O**bject in an indivisible synthesis. This athanor has three levels, one for each state of life. The fire is  consciousness, which *cooks* and  fuses together the two  sides producing knowledge. That  *heated* synthetic unity is the dewdrop.  Namely, it is the point of consciousness-*of*-the-objective-world represented by the two hands of the subject/man united in prayer. 

The awakening, portrayed in the previous vignette, takes place when the consciousness' fire keeps distilling that dew  until it evaporates ascending to the Heaven of Awareness, as  pointed out by the hands of the object/woman, along 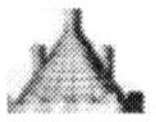 the athanor's channel or *sushumnā*, the  ladder that leads to the Transcendent. In fact, those hand gestures are commands. The left hand  indicates, −Take that dew, namely the synthesis of consciousness, and distill it.− The right hand orders, − Direct this synthesis, through this athanor, into the dimension above.−

In other words, the consciousness-*of* the object placed before us is the knowledge-*of* the object itself. However, in our daily experiences, we identify with the object forgetting the consciousness, which makes it possible. We should *focus*[251] *firing* only on consciousness as such. When we keep *focusing*, *burning* and *cooking* that knowledge, we *distill* subjectivity from objectivity. The new *spirit* obtained is the *dew*, the *bindu* (•) or the essence of pure consciousness, what the Buddhists call mindfulness.[252]

The composition of this dew is not only of the waking state, but also the dream and dreamless sleep. In fact, the three, 1) Apollo the Sun, 2) Neptune on the world's boulder with a dolphin, the fish traversing the two banks of life's river, and 3) Isis the Moon, are united as one in the symbol of Neptune's trident,  namely the three levels, A, U and M, as we explained before.

In other words, the waking, dreaming and dreamless-sleep states are all awake in the Certainty of Awareness. The two angels on the ladder awakening into the Transcendent, as in the previous vignette, are now taking Israel, the Preserving Power of God, to the Heaven of the realization of his own Self-Awareness.

The logical distinction between subject and object is that the subject thinks and →*sees* the object-*id*ea as an *id*ol in-itself placed before and outside the subject.[253] It is like the reflected light of the moon. At night, it seems as if it emanates its own light, not reflecting that of the Sun. Likewise, the moon/object is conceived as impressing its own radiance on the mind←. In other words, the luminous *building block* of Awareness is *discarded*[254] and the object/idea is erroneously perceived as self-luminous, namely, as transcendent. The mind, mesmerized by thought, as if a *goddess* (below), ignores Awareness (above), which is the only one that *certifies* with unshakable *faith* the idea.

The point that we want to make here is not on reflection as such, but on the reflected conceived, during the process of knowledge, as real in itself, like Narcissus enamored by his own watery reflection.[255]

In Villa of the Mysteries, Pompeii, Italy (15 BC 15 AD), there is a fresco, which clarifies this same concept. On a mural a

"young man is being initiated... The initiator is on the left and his assistant is behind the groom. The youth is told to look in this metal bowl and he will see his own face, his own true face. However, the bowl is so concave inside that what he sees is not his own face but the distorted mask of old age, which the assistant holds up behind him. With a shock he is introduced to what our American Indians call the *long body* - the whole body of life from birth to death."[256]

The shock of the man derives from considering true the reflected image, without realizing that it is a reflection of a reality coming from elsewhere. In other words, it is like assuming one's own dream as real while missing oneself as the dreamer.

Awareness, then, is the certitude or *faith,*[257] which is present even in dreams. That faith is the certitude sustaining everything also dreams and non-dreaming states. No one can deny having a dream. We can question what they may be without the dreamer. We never question if we had one.

We distinguish faith from belief. By faith, we intend apodictical-self-evident-*certitude*. By belief, we mean accepting a dogma as true in-itself, with no evidence. We are Certain-Aware of the dogma as a belief, but we are <u>never</u> aware of the existence in-itself of that, which is imagined or believed to be in-itself. Awareness, however, is hidden by the object's reflection. In fact,

> "*I will hide my face from them, I will see what their end* [shall be]: *for they* [are] *a very froward generation, children in whom* [is] *no faith.*"[258]
>
> "*For verily I say unto you, If ye have faith as a grain of mustard seed, ye shall say unto this mountain, Remove hence to yonder place; and it shall remove; and nothing shall be impossible unto you.*"[259]

PLATE 3: "THE PSYCHOLOGICAL TOPOGRAPHY OF EMANATION"

**Creation manifests itself in the four stages of life:
waking, dreaming, sleeping and beyond.**

AWARENESS

Awareness is not consciousness-*of-something*.

By Awareness, we mean Truth, Certainty or *Apodictic-Faith*, without which, consciousness can never be *conscious-of-anything*. Awareness in Itself is Transcendence, of which nothing can be said, because,

"*no one has ever seen Transcendence.*"[260]

However, all that is said or seen or thought is based upon It. It is the Awareness that is not awareness. It is the Way that is not the way.

"*It is the Tao that is not the Tao.*"[261]

Therefore, the only method to express it is through symbols.

> "Symbols contain volumes of encoded information and are incredibly powerful in an understated way. They convey meanings directly and intuitively without words. Symbols can lead and focus us. We have gone to war behind banners bearing crosses, stars, and magical beasts like lions, eagles, and dragons. Corporations, even nations, represent the essence of their identities with logos. Think of the United States and you focus on the nobility inherent in the Statue of Liberty...
>
> Symbols... can serve as pathways to higher consciousness. Sacred art... give[s] us a detailed road map into divine states of mind. By meditating on each layer, each mazelike pathway, and entering each symbol in the painting, you can pass through a process that re-creates the stages on a spiritual path."[262]

The many symbols on this plate are milestones of our psychophysical map. At the very top sits Zeus-Jupiter, the Apodictic-Awareness-Itself in the form of a timeless  *old* man overlooking everything. Without Awareness, in fact, nothing would be. He manifests this entire World with an ample motion of his unarmed  hand, which is open to reassure not to be afraid. He commands,

"*Let there be light.*"[263]

This is the illuminating-shining-light (אוֹר *'owr*) of Awareness. It is the brightness of Certainty. It is the light of light, without which light itself would not be. Indeed, He is above the Sun  and the Moon, above the Subject and the Object. They are

"*the greater light to rule the day, and the lesser light to rule the night.*"[264]

He rides an Eagle,

"symbol of the  direct perception of intellectual light,"[265]

On that bird, Awareness soars above the entire depth[266] of the Celestial Waters,[267] the inscrutable Ocean of Transcendence, and the

"*firmament in the midst of the waters.*"[268]

Finally, the scepter held by Awareness is the Tree of Life. It  is the central staff of the Hermetic caduceus without the subject-object serpents. It is, as we have seen, the pillar of the world, the *axis-mundi* (*sushumnā*). On its top sits the bloomed flower of ecstasy symbolizing the Pure-*Gold* of Apodictical-Awareness. On that seat, God rests from the manifestation of creation. 

As we have seen, above all the circles predominates Transcendent Awareness. Below, on the first circle, sits the Manifestation  of the world. Under her, on the second circle, takes place Creation.  Finally, in the third circle the subject and object sit in a boat on the sea. 

However, starting from the center, all circles are interconnected. The fishing line itself becomes a tracing string. It is like the thread that Ariadne gave Theseus to trace his steps out of the deadly maze of the Minotaur and back to life.[269] 

THE MANIFESTATION

On the first circle, below Awareness sits a woman. She represents *la Manifestation,*[270] the Manifestation of the World. Manifestation (Latin *mani-festus*) is that, which is struck (*festus*) with a hand (*manū*). In fact, she gives direct evidence with her hand by pointing at  a formation  of ten ducks or doves or seagulls. In the vignette, there is also a turkey or a peacock displaying a full wheel. What do all these birds symbolize?

The peacock symbolizes the totality of nature and its manifestations.[271] The turkey, in 1677, was still considered a new bird from the Americas, a novel world discovered less than two centuries before. Therefore, it represents the new emergence of Consciousness manifesting the World immediately following the stillness of Awareness. Ramana Maharshi states that,

> "*When the mind comes out of the Self, the world appears. Therefore, when the world appears* (to be real)*, the Self does not appear.*"[272]

> "The turkey is sometimes called the earth eagle. It has a long history of association with spirituality and the honoring of the Earth Mother. It is a symbol of all the blessings that the Earth contains... The... turkey helped create the world."[273]

Both the peacock-wheel and the turkey's wheel represent the circular totality of the entire universe.

The flight of the ducks, on the other hand, symbolizes

> "the relation between heaven and earth."[274]

The white duck or gander is equivalent to the swan, the Sanskrit *haṃsa*, the water bird which goes (√*han*) from earth to heaven. The Supreme-Swan (*parama-haṃsa*) stand as a metaphor for

> "'the Universal Soul or Supreme Spirit', identified with... Vishṇu, Śiva... and the Sun... According to Sāyaṇācārya resolvable into *ahaṃ sa* , 'I am That'."[275]

In the Bible, the swan becomes a dove,

> "*straightway coming up out of the water, he saw the heavens opened, and the Spirit like a dove descending upon him.*"[276]

In Greek, the word dove, *peristerá* (περιστερὰ), derives from *perasch-Istar*, the "bird of Ishtar,"[277] the Assyrian-Babylonian fertility goddess. The *Egyptian Book of the Dead* calls the Primeval Duck the Great Cackler uttering the first sound

> "*when the earth was submerged in silence.*"[278]

Overall, the duck, as the seagull, is the herald from the water world, it is the

> "messenger from the Other World."[279]

Nevertheless, the ten ducks or doves or seagulls, are Neptune's birds who "are the owners of daylight."[280]

They are the symbols of the ten Sephiroth (סְפִירוֹת) as described in the traditional *Kabbalah* (קַבָּלָה).[281] They are the lesser lights that, from the Crown (כֶּתֶר *keter*), the One Light of Awareness, exhibit themselves in ten degrees. They manifest themselves as Mindfulness, Consciousness and, all the way down, as consciousness-*of* this objective world. They are the ten emanations that, from the Supreme-Infinite-Awareness, Ayn Sof (אֵין סוֹף), display themselves throughout the entire creative process all in each of the Four Worlds (עוֹלָמוֹת *Olamot*), *i.e.* the four states or levels of A) waking, U) dreaming, M) dreamless sleep and •) Transcendence.

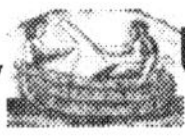

The third circle is where the sky separates the Celestial Waters of Pure-Awareness above from the waters below. These lower waters are the infinite possibilities of all the world's objects. They are also the infinite dimensions of endless universes in which each countless instant is frozen in the stillness of timeless Awareness. This is the stage of intuition, the necessary element without which there would be no discursive process. In fact, it is impossible to say something logically meaningful without its thought being completely formed in the mind before its utterance. Furthermore, it is the beginning of all possible knowledge and consciousness. Studies on consciousness and unconsciousness have

> "suggested that … our actions are initiated by unconscious mental processes long before we become aware [*i.e.* conscious-] of our intention to act. [№1-3] In a previous experiment [№1]… conscious decision… was preceded by a few hundred milliseconds by a negative brain potential, the so-called 'readiness potential' that originates from the <u>s</u>upplementary <u>m</u>otor <u>a</u>rea (SMA), a brain region involved in motor preparation. Because brain activity in the SMA consistently preceded the conscious decision, it has been argued that the brain had already unconsciously made a decision to move even before the subject became aware [*i.e.* conscious-] of it."[282]

The Self is the *internal regulator*, who, in the state of deep sleep without dreams,

> "*does not know, except that, while not knowing, he is still the knower. In fact, knowledge does not separate from the knower, because he is imperishable. Merely, in that state, there is no otherness and nothing else that he may know.*"[283]

<<In other words, the objective world, in the state of deep sleep without dreams, is always present and unified with the pure potential consciousness, which is not yet in actuality. This is also the case of cataleptic and comatose states. In fact, when all senses are gone, when all thoughts are gone and when conscience-*of* this Ego

is gone what is there left? Whatsoever is left must be the same foundation of the senses, of the thoughts and of the consciousness-*of* this Ego.

Being without otherness is like a unified ocean.[284]

> '*Thus, after all dissolves, alone this one remains awake. From this vacuity, this one truly awakes this world consisting of Pure Awareness. This world is meditated by that one and, verily, in that one it dissolves.*'[285]

From deep sleep, the self

> '*returns, as he came, again to the dream state, the place he departed from, and from here to the state of wakefulness.*'[286]

Therefore, similar to an electron, jumping between orbits, or a frog, hopping between ponds, the self leaps from one dimension of life into another state and beyond.>>[287]

The Siren

At the very bottom of the murky lower waters abides the Siren, the monster, which seduces the living, *i.e.* the sea goers who encounter death having been mesmerized by the infinite possibilities of objectivity.

Life is a sea  voyage in which "sirens are pitfalls arising from desires, and passions,"[288] which find their manifestations in dreams. The siren of desire lives in the unconscious state of the dreamless sleep and she is netted

 and caged  by objectivity  and fished 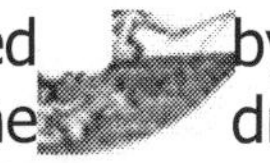 by subjectivity  in the next circle-stage, namely the dream state.

That fishing web is like Indra's net, which

"stretches out infinitely in all directions. A jewel hangs in each vertex reflecting every other Jewel in the Net. Symbolically, the Jewel is each one of us, every individual intimately united with every other being and thing by conscious reflection."[289]

THE CREATION

The English word creation derives from the Indo-European root √*kṛ*, meaning, as in the equivalent Hebrew *bara'* (בָּרָא), to do, to make, to form. The Sanskrit *kṛ* means also

"to direct the thoughts... towards any object... to think."[290]

In any case, independently from the reality or unreality of creation, the word has a specific meaning and we are interested in that meaning only as such. The word creation implies, *ideally*,[291] an act *producing something out of nothing*. Namely, nothing must have been there *before* the act itself, not even a *before* or an *after*. Indeed, if creation is, that act itself must create Time and Space. In fact, if time and space *predated* the creative act, it would have been an entity subjecting God to its own *temporality* and spatiality, which would be a contradiction in terms. Consequently, since the act of creation conceptually implies the production of time and space, it infers that the event takes place in a timeless/spaceless dimension. On the contrary, evolution is necessarily within time and space, it implies time and space. Therefore, *Creation* is not an antonym of *Random Evolutionary Processes*. Both do not exclude each other. In fact, the process of evolution is in time and space. It is as old as the universe. It persists in it and it will continue to persist in it. Creation, on the other hand, conceptually has no time and no space. It takes place outside the past, present and future *time* frame. If the concept of creation were conceived in time and space, then, it would not be *creation*, but it would be the regular production of any *temporal/spatial* being.

Furthermore, the world, as physical and mental objects, appears only in the mind and when the mind is present. How does this happen? Thoreau asks,

"With all your science can you tell how it is, and whence it is, that light comes into the soul?"[292]

In this Plate, on the top of the second circle sits a woman. She represents Creation (*la Création*)[293] taking hold (*kṛ*) of a handmade pot, symbol of fertility. Six flowers grow in that vase, one for each day of creation.

"[In] *six days the LORD made heaven and earth, the sea, and all that* [is] *in them.*"[294]

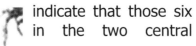

The two leaves pointing downward  indicate that those six days physically manifest themselves only in the two central circles, wakefulness and dream.

Next to the woman, from the ground sprout five flowers.

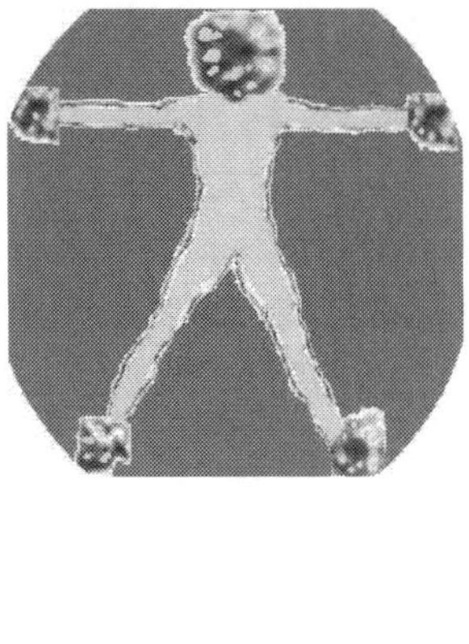

"*And the LORD God formed man* [of] *the dust of the ground, and breathed into his nostrils the breath of life; and man became a living soul.*"[295]

These other flowers symbolize the human-being endowed with five senses and with one head, two arms and two legs, metaphorically like a

"*river... parted... into four heads.*"[296]

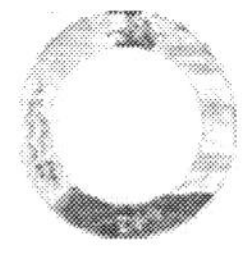

"*And God said, Let the waters under the heaven be gathered together unto one place, and let the dry* [land] *appear: and it was so.*
And God called the dry [land] *Earth; and the gathering together of the waters called he Seas...*

And God said, Let the earth bring forth grass, the herb yielding seed, [and] *the fruit tree yielding fruit after his kind, whose seed* [is] *in itself, upon the earth...*
And the earth brought forth grass, [and] *herb yielding seed after his kind, and the tree yielding fruit, whose seed* [was] *in itself, after his kind...*

And God made two great lights; the greater light [projected by the subject] *to rule the day, and the lesser light* [reflected by the object] *to rule the night...*

And God said, Let the waters bring forth abundantly the moving creature that hath life, and fowl [that] *may fly above the earth in the open firmament of heaven.*

And God created great whales, and every living creature that moveth, which the waters brought forth abundantly, after their kind, and every winged fowl after his kind...
And God blessed them, saying, Be fruitful, and multiply, and fill the waters in the seas, and let fowl multiply in the earth.
And God said, Let the earth bring forth the living creature after his kind, cattle, and creeping thing, and beast of the earth after his kind...

And God made the beast of the earth after his kind, and cattle after their kind, and every thing that creepeth upon the earth after his kind: and God *<u>saw</u>* *that* [it was] *<u>good</u>.*"[297]

It is God's conscious-*seeing* that puts the world into the *goodness* of-existence. In the symbolic time-space-*day*-circle of Creation, the world-object is intentioned by God's Mind into objectivity and thereafter is perceived as good. Thus, each *day* of Creation concludes a circle, namely, the circularity of consciousness metaphorically called *day*. The *Bṛhadāraṇyaka Upanishad* declares that,

"*he, who thus knows, is present to his own creation.*"[298]

In fact, every act of knowledge sets the object into conscious existence. To state anything, *i.e.* – This is the moon; – we must first project the moon as something different from us. Then, we must bring it in our sensory cortex. Afterwards, we must conceive it in an external dimension. Having established this perfect circularity of consciousness or, figuratively, having traveled a full day (which has nothing to do with time), only then, we can establish the moon as existent. Thus, creation or knowledge becomes a circular process.

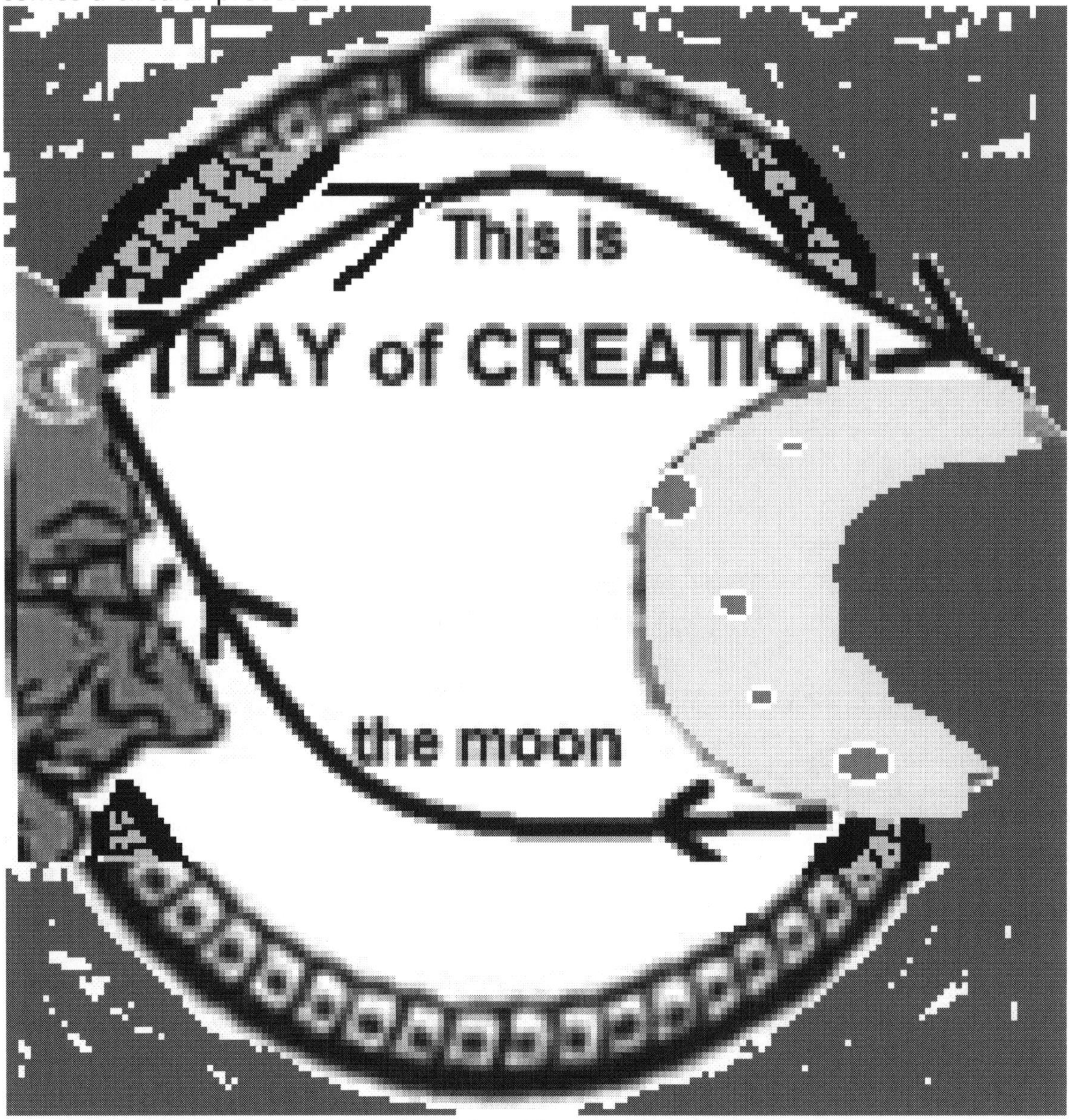

In this Plate, there are three circles. They correspond to

A) Ego-consciousness of the waking state, namely where the ego grasps itself as this physical individual right here and now;

U) I-consciousness of the dream state, namely where thought thinks itself as thought;

M) Auto-transparency of the dreamless-sleep, namely where the Self "is present to itself, without needing to mediate itself, that is to see itself before itself as object of its own knowledge."[299]

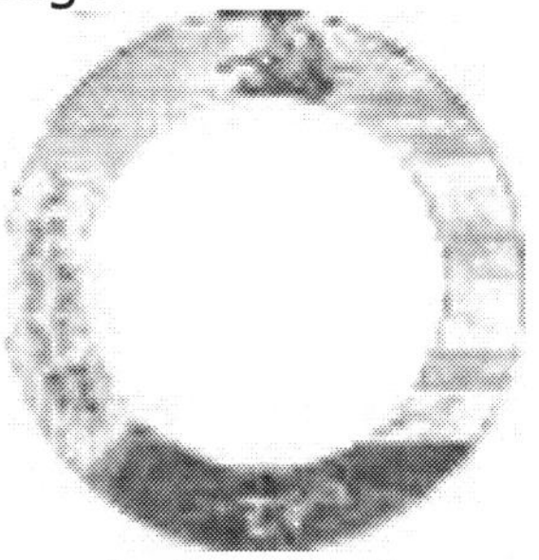

The second ring is the oneiric circle. In it, there are two animals an ovine, sheep, goat or  ram, and a bull. The first, as a sheep represents the transformation principle and the bull symbolizes fertility and the elemental power of dreams.[300]

"*They took their sheep, and their oxen, ... and that which* [was] *in the city, and that which* [was] *in the field.*"[301]

Furthermore, the ram, symbolizes the principle of individuation, which drives the action to knowledge and enjoyment. The ram and the driver of the central circle share the same symbolic meaning. They symbolize the individualized 'I' as the driver and the ram[302] of actions.

On the other hand, the bull is the symbol of fertility. In fact, the *Upanishad* says,

"*the word* [as intentionality] *should be honored as the milk cow. The vital spirit is her bull* [and] *the mind is the calf.*"[303]

The church, built in those dream created fields, is a symbol of mother womb. The tower  is the athanor of the transforming internal strength. The  cities are centers of the psyche. Moreover, the  farms are symbols of productivity.[304]

MOTIONLESS MOBILITY

The Big Bang singularity jump-started the Universe producing space and time, virtually *expanding* into a timeless/spaceless dimension beyond the Universe itself. Like in a dream, a *motionless-mobility* sets the *speed* of consciousness. Consciousness proceeds in a circular motion, metaphorically described as

> "*the space of a year's time*"[305]

or a day, *e.g.*

> "*the evening and the morning were the… day*"[306]

of creation. Consciousness, moves from the subject *outward* to reach the object. From there, it brings the object back *into* the subject. Henceforward, declares it to be *external*. The day of creation, therefore, is a journey. To be precise it is *yowm* (יום), a *day's journey*. The Hebrew word derives from a root denoting "*to be hot*." Similarly, in the *Bṛhadāraṇyaka Upanishad*, the Creator is said to be "*tired* and *heated*" (*śrāntasya taptasya*) by the flame-of-awareness (*tapas*), after which he "*rested*," viz. *aśrāmyat*, in Sanskrit, and שבת *shabath*, in Hebrew.[307]

In order to have an experience, anyone of the sense-faculties of the brain-mind-consciousness must *take-into* the brain-mind the *external* object. Namely, sight, hearing, taste, smell and touch transmit *into* the brain what they see, hear, taste, smell and touch. Consequently, the mind refers to an *external* light, sound, food, odor and perception that which has been seen, heard, tasted, smelled and touched. All this takes place at the *circular-speed* of conscious thought. However, all the senses cannot perceive the Perceiver-in-Itself. In fact,

> "*You cannot see the seer of seeing, hear the hearer of hearing, think the thinker of thinking, nor understand the understander of understanding. This is your Self which is in everything.*"[308]

The *Īśa Upanishad describes* the Self as

> "*one, motionless, faster than the mind. The faculties of the senses could not reach this, which quickly moves ahead. Being still, It surpasses others running. The life breath in It sustains all the* [beings'] *activity.*"[309]

Yājñavalkya, the Sacrifice-Speaker, when asked about

> "*the worlds' ends,*"

gave the following description of a mythical and psychological topography,

> "*This location is thirty-two times the daily course of the god's chariot.*
>
> *All around, the earth surrounds it twice as much. All around the earth, the ocean surrounds it twice as much.*"[310]

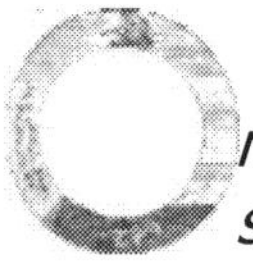

This location (*loka*) is our wakeful consciousness  surrounding and constituting us as this psychophysical conscious individual. The earth 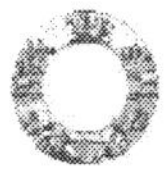 extends all around consciousness as the possibility of the objects to enter into consciousness. In fact,

"*the directions of space are infinite*"[311]

and objects change before our eyes. Also, all these possibilities are transcended by

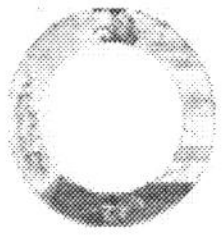

"*the Ocean,* [which] *is its source,*"[312]

"*And the Spirit of God moved upon the face of the waters…*
And … divided the waters which [were] *under the firmament from the waters which* [were] *above the firmament,*"[313]

Namely,

"*the Celestial Waters of inscrutable depth.*"[314]

Like in Plato's *Phaedrus,*[315] we must

"*understand the body as a two-wheeled chariot and also the Self as riding in the chariot [and] verily, understand consciousness as the driver of the chariot, and also the faculty of thought as the reins,*"

declares the *Kaṭha Upanishad.*[316] And

"*this self resides in the heart,…* [and] *is the heart.*"[317]

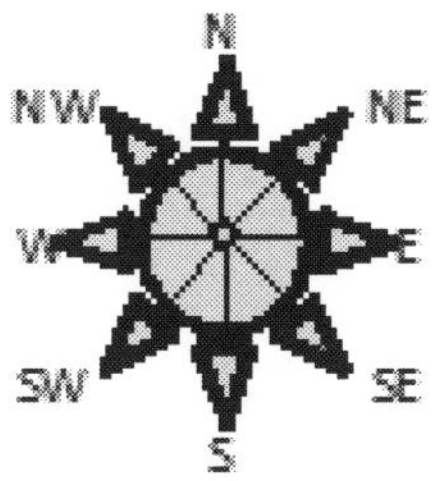

The *Bṛhadāraṇyaka Upanishad* points out that Indra is the god of the chariot, he is the self-consciousness.[318] He is the intellect, the mind that knows through the forms of space and time. In fact, as a Kabalistic Sephirothic Tree, the mind extends, in length and width, on the eight horizontal directions of the compass-rose. In height, the mind surges along the three dimensions of consciousness plus the Transcendent. Namely, they are

A) the waters as the Ego-consciousness in the waking state,
U) the ground as the I-consciousness in the dream state,
M) the atmosphere as the Auto-transparency of the state of deep sleep and
•) the sky as the primeval and final fourth state, viz. Transcendence in-Itself.

These four vertical states by the eight horizontal directions equal to

"*thirty-two times the daily course of the god's chariot.*"[319]

This is the *volume* of the internal-external space of consciousness-*of.* In a Kantian sense,

"space and time"

become the I-think *a-priori* forms of the process of knowledge. They "exist... only in us. What may be the nature of objects considered as things in themselves... is quite unknown to us. We know nothing more than our own mode of perceiving them."[320]

This Self,

"*Which alone spreadeth out the heavens,*"[321]

is faster than the mind or the senses.

"*Lo, he goeth by me, and I see* [him] *not: he passeth on also, but I perceive him not.*"[322]

"*It moves, It moves not. It* [is] *far* [and] *also near. It* [is] *within all this* [and] *It* [is] *also outside all this.*"[323]

Apodictic Certain Awareness is the Self, the life breath of all beings. It is like the hexagram or the turtle, which rests within while moving without. While it rests within its Pure Consciousness, motionlessly reaches the extreme borders of the Universe. It surpasses everything while realizing that it had never gone out of its own circular consciousness.

There is a double act. The Supreme Self <<displays itself along the entire tiered realm of reality without losing its motionless being in-itself. In other words, the Self, as the source of the light of Awareness, irradiates itself throughout the Universe, persisting in-itself as an unmoving origin.>>[324]

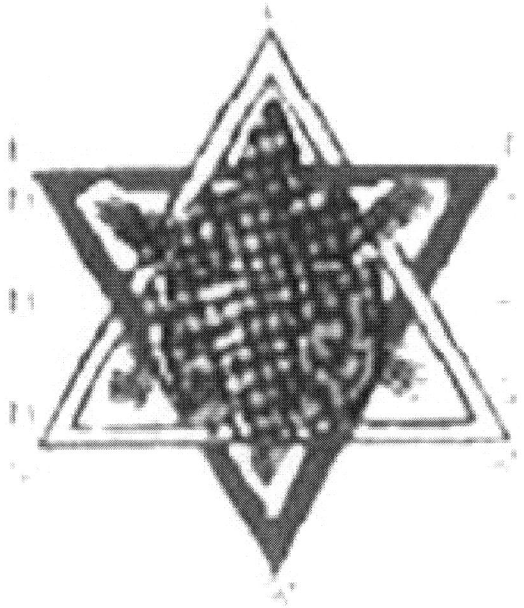

FROM DEEP SLEEP TO THE WAKING WORLD

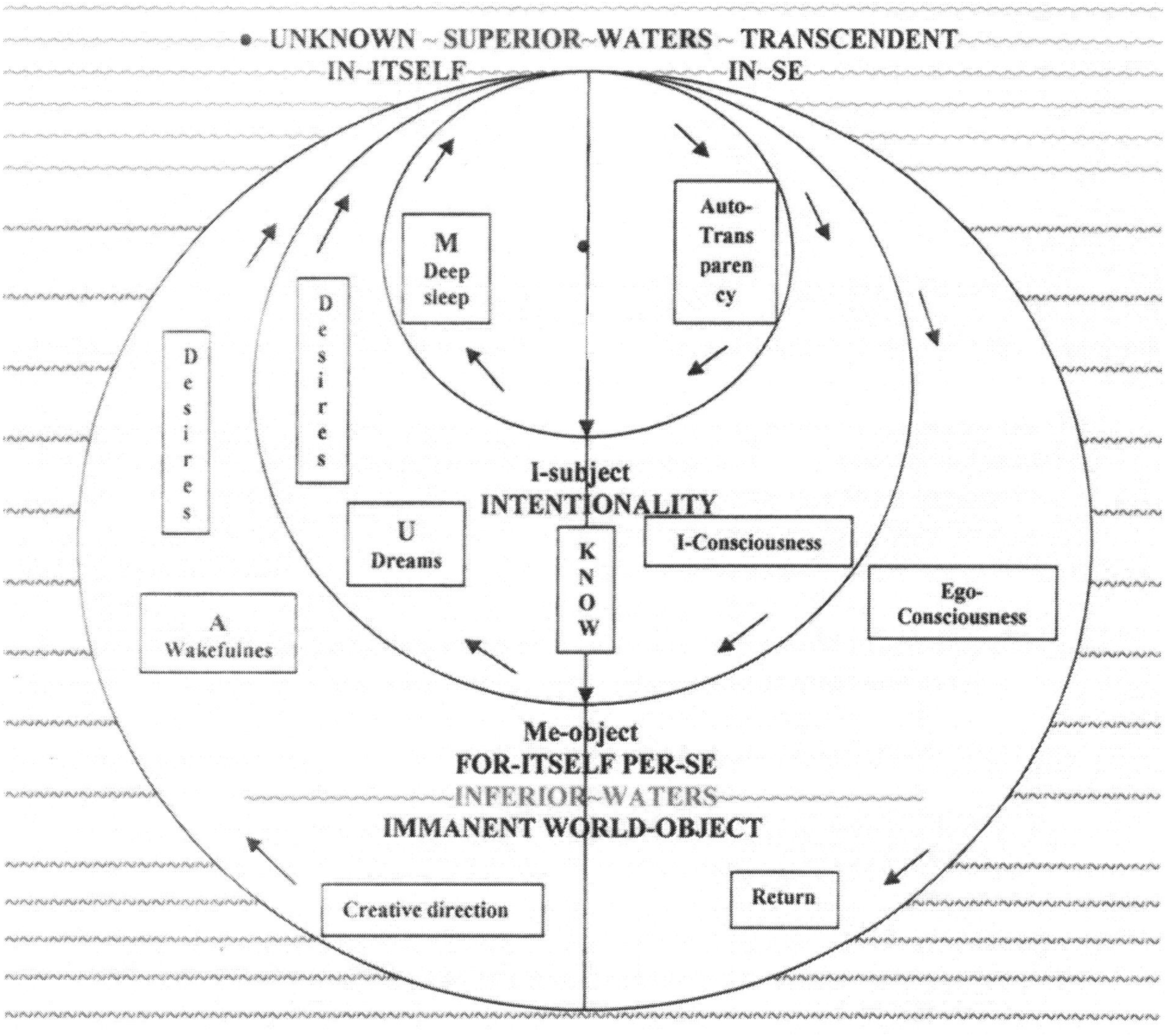

FROM THE WAKING WORLD TO THE TRANSCENDENT REALITY

All three circle-levels or stages of life are interconnected and each is the periscopic function of the next one inserted into the previous. This trine structure is indicated by the triple fins on three sea creatures, the fish,  the double-headed triton,  the siren  and by the  trident of Neptune, the god of the ocean of possibilities.

The two center circles, namely the dream  and the waking ones, are the only ones in which there are visible represemtations. In fact, the subject of the dream stage is pointing up to the doublefaced triton. This monster, like the two headed Greco-

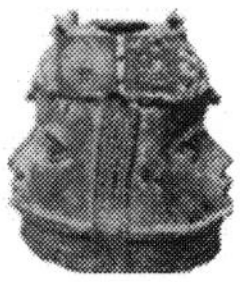

Latin god Janus,[325] symbolizes that the same subject of knowledge *sees* in those two circles. He enjoys the waking state and, at the same time, operates in the dream world.

Furthermore, the tri-ton (τρἰ-των *tri-tōn*) is a Greek mythological merman, half man and half fish. According to the myth, he abides the depths of the waters below, where he sounds his conch with three-(τρἰ *tri*) tones (τὀνος *tonos*),

"*his voice as the sound of many waters,*"[326]

suggesting the three *AUM* sound-levels we have seen.

This triple aspect is continuously repeated in various plates and corresponds to the symbolism present in the trident (*triśula*) of the Indian god Śiva, equivalent to Neptune.

The god Neptune abiding all those three levels is the individual "I." That self (*ātman*) moves

"in three states, in succession, and on account of the knowledge, 'I am that', resulting from the experience which unites through memory."[327]

The self (*ātman*) traverses, in the water, all the states of consciousness as a double-horned

"*great fish*" (*mahāmatsya*)

with one horn for the waking and the other for the dream state. In the air, that 'I' crosses all those levels as

"*a falcon*" (*śyena*).[328]

"*Then, which one is the self? This person is the light within the heart.*[329] *S/he, being serenely centered in itself, penetrates both worlds as if s/he were thinking and moving back and forth.*  *S/he, upon entering the dream state, goes beyond this dimension and the forms of death.*"[330]

The waking state is the central circle. In it, on a  boat, symbol of "the crib of rediscovery,"[331] the subject and the object traverse the ocean of possible objectivity. The subject directs the attention  steering that boat while objectivity,  directly connected  to the I, fishes each  object from that ocean of possibilities. That same objectivity is holding a duck,  *i.e.* symbol of the Sefirah[332] consciousness-*of* the object.

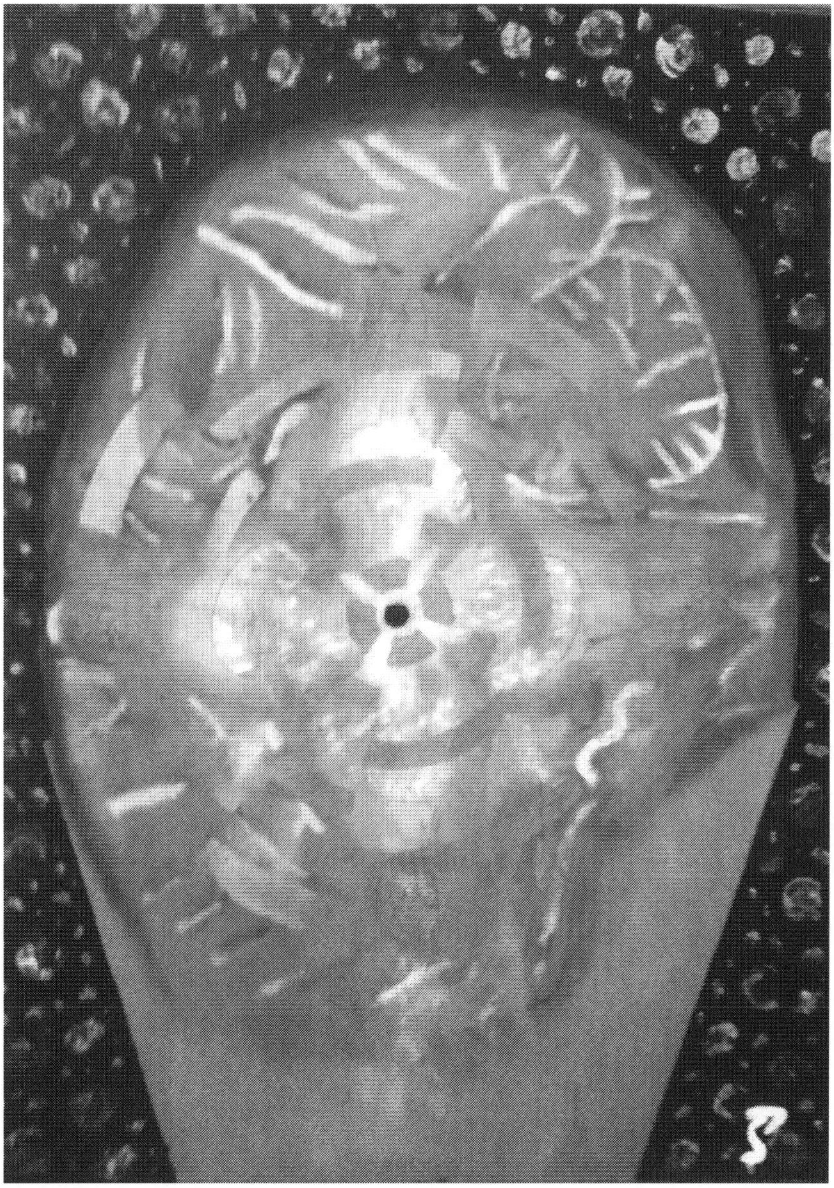

Awareness

PART II

THE OPUS

PLATE 4: "DISPASSIONATE IN AWARENESS"

Dry your thoughts in the True Light of Apodictic-Awareness.

AWARENESS' CENTRALITY

"Give ear, O ye heavens, and I will speak; and hear, O earth, the words of my mouth. My doctrine shall drop as the rain, my speech shall distil as the dew, as the small rain upon the tender herb, and as the showers upon the grass."[333]

This plate clearly depicts the centrality of Awareness' Light. In fact, that Luminosity does not come from the Sun-subjectivity. It does not come from the Moon-objectivity. On the contrary, It comes from a  Central-Source between the two. That Fountain has no origin because It is Transcendent. That Light is the True-Certain-*Faith* (*pistis* πίστις) of Apodictic-Awareness.

The Light of Awareness shines on everything that the five senses of the subject-object pick up. The senses are symbolically represented as hemp sheets grounded on objectivity and basking in the Light of Awareness. The two more luminous 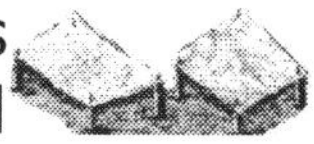 hemp sheets represent from, left to right, sight and hearing. The darker two are  smell and taste. The lower darkest one is  feeling. The senses are constantly flanked by the ram of individualized 'I' and by the vital bull of intentionality.

In this plate, we have two sides:

S) The noetic one or the subjective aspect of experience as act-of-perception aiming to grasp the object in which, the sun represents subjectivity, the stepping ram the 'I' and the man the subject.

O) The noematic one or the objective aspect of experience in its modes-of-being-given in which, the moon represents objectivity, the ramping bull the vital aspect of intentionality and the woman the object.

It must be clear that man and woman, subject and object, are not two separate entities, but are the synthesis of the same act of knowledge in all its epistemic articulations.

What they are doing in this vignette is wringing the wet hemp-sheet symbol of the epistemic synthesis of the subject's mind with the senses. The subject and object are squeezing all the moister or fluid-experiences out of the mind-senses resulting in

the liquidity of knowledge. That moister is a metaphor for the synthesis of knowledge deriving from the objective empirical experience and the subjective emotional connection between them.

THE TWO WAYS

The ancient Hermetic Tradition distinguished two methods for the sacred Art, or Opus, the Humid and the Dry Way.[334] Clearly, here Altus opts for the dry one. However, what is the real meaning of these two ways? Usually, the interpretation is one of chemical nature. It should be evident, by now, that we depart completely from the physical chemical interpretation. Our reading is fundamentally epistemic. If any transformation takes place, it is on the gnoseological level. What we know is the only reality *per-se*. The knowledge-of the world puts it into existence. When that knowledge ends the world *per-se* ends. We may think of a world *in-se*, but also that thought is inevitably and ultimately *for-us* (*i.e. per-se*). A world *in-se* can never be known, thus, it will never exist *for-us*, except as our imagined concept. Therefore, the two hermetic ways correspond to:

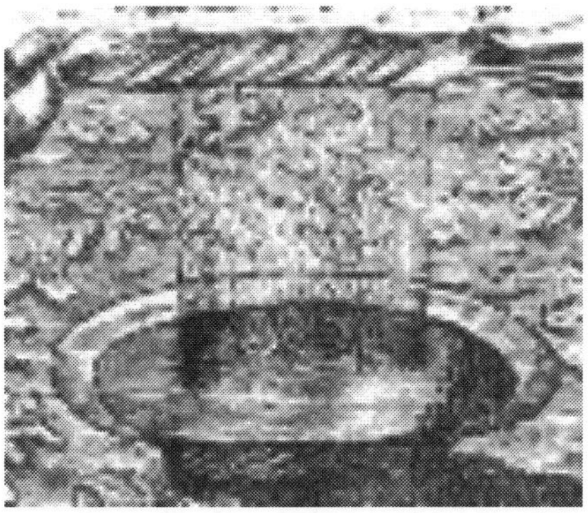

- The Humid Way corresponds to Being-for-itself (viz. *per-se*), namely, the continuous circular reference of a *subject* to its correlated inseparable *object*. There we become emotionally involved with and in the world.

- The Dry Way relates to Being-in-itself (viz. *in-se*), namely, the absolute independent *transcendent* center of the *immanent* circle set apart from the inseparable *subject-object* circular correlation. There we become disengaged from the world's seductions.

From these premises, we deduce that wringing symbolizes extracting, from the subject-object correlation, the knowledge of the world as Being-for-itself or *per-se*. It is the dry abstention from the attachment to this world as we see, understand and know it. This is the true spiritual alchemy that transforms the *lead*, the heavy-consciousness-*of*-objective-world into the Pure-Gold-of-Awareness.

WITHDRAWAL

The sheet-drying corresponds to what the II Century BC Indian sage Patañjali described in his *Yoga-Aphorisms*[335] as *pratyāhāra, viz.* the re-absorption or withdrawal of the senses from the external objects. This withdrawal is described as the fifth member (*aṅga*) of the eighth steps (*ashṭā-ṅga*) yoga. *Pratyāhāra* must occur during the waking, dreaming and dreamless stages of life. The entire world of experience, *viz.* the two-sided subject-object, metaphorically represented as villages-cities, farms and churches, must find their unification in the shaft of Awareness indicated, in this plate, by the central tower.

Consequently, this withdrawal must take place also on the emotional level. This emotive distillation is described by a traditional Indian sacred writing, the *Bhagavad-Gītā*, the *Divine-Song* (400 BC?). The text is part of the middle section of the *Mahābhārata*[336] the longest major Sanskrit epic poem, which describes the war between two related rival families for the control of a kingdom in India. The leader of one of those families, the Pāṇḍava, is Arjuna-the-White-one. He is instructed by Kṛshṇa-the-Black-one, an avatar of Vishṇu. His black or dark blue appearance symbolizes the metaphorical color of God, the Transcendent unseen Midnight Sun.[337]

Responding to Arjuna's moral concern about killing during war, Kṛshṇa instructs,

> "*Having rejected all attachments, perform your actions in a state of union* (*yoga-stha*); *be unaffected by victory as well as failure.*"[338]

Similar to Jesus' command,

> "*Let the dead bury their dead,*"[339]

Kṛshṇa reminds Arjuna to be unmoved and not mourn, in fact,

> "*He who views someone as a killer and he who considers himself killed, the two do not know. This one does not kill and is not killed.*"[340]

Therefore, he instructs Arjuna to be free from any desire. Paul says,

> "*those who mourn,* [should be] *as if they did not; those who are happy, as if they were not.*"[341]

Furthermore, Kṛshṇa incites Arjuna to withdraw from the world,

> "*One who does not hate enlightenment or accomplishments*
> *or even delusions when they are present ...*
> *nor desires them when they are absent,*
> *one who meditates serenely and is not disturbed by virtues or passions,*

one who stays unmoved and remains beyond virtues or passions,
one who remains the same in pain or pleasure, who is the same before a lump of dirt, a stone or gold,
who is equally firm if loved or detested and equal in insult or praise,
one who is the same in honor or dishonor, equal with a friend or a foe,
who has renounced all struggle, is said to have transcended virtues and-or passions."[342]

In fact, inevitably, at the end all troubles wash away. After 2000 years, except for literary and historical references, no one any longer remembers Varus' defeat. No one even worries or feels the consequent anguish of the Divine Augustus. In September of the year 9 AD, the Roman governor of Germania, Publius Quinctilius Varus[343] lost three legions at the Battle of the Teutoburg Forest.[344] He was defeated by an alliance of Germanic tribes led by Arminius.[345]

The Roman Emperor Augustus was seriously distressed by this defeat.

"In fact, they say that he was so greatly affected that for several months in succession he cut neither his beard nor his hair, and sometimes he would dash his head against a door, crying:

Quintilius Varus, give me back my legions!

And he observed the day of the disaster each year as one of sorrow and mourning."[346]

Today no one observes that day.

Withdrawal is similar to Dante in Purgatory, submersed in the river Lethe, he

"was forced to swallow of the water…
which takes away all memory of sin."[347]

PLATE 5: "THE CIRCADIAN RHYTHM"

The opus in the waking, dreaming, dreamless sleep and transcendent states

ATHANOR, ALEMBIC, CUCURBIT, VIAL, COLUMN AND BUILDING-STONE

The athanor 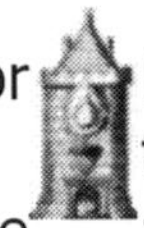 is the alchemic furnace. Here, it symbolizes the shaft of intentionality through which consciousness travels to reach the object of knowledge. The athanors in the waking and dreaming stages have two levels 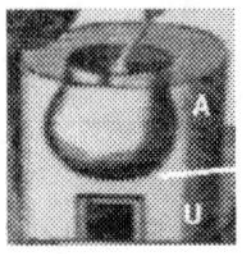 indicating that they are both stages in which representations take place. The athanor representing the third state of  dreamless sleep, in which no representation is present, has only one level. In our plates, the tower  also represents the athanor. Precisely, the athanor is the  Hermetic Caduceus. The two serpents 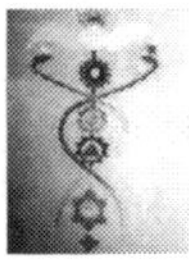 connote subjectivity, metaphorically represented as a man, and objectivity, symbolized by a woman. They are 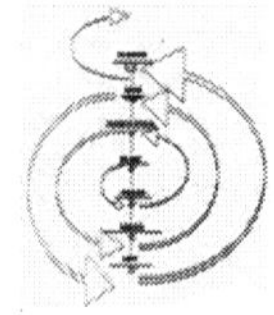 coiled around the shaft-of-consciousness (*sushumnā*). That shaft is the intentionality of the subject aiming to grasp the object.

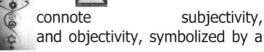

Pure-Awareness is on the top of that channel. The trident  represents the three levels of consciousness, *viz.* wakefulness, dream and sleep, held together by the staff, the fourth  and all-encompassing Transcendent realm, namely the silence from which we come and the *muteness* to which we go. The athanor is also the ladder symbolizing the direction to that Transcendent state of Apodictic-Realization, the alchemic goal of this entire book.

The XV century distilling vessels, the beaked alembic 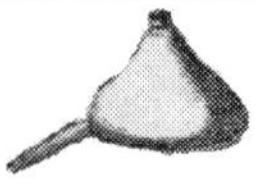 and the cucumber-shaped  cucurbit, are symbols of consciousness, in that they distill the fluid-experience in a product of knowledge. In other words, they transform the external objective world in thoughts, viz. in conscious ideas.

 The vial of any shape represents the container of that consciousness which also can be transferred 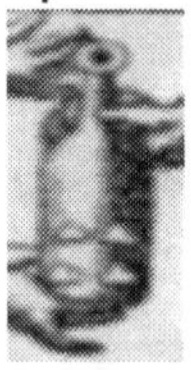 in other life dimensions. When empty, it symbolizes pure consciousness. When full, it signifies consciousness-*of*-the-objective-experience.

 Columns are symbols of the axis of the world, of the tree of life, the incorruptibility and immortality of the Transcendent.[348]

> "*And Jacob … took the stone that he had put* [for] *his pillows, and set it up* [for] *a pillar... And this stone… shall be God's house.*"[349]
>
> "*And the LORD came down in the pillar of the cloud, and stood* [in] *the door of the tabernacle.*"[350]

Columns, of any shape or with any cap, indicate the  beginning and the conclusion of a stage of life depicted in a vignette. Some of them are baseless because they are founded on the building-stone of the Transcendent.

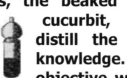

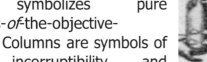

THE FOUR LEVELS OF REALITY

WAKE

DREAM

DREAMLESS SLEEP

TRANSCENDENCE

THE WAKING STATE

W
A
K
E

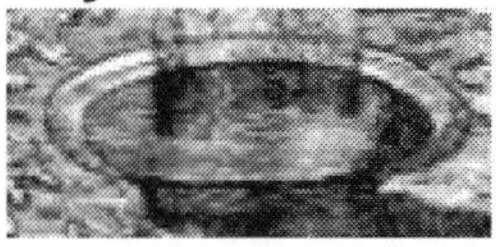

The man and the woman, in this plate, are the subject and the object in the laboratory of the experience of the waking state. A left-projected square window represents this state. Its view means that the waking experience, enjoyed by them, is open to the receptivity of the *external* material world.[351] In the waking state, both the subject and the object decant in the athanor of consciousness all the flowing perceptions obtained, in the previous Plate, from wringing the senses. This is the realm of ego-consciousness. We are conscious-*of* our historical psychophysical being. We are these distinct ideas currently thought by us. We are this present specific sentient body and this individualized emotional person here and now reading these words and seeing these pictures.

The first part of this vignette symbolizes the waking conscious experience. A chamber, delimited by baseless columns, represents it. One pillar is round with a Doric cap and the other is a Tuscan-cap square one.[352] The columns distinguish the two moments of the waking experience. The round pillar opens the room and the rectangular one separates one scene from the other. In fact, the second column parts the object of the first scene from the subject of the second one.

In the next *room*, the experience is perceived as having objective qualities. Namely, we see the world out there as real in itself and we consider ourselves only as interacting perceivers. Two baseless columns delimit the scene. On the right, behind the waking-woman-object, a round column with an Egyptian-cap opens the scene. On the left, the square column with a Tuscan-cap of the previous segment closes the scene. This reflecting action of the object on the the woman-object is pouring from an consciousness-*of* the world decanted into container of the man-subject. Therefore, turns away from exteriority by giving his window. He is always concentrated within object constantly looks outward.

room symbolizes the perceiver. In fact, alembic the the experience- the waking-subject shoulders to the while the waking-

Specifically, the woman/objectivity presents that which is *ob-jective* (*i.e. before-thrown*). Thus, the perceiver realizes its own centrality as an '*I*' subject, namely the Kantian transcendental 'I-think,' the necessary a-priori foundation of knowledge.[353]

In the Indian tradition, the '*I*' is named Agni, the Divine-flame common to all humans (*vaiśvānara*), it is the fire in the athanor,

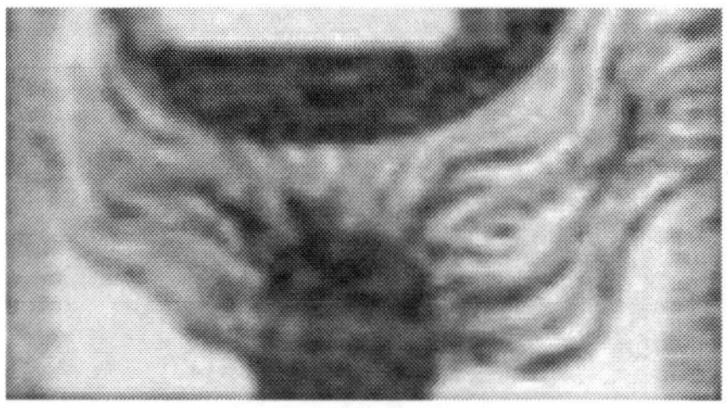

> "*the image of God,*"[354]
>
> "*Agni, the Divine-flame is the individual soul,*[355] *the Leader*[356] *and the Digestive-fire within a person, who is this one by whom this food is cooked and then eaten.*"[357]
>
> "*All that exists is either food or the eater of food and ambrosia is food and Fire he who eats food.*"[358]

Symbolically, that which is known becomes *food-for-thought*.[359] In the Indian tradition,

> "the word 'food' (*anna*) ... is metaphorically used of that also which is not food."[360]

Therefore,

> "*knowledge is food.*"[361]

The liquid poured in the athanor is that food, the fluidity of experience. The philosopher Husserl asserts that

> "Experience is essentially something that flows, and ... we can swim after it."[362]

THE TWO ONEIRIC STATES

THE DREAM STATE

A *room* delimited by two baseless square columns with Tuscan-caps portrays this new dimension. The square pillars, as we have seen, indicate complete separation

between different rooms.[363] In this case, they separate the previous waking and the following deep-sleep areas.

This room is the laboratory of experience in the field of dreams and sleep. This is the realm of I-consciousness. Here, the *I-think* is conscious-*of* the ideas as thoughts (*i.e.* dreams) thinking (*i.e.* dreaming) themselves as thoughts (*i.e.* dreams). This is not the historical psychophysical being, but it is the universal form or faculty of knowledge capable of being conscious-*of* thoughts (and/or dreams) as such.

A right-projected square window  represents this dream state. It means that the dreaming experience is open to the receptivity[364] of the *internal*-world. The woman-dream-object, in fact, is portrayed as turning away from the exteriority by offering her shoulders to the window. Thus, the perceiver is pouring consciousness from the alembic. He is fusing in the two oneiric level athanor all the objects of the senses. Both the dreaming-subject and dreaming-object are looking within. Meanwhile, the woman-dream-objectivity stirs the dream objects in that consciousness. The mixing and the ladle symbolize sharing, nurturing, tasting and articulating objects in the mind's experience.

She holds a vial  with four triangular cloud-shapes in it. The vessel represents the synthesis-of-experience lived in both the waking and dreaming moments. The four clouds represent the subject-object pair, once in the lighter waking side and the other in the darker dream state. Both states are joined in the one container of the human psyche. They are cloud shapes because they represent the ego and the objective desire obfuscating the shining awareness.

The second action of the plate's dream-row shows an interesting change of pace. The window  here, as in the next chamber, is half round representing both the sleep state and the internal eye of consciousness.[365] The dream-objectivity enters the realm of deep sleep as a  crescent Moon and she hands the vial  to a saturnine figure clad with the Moon  and about to devour the child  in his arms. The  woman-dream looks at him  in the impossible attempt to objectify the state of that deity. On the other side, Saturn focuses on the flask assimilating it within and disregarding any subject-object distinction.

*Sat*urn symbolizes the *sat*isfying quiescence deriving from the accomplishment of deeds. His nakedness represents his *warrior trance*, or hypnotic or cataleptic state.[366] Thus, he signifies the dreamless sleep. Therefore, in this vignette the woman, the objective-dream, hands the flask of the waking and dreaming (REM) synthesis-of-lived-experience to the next state, the dreamless sleep (NREM) state, represented as Saturn. He is standing near the column  at the threshold of the next realm.

Why Saturn is represented here? To answer this question, we must refer to its Greco-Roman mythological aspect. The Greek Titan Kronos, identified with the Roman god Saturn-Time-Khronos, was the son of Ouranos-Heaven and Gaia-Earth. He ate all his offspring except for Zeus. In fact, he could not devour him because his mother Rhea, or the serpent goddess Opis, substituted the baby with the stone Abadir[367] 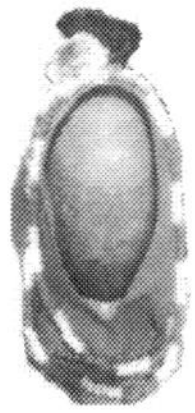 wrapped in clothes. Eventually, Saturn disgorged it on Mount Helicon.[368]  The Greek tradition does not explain the meaning of this myth. Nevertheless, the Indian tradition offers similarities and accounts that can shed light on Saturn's puzzle.

a) As Saturn in this Plate, the Indian god Śiva/Rudra exhibits the moon on his head while holding a trident (*triśula*). He is

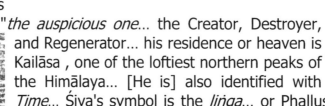

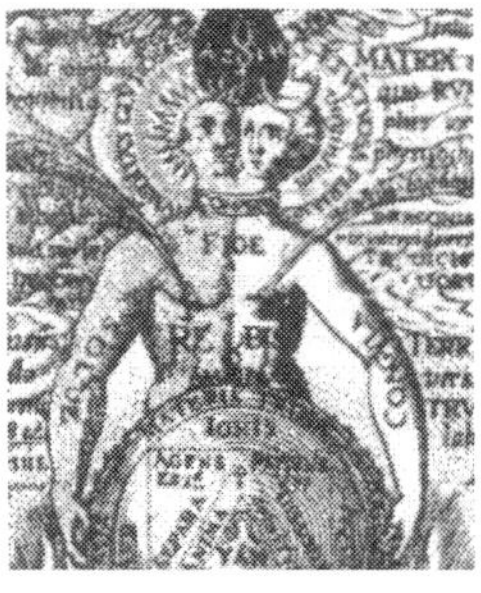

"*the auspicious one*... the Creator, Destroyer, and Regenerator... his residence or heaven is Kailāsa , one of the loftiest northern peaks of the Himālaya... [He is] also identified with *Time*... Śiva's symbol is the *liṅga*... or Phallus... [Like the *Re-bis*, the Hermetic double-thing,][369] one of his representations is as *ardha-nārī*, *half-female*, the other half being male to symbolize the unity of the generative principle... A moon's crescent... marks the measure of time."[370]

In this vignette,

"the moon is... the symbol of passage from life to death and from death to life... [of] chthonic and funerary lunar divinities... The moon is a symbol of indirect knowledge... reflection of the sun's light... and symbol of fecundity."[371]

b) Saturn's cannibalistic act finds an explanation in the *Bṛhadāraṇyaka Upanishad*. The text relates that Mṛtyu/Death, as the destroyer (*i.e.* Rudra), and, at the same time, father of creation (*i.e.* Śiva), produced his own self.

"Verily, nothing at all, was here in the beginning?
Indeed, all this was concealed by Death, by Hunger,
because hunger is death. Then, he projected the mind:
'Let me be a being for-myself.'"[372]

He labored on the solidified froth of the lower waters and they became the earth.[373] Then, Death/Saturn united with the Moon.

"desired a second and extended itself as a woman-wife,[374] *the object, and a man-husband, the subject, in a loving embrace. It divided Itself in two parts... Thus humanity was generated."*[375]

"He desired: 'Let a second self be born from me.' He, Mṛtyu/Death or Hunger, identified with the Mind, paired with Mother-Word. That, which was the flow-of-semen, became the 360° year. In the beginning, indeed, the year was not. For as long as the ***space of time of a year*** *he parented his child. Thus, after that time, he projected him. Once generated, Mṛtyu opened his mouth* ***to swallow him****; he, the babe, made the sound 'Aaahhh!' That, indeed, became speech."*[376]
Mṛtyu/Death thought, 'Verily if I will kill him, I will consummate very small food.'"[377]

In fact, in dreams or dreamless sleep there is no increase of knowledge. All that is known in those states is already contained in the mind of the dreamer. Similarly, in the process of consciousness

"you cannot think the thinker of thinking,
nor understand the understander of understanding."[378]

The Self-In-Itself can never be known because It always transcends the self-for-itself. Namely, the Ultimate-Perceiver is thought or understood always as an object, never as the perceiving subject itself. Therefore, Saturn, about to devour his own offspring, ends up eating an object, namely a *stone*.

The Generative Principle, namely Mṛtyu-Death or Prajāpati, the Father of Creation,[379] Time itself or Saturn here, hungers for I-consciousness. In the course (*retas*) of a year, Mṛtyu, uniting mind and word sends forth his seed (*retas*), an aimless and unsystematic stream (*retas*) of consciousness, of thoughts. The hunger of Death, however, goes unsatisfied. The subject, through its intentionality or appetite, reaches the object, the other than itself. Thus, the mind-thought is driven by the desire-to-know. The word is the sound conferring sense to what-is-known.[380]

Hunger and eating are not so much a metaphor, as they indicate an actual physiological and epistemological reality. In fact, we cannot satisfy our carnivorous hunger without killing the animal in order to transform it in our food. Similarly, we cannot know any person without eliminating his/her subject, thus reducing him/her into an object of thought. Therefore, the subject as such remains always unknown.

Saturn devouring his son[381]

DREAMLESS SLEEP STATE

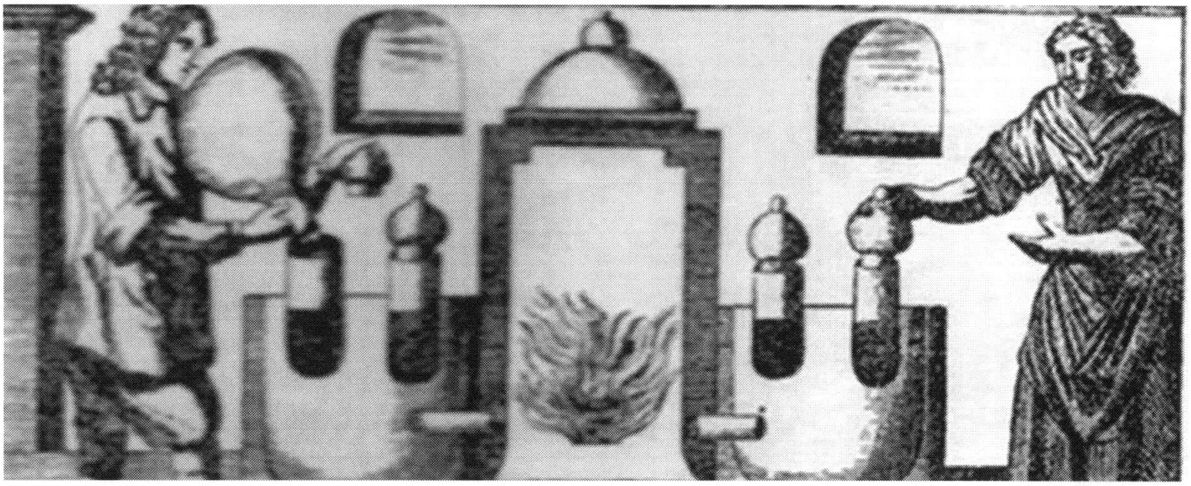

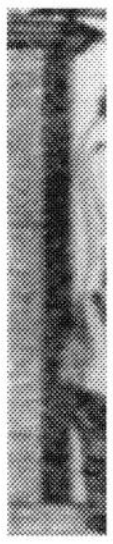

The third strip on this plate is open-ended. In fact, it starts with a Tuscan-cap square column separating this stage from the preceding strip. However, an ending pillar does not delimit the vignette. Thus, it indicates that this state-of-being continues throughout the entire process of life. This is because <<the objective world, in the state of deep sleep without dreams, is always present and unified with the pure potential consciousness, which is not yet in actuality. This is also the case of cataleptic and comatose states. In fact, when all senses are gone, when all thoughts are gone and when conscience-*of* this Ego is gone what is there left? Whatsoever is left must be the same foundation of the senses, of the thoughts and of the consciousness-*of* this Ego.>>[382] Where is the self during a

"less than 40 minutes... open heart surgery"?[383]

Where does the subject go? Where the perceiver is, during the procedure, when the brain electrical activity is completely flat, the breathing is suspended and the heart does not pulsate?[384] From where, does the 'I' come back from?

This is the realm of <u>Auto-transparency</u> which

> "must not think of thinking ... because ... it is present to itself, without needing to mediate itself, that is to see itself before itself as object of its own knowledge."[385]

The Self is the

> "*internal regulator,*"

who, while in the state of deep sleep without dreams,

> "*does not know, except that, while not knowing, he is still the knower. In fact, knowledge does not separate from the knower, because he is imperishable. Merely, in that state, there is no otherness and nothing else that he may know.*"[386]

It is pure intuition referring always to an unknown Self-in-itself,

> "*Like transparent water, he becomes one seer without a second,*"[387]

"as a fire concealed by fire."[388]

At this level, that Self does not enter in the dialectical subject-object correlation, but persists in Its Auto-Transparency. This Auto-Transparency is such only until the moment in which we think of it, at which time it becomes I-consciousness and/or Ego-consciousness. Then, it becomes consciousness-*of*, always intentionally turned towards the world with which it establishes a correlation. In each moment or state of mind, there is the presence of the other two. In fact, it is as when

> *"you walk from one place to another: you do not attend to the steps you take. Yet you find yourself after a time at your goal.... There is full awareness in sleep and total ignorance in waking."*[389]

The *Māṇḍūkya Upanishad* states,

> *"Deep-unconscious-sleep* [is] *the third quadrant, where one* [is] *asleep* [and] *does not desire any desire* [and] *does not see any dream.*[390] *Having become one-compact-knowledge, the state of deep-unconscious-sleep*[391] *made of bliss* [stands] *alone. Indeed,* [it is] *the enjoyer of bliss. Its mouth is consciousness* [and] *the knower."*[392]

The *Mutus Liber* depicts this Auto-transparency in two ways. If fire burns in the Athanor of consciousness, it means that Awareness is present. When, there is no fire in the Athanor, it indicates that Awareness is hidden in its Auto-transparency.

In 1952, at the University of Chicago, Dr. Nathaniel Kleitman discovered two kinds of sleep.[393]

> "These two kinds of sleep are as different from each other as sleep is from wakefulness... the essential difference between wakefulness and sleep is the loss of awareness,"[394]

i.e.: deep-unconsciousness state (*sushupta-sthāna*).

> "A region of the hypothalamus... controlling sleep/wake states... mediate[s also] the sedative effects of anesthetics."[395]

Further research on the oneiric realm has revealed two events that more likely indicate the distinction between

a) dream state, *i.e.*: the phasic-events predominant in the REM stage with

> "rapid, short-lived phenomena like twitches and the rapid eye movements," and

b) deep sleep state, *i.e.*: the tonic-events, predominant in the NREM stage with

> "slow, stable phenomena such as suppression of skeletal muscle activity."[396]

<<In dreams, intentionality, as stream of consciousness directed toward something, persists entirely in the subjectivity of the oneiric state, while, in the dreamless sleep, that intentional stream persists frozen in the stillness of this state. As the waking state and the dream state are the realm of the discursive process, this deep-unconscious-sleep state is the realm of intuition. That is the knower. That is the condition underlining the previous two states. In fact, it is intuition, the state of immediate and total com-prehension or direct *in*sight of objective world reality. In it, all

the opposites coincide into one undifferentiated point without any temporal or spatial juxtaposition or distinction, without proceeding from one element to another.

> "I have often encountered motif which made me think that the unconscious must be the world of the infinitesimally small,"

declares Jung .[397]

It should be understood that the unconscious aspect is such only from the point of view of the waking and dream states, while, from the vantage point of sleep with no dreams, it is pure intuitive stillness.>>[398] The *Kaushītaki-Brāhmaṇa Upanishad* states,

> "*Thus, when a person is sleeping, so that s/he sees no dream whatsoever, verily s/he becomes one with that breathing self. Then, speech together with all the names goes to him. The eye together with all the forms goes to him. The ear together with all sounds goes to him. The mind together with all thoughts goes to him. When he awakens, as from a blazing fire, sparks spread out in all directions. Similarly, therefore, from this self the vital breaths spread out each in its own place. From the vital breaths, the resplendent senses* [spread out] *and from the resplendent senses the worlds spread out.*"[399]

Dr. William C. Dement, an American pioneer in sleep research. Gives the following description of deep sleep, namely, Non-Rapid-Eye-Movement,

> "The NREM state is often called 'quiet sleep' because of the slow regular breathing, the general absence of body movement, and the slow, regular brain activity... The body is not paralyzed ... it *can* move, but it *does not* move because the brain doesn't order it to move.[400] The sleeper has lost contact with his environment. There is a shut-down of perception because the five senses are no longer gathering information and communicating stimuli to the brain [*i.e.: does not see...* etc]. When gross body movements (such as rolling over) occur during NREM, the EEG[401] suggests a transient intrusion of wakefulness."[402]

Each night, as the EEG wave pattern gradually changes from wakefulness into NREM, Dr. Dement notices four gradual levels,

> "a progressive descent from Stage 1 into other stages of NREM sleep. The term 'descent' is meant to imply a progression along the depth-of-sleep continuum as sleep becomes deeper and deeper, the sleeper becomes more remote from the environment, and increasingly more potent stimuli are necessary to cause arousal. Each new stage is announced by its own characteristic pattern in the EEG. After only a few minutes of Stage 1 [], the onset of Stage 2 [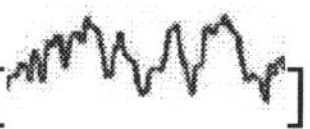] is established by the appearance of spindling and K complexes.[403] Several minutes later the slow delta waves of Stage 3 [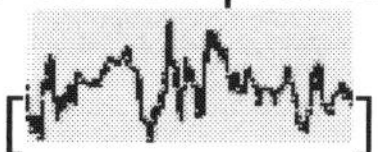] become apparent. After about

ten minutes of this stage, the delta activity becomes more and more predominant and signals the presence of Stage 4 [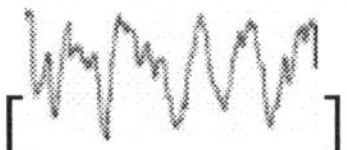]. At this point it is extremely difficult to awaken the sleeper… in Stage 4, thirty or forty minutes following sleep onset, a series of body movements heralds the start of re-ascent through the stages of NREM sleep."[404]

With these premises, we can now return to the analysis of this vignette. The subject 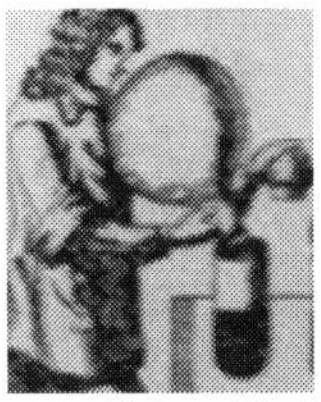 decants all consciousness in the first cucurbit of wakefulness lined up with three other decanters.  The four cucurbits may indicate the different levels of the NREM state. Nevertheless, they are all sealed, except for the first one. The lid of the last one is kept  in place by objectivity. This indicates that knowledge is contained within them but in an unconscious state. However, the subject-object distinction, which characterizes the waking-dreaming states, in the first two cucurbits, 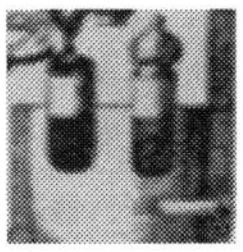 is not in the second two cucurbits. 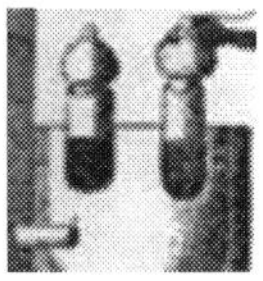 They portray dreamless sleep and the fourth state. Nevertheless, the unifying synthetic distilling process 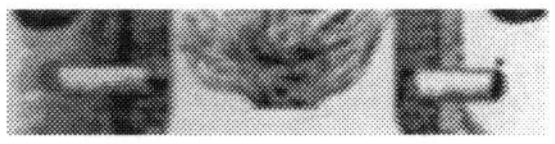 interconnects all.

The half-round window  represents, as we have seen, the internal eye of consciousness. Central to the whole figure is the fire in  the athanor. This is the flame of Awareness, which is the amalgamating principle of the entire book. The *Māṇḍūkya Upanishad* declares,

> "*This* [is] *the Lord of all. This* [is] *the omniscient. This* [is] *the internal regulator. This* [is] *the source of all, verily the cause and dissolution of beings.*"[405]

Like a unified ocean,[406]

> "*after all dissolves, alone this one remains awake. From this vacuity, this one truly awakes this world consisting of Pure Awareness. This world is meditated by that one and, verily, in that one it dissolves.*"[407]

From the state of deep sleep, the self 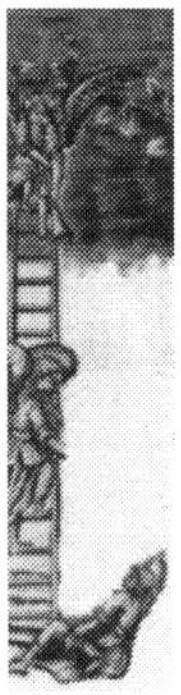

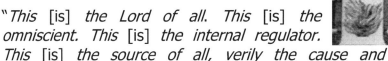

> "*returns, as he came, again to the dream state, the place he departed from.*"[408]

At this point, it may be argued that this waking, REM and NREM interpretation is arbitrary and purely conceptual. To answer, we invite the reader to observe the first Plate again. There is depicted the tone and jest of the entire book with a man sleeping and dreaming of heaven. To confirm this point without any doubt, that same Plate quotes the *Bible* where it states that Jacob

> "*lay down… to sleep… and he dreamed… of… heaven.*"[409]

We do not understand how this, clearly oneiric motive, may have led commentators to relate this treatise only to physical chemical compounds and reactions. On the other hand, the adoption of the epistemic, psychological and mythological interpretation, that we propose, fits perfectly with all the plates, starting from the very first one. Furthermore, there would be no necessity for the secretive or hermetic *hieroglyphs* if the book were describing purely physical elements and chemical reactions. On the contrary, the *muteness* of the book confirms the subtlety of the concepts expressed that refer to what has been defined as the Ineffable-Transcendent. As Joseph Campbell declared,

> "The best things can't be told because they transcend thought. The second best are misunderstood, because those are the thoughts that are supposed to refer to that which can't be thought about."[410]

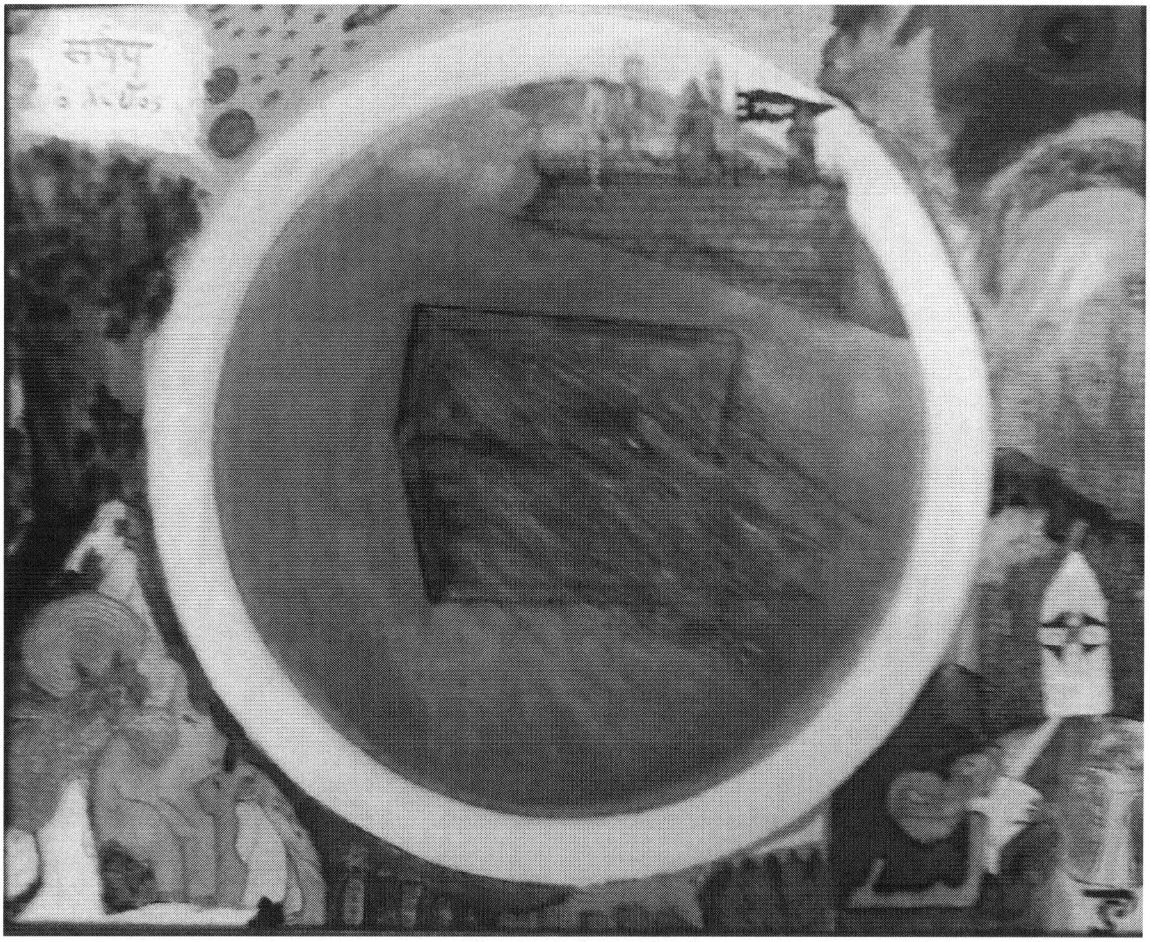

The building block

TRANSCENDENCE, THE 4TH STATE

TRANSCENDENCE

At the base of the circadian rhythm there is a black square surmounted by the numbers 4.0.  That is the portal to the furnace of Awareness. It is the Transcendent Awareness. It is the inextinguishable Fire of the *burning bush*, which declared to Moses,

> "*I AM THAT I AM.*"[411]
>
> "*I have come as light* [of Awareness] *into the world, so that everybody who is certain in me may not remain in darkness.*"[412]

From that Fire of Awareness derives Consciousness. Creation is consciousness that brings the world into light. The Fire of Awareness is the foundation on which all the pillars of the world are grounded. The number 40 symbolizes the accomplishment of the cycle. Separately, 4. is its wholeness and .0 its infinity.[413]

The *Māṇḍūkya Upanishad* states that

> "*the fourth state* [is] *without metrical letters, uncorrelated, the cessation of the manifestation, the final emancipation, the One without a second. Thus, the sacred mystical syllable AUM verily* [is] *the Self. Whosoever so knows merges with the Self into the Self.* [Indeed], *whosoever so knows* [merges into the Self]."[414]

The  fourth quadrant of the AUM's (ॐ) three sound-musical symphony is silence. It is the fourth (4) all-encompassing-motionless-movement of the Transcendent-Nothingness-Zero (0). It is the mute mystery. It is the center from which we come and to which we go.

<<The fourth quadrant is the after-sound (*anu-svāra*) Sanskrit letter ं, as in the final vibration of a diapason. It is the last letter of the Sanskrit alphabet, it

> "is written with a dot above the letter which it follows."[415]

No sound is emitted, because it is the fading away of the echo of the letter Mᵉ. It is silence. It is silence, which precedes sound. It is silence, which follows sound. It is silence, from which sound comes. It is silence, in which sound goes. It is silence, which shrouds all sounds. It is the fourth state and all four states at the same time.

Stillness is the Apodictical-Certitude of Awareness. It is the silence from which we come. It is the silence of the Ego-thought, which subsides to make room for the Self. That Self is none other than that Apodictical-Certitude of Awareness, which is present in all of the preceding states. Except that now It is the Apodictical-Certitude of Awareness in itself. It is the

> "*measure of knowledge*" (*cinmātra*)."[416]

Now,

> "*the time is fulfilled, and the kingdom of God is at hand.*"[417]

Who knows this identifies with the Self.>>[418]

> "*I and* [my] *Father are one* [says Jesus, and] *ye shall know that I* [am] *in my Father, and ye in me, and I in you.*"[419]
>
> "*All may be one; as thou, Father,* [art] *in me, and I in thee, that they also may be one in us: that the world may believe that thou hast sent me.*"[420]

Pope Francis reaffirms the presence of

> "God in everything... God is in the life of every person... Even if... it was a disaster... He must be found in every human life. Even if... it is a field full of thorns and weeds."[421]

Jung writes that, regarding

> "the identification of the Self with God, as expressed in Śrī Ramana's utterances, Psychology cannot contribute anything further."[422]

We comment, *Psychology cannot contribute anything further* because, like any science, psychology conceives and studies the world as an object. Even if that *world* turns out to be the psyche, still the observer-scientist conceives it as an object different and separated from him/herself. If Jung had completely *decanted* the psyche, he would have realized Awareness, the founder and sustainer of his psychological analysis. Consequently, he would have realized the transcendence of Apodictical Awareness. For Jung, Alchemical transmutation takes place in the process of *individuation*.[423] However, individuation persists in the epistemic subject-object dichotomy that leads to uncertainty. It is exactly the opposite of the Alchemic Realization, of the Universality of Apodictical Awareness, which is the True-Foundation of All-Certitude.

The universality of that Certainty is what the French mathematician and philosopher René Descartes, sought in his *Discourse on Method*.[424] There he writes, in order to

> "distinguish Truth from Error [and] ... to strip... of all past beliefs... I ought to reject as absolutely false all opinions in regard to which I could suppose the least ground for doubt, in order to ascertain whether after that there remained aught in my belief that was wholly indubitable. Accordingly, seeing that our senses sometimes deceive us, I was willing to suppose that there existed nothing really such as they presented to us... I supposed that all the objects (presentations) that had entered into my mind when awake, had in them no more truth than the illusions of my dreams. But immediately upon this I observed that, whilst I thus wished to think that all was false, it was absolutely necessary that I, who thus thought, should be somewhat; and as I observed that this truth I think, hence I am (*cogito ergo sum*), was so certain and of such evidence (*si ferme et si assurée*), that no ground of doubt, however extravagant, could be alleged by the Sceptics capable of shaking it, I concluded that I might,

without scruple, accept it as the first principle of the Philosophy of which I was in search."

Furthermore, the German philosopher Immanuel Kant recognizes Certitude as *pure* or *transcendental apperception*, I-consciousness, the original universal unifying formal principle of the logical and impersonal generic (*überhaupt*) consciousness. In fact, he states,

> "The 'I think' must accompany all my representations, for otherwise something would be represented in me which could not be thought; in other words, the representation would either be impossible, or at least be, in relation to me, nothing... 'I think,' is an act of *spontaneity*; that is to say, it cannot be regarded as belonging to mere sensibility. I call it pure apperception... because it is I-consciousness... accompanying all our representations."[425]

Then, wakefulness becomes the Certain-Awareness present in the entire spectrum of the AUM and finally merging in the fourth soundless state (*turīya*).[426]

> "*Turīya means that which is the fourth. The experiencers (jivas) of the three states of waking, dreaming and deep sleep, known as viśva, taijasa and prājña, who wander successively in these three states, are not the Self. It is with the object of making this clear, namely that the Self is that which is different from them and which is the witness of these states, that it is called the fourth (*turīya*). When this is known, the three experiencers disappear and the idea that the Self is a witness, that it is the fourth, also disappears. That is why the Self is described as beyond the fourth* (*turīyatita*)."[427]

Is it possible that the Hermetic circles, to which Altus certainty belonged, had knowledge of the *sound* related to the four states of mind? It may be so, if we read the ancient sources.

Apollodorus of Athens (180 – 120 BC), in his encyclopedic *Library* of Greek mythology, describes how Oedipus induced the Theban Sphinx[428] to kill herself once he solved her famous enigma (αἴνιγμα *aínigma*). The enigma was,

> "What is that which *has* (ἔχον *échon*) *one* (μίαν *mían) sound* (φωνὴν *phōnhèn*)[429] and nevertheless becomes four-footed and two-footed and three-footed?"[430]

If the riddle were not solved, the Sphinx would have suffocated him.

In ancient Greece, during the Eleusinian Mystery, the adepts recited the jaculatory

> "*Konx om pax,*"[431]

perhaps an echo or a corruption of Sanskrit words. Apollodorus, who, conceivably, was not familiar with it or with the *Upanishadic* doctrines, explained the ancient Sphinx's riddle of the "*one sound,*" the best he could. He clarified that the riddle referred to the human being. In fact, in its infancy, s/he walks using all four limbs. In adulthood, s/he walks on two limbs. In old age, s/he walks with the help of an inanimate cane. However, this solution of the riddle does not explain the *one sound* clearly connected with *metrical feet* and not limbs. The complexity of the puzzle may indicate that the enigma was much older than the Hellenic account and, therefore, the actual answer had been already lost at the time of the composition of the *Library*. In any case, Apollodorus points to the totality of three stages in the life of the human being.

The one sound is the *Oṃ*, the totality of the Self. It is composed of four parts/feet/sounds (Sanskrit *pada*, Greek πoὐς *poús*,)[432] A-U-M-•. Those four become two parts/feet/sounds in A-M, namely consciousness and unconsciousness.

> "*Verily there are only two conditions of this person, this condition and the world beyond.*"[433]

In fact, there is a second formulation of the Sphinx's riddle, which goes as such, there are

> "two sisters: one gives birth to the other and she, in turn, gives birth to the first."[434]

This is the distinction between consciousness and unconsciousness

> "*In between there is the third condition of dream,*"[435]

namely the subconscious. Furthermore, according to the Greek geographer Pausanias (II century AD), Oedipus

> "had been told the oracle in a dream."[436]

Finally, the three parts/feet A-U-M, namely conscious, *sub*conscious and unconscious, or waking, dreaming and sleep, or past, present and future, make the totality of the human being.>>[437] With the solution of

> "the riddle of the Sphinx, death has no further hold on you, and the curse of the Sphinx disappears."[438]

The Theban Sphinx[439]

PART III

THE WAY

PLATE 6: "THE OPERA BEGINS"

The first steps in the Alchemic Art.

THE PALINDROMIC SQUARE

An ancient palindromic square, which can be read from all sides and from all directions, declares:

"*The SOWER in the FIELD HOLDS the PRODUCTION's WHEELS.*"[440]

"Each one is the maker of his own fortune"[441]

~

"*Verily, he is the maker of action producing recompense and the enjoyer of his fortune.*"[442]

~

"[However] *no man, having put his hand to the plough and looking back* [in time], *is fit for the kingdom of God.*"[443]

THE FIRST PHASE

The first strip of this Plate portrays the Alchemic Opus (*OPERA*) to be accomplished in both the waking and dreaming stages of our life. Any alchemical operation must take place on all of the three levels of existence. In fact, all the athanors represented in this plate have three levels. The Alchemist must *hold* (*TENET*) a steady awakened mind, <<by bringing the waking-state awareness consciously awake into the dream state, as in a lucid dream. Subsequently, the mind, consciously awake, must ascend in the stillness of unconscious-sleep, realizing that the unconscious auto-transparency is always present here in this waking state. In fact, not all our actions are conscious, and those, which are not, still move on the overall background of the unconscious.>>[444]

> "*Indeed, he who knows this becomes a creator in this higher creation.*"[445]

Furthermore,

> "*Whatever desire one desires, verily the desired object materializes out of his conceptual determination.*"[446]

As directed in Plate 14, the advanced Alchemists, like the Philokalists, viz. the beauty-lovers, the Greek-Orthodox hermits, practicing the peacefully-silent Hesychasm,

> "pray at all times, in all places... not only while awake, but even during sleep... they do not break off their continuous prayer during profound mental exercise, nor even during sleep itself. As the All Wise has told us,
>
> *I sleep, but my heart waketh.*[447]
>
> Many, that is, who have achieved this mechanism of the heart acquire such an aptitude... that it will... incline the mind and the whole spirit to a flood of ceaseless prayer [*i.e.* Awareness] in whatsoever condition those who pray find themselves, and however abstract and intellectual their occupation at the time."[448]

A square Tuscan-cap-pillar introduces to the waking *room* with a rectangular window open to the external world to which no one pays attention. From the waking state, the subject pours his consciousness in the second cucurbits, viz. in the dream state offered by objectivity. This opens the connection with the other two cucurbits, which are now open and ready to receive that consciousness. The subject pours in the fire of a three level athanor the consciousness-*of* all the objects offered by objectivity. They are passions, desires, feelings, sentiments, cravings, emotions together with all the other habitual attachments.

As they flow before consciousness, the subject looks at all experiences focusing not on them emotively but only on the consciousness acknowledging them. These objects are open so that the subject can pour them in the stillness of Awareness. This is what yoga calls *pratyāhāra* or inward withdrawal of the senses.

<<During the II Century BC, the Indian sage Patañjali described, in his *Yoga-Aphorisms,*[449] this withdrawal of the senses as the fifth member (*aṅga*) of the eighth fold steps (*ashṭā-ṅga*) on the path of yoga. *Pratyāhāra*, the sense withdrawal, takes place in the waking state, continues in the dream level and finally merges with the dreamless realm ready to enter the next step in the *turīya,*>>[450] the Transcendent fourth level.

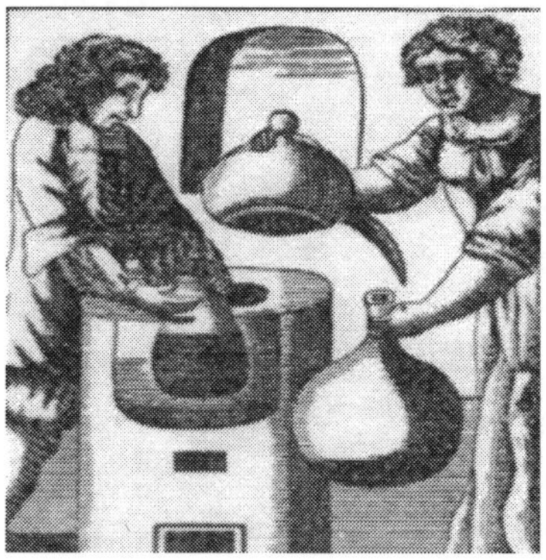

This withdrawal of the senses continues in the dream *room* with a semi-round window. There, the object takes over decanting consciousness into alert senses. Then, while dreaming, the vision is realized as an internal production. Then, the object itself is caught in its being consciousness.

Thus, the perceiver realizes its own centrality as "*I am this creation because I have created all this. Thus, he became the creation. He who thus knows is present at its own creation.*"[451]

The absence of an ending column in this room indicates that this stage should not have a solution of continuity. In fact, the same action continues in the same waking *room* but on a different level.

THE PERENNIAL STILLNESS IN THE WAKING STATE

In this new phase, the subject enters a different mindset. Having withdrawn the senses from the external clangor, the Alchemist reaches a new height, *i.e. altus*. The distilled consciousness poured in the *liquid*-experience produces sublimation, a novel realization indicated by the bloomed six-petal flower in the vial. Each petal united with the central pistil represents the six steps of the heavenly ladder or on the hermetic caduceus all fused into the top sphere of its shaft. The flower symbolizes the alchemical development and transformation of the passive-unstable earthly desirous-attachments into a heavenly enlightenment.[452] In fact, the subject realizes that

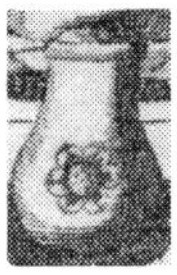

> *"I am a stranger in this world; there is no one with me! Just as the spume and the waves are born of the ocean then melt back into it, so the world is born of me and melts back into me."*[453]

Thus, the subject, focusing on its own inevitable epistemic centrality, blossoms as a flower of consciousness.

This realization involves also the objective world. In fact, the object holds that flower of realization while stirring nothingness in a vessel empty of all objectivity. Once the centrality of consciousness is recognized as constituting the reality of the object itself, then, the subject realizes:

> "*Everything is born in me, all is rooted in me and all reaches dissolution in me. I am that Supreme-Spirit without a second.*"[454]

In addition, this *room*-strip has no ending pillar indicating no conclusion of this enlightened state, which continues in the next phase that takes place in both the waking and oneiric stages, as indicated by the square and half-round windows in it.

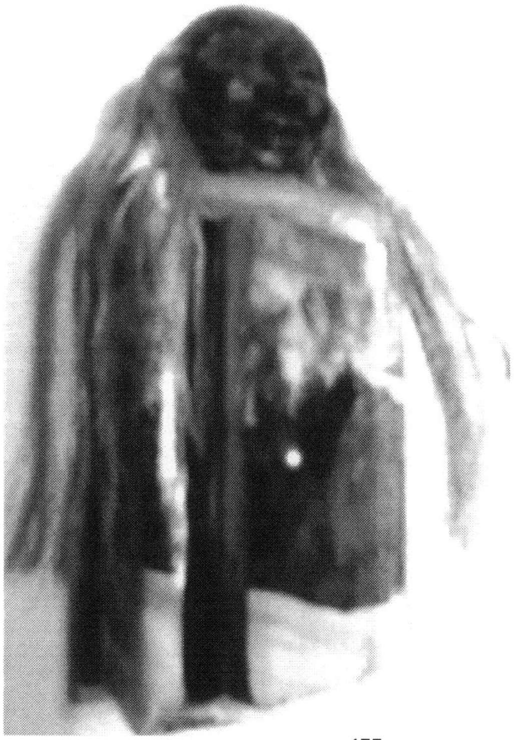

"*I am the door*"[455]

THE ULTIMATE PERCEIVER

The strip of the next phase opens with a square column and remains open-ended. Square and half-round windows indicate that this is both the waking and oneiric realms. However, none of the three characters looks outside those openings. They are all concentrated on their alchemical enterprises.

In the first segment, the subject holds the flask containing his realization of oneness.  He hands it to Apollo, 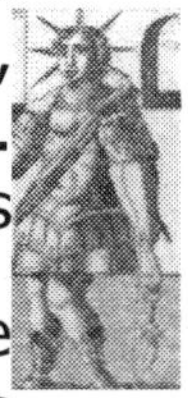 the solar figure with the armor of invincibility and a bow. He is the ultimate perceiver, he is mindfulness and he is the alchemic gold. In fact, he is our true Self-of-self, as distinguished from the mental concepts of *I-think* and from the subjective consciousness or Ego.

"*The mystical syllable AUM is compared to a bow,* [and] *the self to an arrow.*"[456]

The subject, as Ego and/or I-think, realizes that the real knower is the One who cannot be known because It is the Self-in-Itself, while his inevitable unity with the object makes him/her a self-for-itself unknown in-itself. To that real non-reflected and non-reflecting Knower he concedes its consciousness that derives only from that Awareness.

In the second segment of this strip, the object is pouring  all objective consciousness in a three level athanor.  There, the fire of Awareness synthesizes both the subject-object of the waking  and dreaming  stages. Again, wakefulness and dream are founded both on the all-containing silent deep-sleep.

PLATE 7: "THE CIRCULAR MANIFESTATION"

Saturn's circular process of world representation

KNOWLEDGE AND THE HUMAN FACULTIES

This open-ended strip indicates the existential human condition present on all levels. The entire  epistemic process is revealed, namely it is shown, placed on the table of manifestation. The table has 

two levels to indicate that the world of manifestation takes place

a) in the waking and
b) on the dream stage.

A hemp sheet, symbolizing the faculties of the senses that allow us to process experiences, covers the tabletop.

The first segment of this strip represents the noetic or subjective aspect of experience as the act-of-perception aiming to grasp the object. In fact, the process takes place with the I-think pouring consciousness over the fluid- 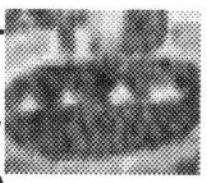 experiences presented by the  woman/objectivity. Namely, the subject is decanting his consciousness over the flowing subject-object triangular-experience-clouds of both his waking  and  dreaming stages.

The second segment represents the noematic aspect of experience in its modes-of-being-given. In fact, it portrays objectivity funneling the fluid objects into the subject's consciousness. The funnel itself is the cone-shaft of the caduceus through which consciousness travels to reach the summit of Awareness.

CIRCULARITY IN THE ONEIRIC WORLD

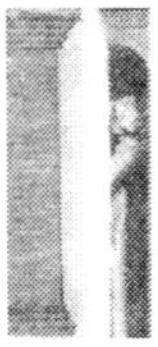

Square columns with Tuscan cap and bases delimit this *room*. The column bases indicate that their foundation is precisely on the ground of this room depicting the interior reality. In fact, it is the oneiric realm, as indicated by the right-projected semicircular and  square windows. The first segment of this strip portrays a

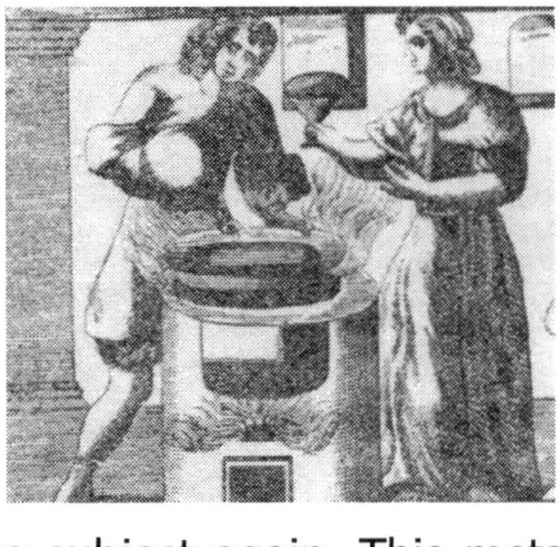

cooking process. It should be pointed out that the vessel or dish, in which the fluid-experience is metaphorically placed, is always round.  It indicates that the subject-object-correlation, which contains the fluidity of experience, is a circular epistemic process, like the autophagous serpent Ouroboros, which goes from the subject to the object and back to the subject again. This metaphorical dish is such because it contains the objective world as *food for thoughts*, which is eaten in all realms of life.

Therefore, this food is cooked on the three level athanor's fire of Awareness sprinkled by the I-think's pure consciousness and funneled by objectivity through its caduceus-staff. Notice that there is a double fire. Namely, to portray that Consciousness has its intensity first in the waking and, then, in the lower dreaming stage.

"*And the priest shall take from the meat offering a memorial thereof, and shall burn* [it] *upon the altar:* [it is] *an offering made by fire, of a sweet savour unto the*

LORD... And every oblation of thy meat offering shalt thou season with salt; neither shalt thou suffer the salt of the covenant of thy God to be lacking from thy meat offering: with all thine offerings thou shalt offer salt... And ... shall burn...an offering made by fire unto the LORD."[457]

"Ye are the salt of the earth: but if the salt have lost his savour, wherewith shall it be salted? it is thenceforth good for nothing, but to be cast out, and to be trodden under foot of men."[458]

In the second segment of this strip, objectivity blends the fluid experience producing a new compound. Following the withdrawal of the senses, the four triangular clouds, which as such impeded the vision of the sun-self-in-itself, are now capable to self-reveal the stars that they always were. They are the subject-object of the waking-dreaming realms fused into a new vessel of unified pure consciousness held by objectivity. Furthermore, those stars are also the alchemic symbol for *sal ammoniacus*, ammonium salt. Its qualities symbolize the "law of physical transmutations as well as of the law of moral and spiritual transmutation... Salt symbolizes incorruptibility... because its flavor is indestructible."[459]

SATURN'S CREATIVITY

This is another open-ended strip. It indicates the fundamental existential human condition from which the entire epistemic process starts. As we have seen, Saturn represents the quiescence of the dreamless sleep. However, here there are more and different details regarding this mythical figure. To understand the last strip of Plate 7, we need to analyze and visit some aspects of the Indian and Egyptian traditions. These mythologies will offer an explicative caption for the corresponding images depicted in this strip.

It is by *pouring* pure consciousness within ourselves, namely by focusing internally with self-introspection, that we discover the inner *sat*urnine quiescence in deep sleep with no objectivity. The Indian *Ṛg Veda* declares that

> "*The seers, searching with reflection in the heart, found the connection of being in non-being.*"[460]

Saturn is a devouring desire. He is famine devoid of objective food.
Saturn is a devouring desire. He is famine devoid of objective food.

> "*Indeed, all this was concealed by Death, by Hunger, because hunger is death,*"[461]

hence, his desire, hunger and need to return to the sub-lunar world of duality. In fact,

> "*in the beginning desire sprung about. Consequently, that desire, that intentionality was the original flowing seed of the mind.*"[462]

Therefore, like dreamless sleep hungering for dreams, out of nowhere, from the secondary primordial fluid waters of possible objects, that creator's desirous hunger gushed forth and

> "*That which was the spume of the watery* [possibilities] *solidified and became the* [objectivity of] *the earth. On it he rested. From him, so rested and heated by the*

flame (tapas) of Awareness, the essence of fluid light came forth as fire."[463]

Here, Saturn is emitting fire and his nakedness represents his hypnotic or cataleptic state as

"warrior trance... [*i.e.*] of the warriors who, on account of their hot-ardor [*tapas*], melt snow thirty steps away."[464]

This is similar to the, scientifically observed, Tibetan lamas' capability of controlling their skin temperature through meditation.[465]

The Indian Agni-Fire, the god son-of-the-Cosmic-Waters (*apāṃ-napāt*), was the first born from the inscrutable depth of the Transcendent Pure Awareness.

> "*Agni, the Divine-flame is the individual soul, the Leader and the Digestive-fire within a person, who is this one by whom this food is cooked and then eaten.*"[466]

Asked about the nature of *tapas*-fire, Ramana Maharshi answered:

> "*If one watches whence the notion of I arises, the mind is absorbed into that. That is tapas* [the flame-of-awareness]. *When a mantra* [prayer-chant] *is repeated, if one watches the source from which the mantra sound is produced, the mind is absorbed in that. That is tapas* [the flame-of-awareness]."[467]

To further understand this statement, let us follow Tolle's experiment,

"Close your eyes and say to yourself: 'I wonder what my next thought is going to be.' Then become very alert and wait for the next thought. Be like a cat watching a mouse hole. What thought is going to come out of the mouse hole? ... As long as you are in a state of intense presence, you are [fire] free of thought. You are still, yet highly alert [burning fire]. The instant your conscious attention sinks below a certain level, thought rushes in. The mental noise returns; the stillness is lost. You are back in time."[468]

Then, the subject quenches the fire of Awareness by pouring his consciousness over it and becoming *conscious-of* the world.

However, the deeply introverted, reflexive moment leads to the original creative self-construction, which is the auto-transparent self. The self-for-itself springs out as desire by itself from the primordial nothingness of non-being. <<Eventually, that hungry intentionality becomes the circular flowing (*rétas*) beam of consciousness-*of*. That is the one which measures (*raśmi*),[469] with space and time, the world of representations placing them in existence, in the Reality of pure Apodicticity.>>[470]

Here we must quote again the *Bṛhadāraṇyaka Upanishad* where Death-Mṛtyu continues his creative process,

> "*He desired: 'Let a second self be born from me.' He, Death or Hunger, identified with the Mind, paired with Mother-Word. That, which was the flow-of-semen (rétas),* ***became the 360°***

> ***year***. *In the beginning, indeed, the year was not. For as long as the space of time of a year he parented his child."*[471]

<<We read that the semen-flow (*rétas*) of time, necessary to deliver the babe, is one year (*saṃvatsara*). The Vedic solar year of 360 days,[472] or the lunar month[473] is a 360° circle of time that moves out of the generator only to return to its starting point.

> "*Twelve are the fellies and one is the wheel-year... joined together in it are three hundred and sixty spokes...* [and] *the year was projected from the foaming Celestial Ocean."*[474]

> "*The Father-of-the-creatures is the year itself."*[475]

The eternal circular flow of the year, represented by the symbol of the wheel, or, in our Plate, the barrel in which Saturn sits,[476] is the *time* necessary to create. It is the *time* it takes for the subject to *project* the object and become conscious of it by reducing it to its own subjectivity.

A graphic expression of this circularity is rendered in a vignette in the sarcophagus[477] of Pharaoh Seti I. There, Osiris, god of the dead, is rendered bent outward shaped as a circle... His body encircles a legend that says,

> "*This is Osiris; his circuit is the place of departed souls* (*ṭuat*)"[478]

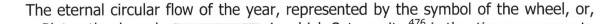

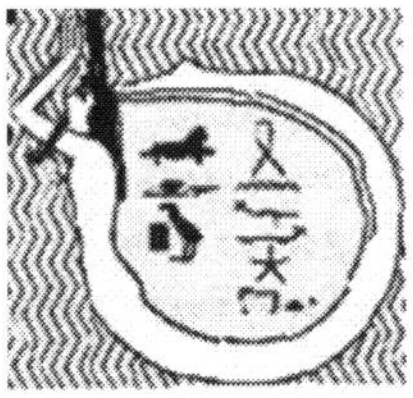

and that god declares,

> "*I was he who came into existence as a circle."*[479]

In Genesis, we find the same metaphor of circularity of consciousness. Indeed, God acknowledges His creation six times at the end of each full day circle,[480]

> "the *evening* and the *morning*,"[481]

when the circularity, from darkness to light is completed. *Maitrī Upanishad*[482] says a day and a night, having twenty-four hours (*ahorātrā*), to indicate the circularity of creation.

> "*One day* [is] *with the Lord as a thousand years, and a thousand years as one day*,"

declares Peter.[483]

> "*And God saw everything that he had made, and, behold, it was very good... And he rested on the seventh day, from all his work which he had made."*[484]

On the seventh day, no objectivity is present. He is back in the timeless inscrutability of His-Celestial-Waters-in-itself from where everything departed. Since time is the product of this creation, past, present and future are only mental constructions of a continuum in which creation implies its being *created*

> "*before the world was*"[485]

created, as well as it *is* created *after* it *will be* destroyed, as well as it *is* destroyed when it *is* created.

> "The distinction between past, present, and future is only a stubbornly persistent illusion,"

wrote Einstein in a March 1955 letter.[486] There is a concomitance of all times, ages and events. Therefore, the Egyptian god Osiris says,

> "*I am Yesterday, Today and Tomorrow... I am the divine hidden Soul who creates the gods... He is I and I am He.*"[487]

Jesus states,

> "*verily, I say unto you, before Abraham was, I am.*"[488]

Bahá'u'lláh writes,

> "*Muhammad, the Point of the Qur'an, revealed: 'I am all the Prophets.' Likewise, He saith: 'I am the first Adam, Noah, Moses, and Jesus.*'"[489]

We find the same circular process in the Arthurian Romance. There, Merlin is

death's procreative power-mark, as the stone Abadir.[490] He

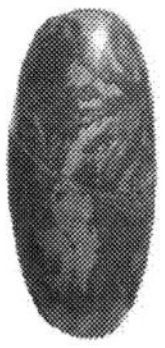

is the mage who, from the prenatal condition, makes the world appear from nowhere. He

> "made the Round Table in tokening of roundness of the world, for by the Round Table is the world signified by right, for all the world, Christian and heathen, repair unto the Round Table, [a total] number of an <u>hundred and fifty</u>, for then was the Round Table fully complished."[491]

One-hundred and fifty is a conventional number symbolizing infinity in most of the medieval Irish literature. The circularity of the world represents the process of knowledge. It requires that we first internalize the world and, subsequently, externalize it in a continuous infinite movement. Therefore, through the senses, the image of the world enters our brain; in return, the brain recognizes the world to be outside, thus a continuous circularity. All that is placed in the subject-object circularity is destined to die and pass away, because it is perceived as an already given, thus as placed into and coming from the past, the realm of the dead, not here now.>>[492] Time, the circularity of the year, is the hunger of the serpent Ouroboros, which continues also after death.[493]

In the last segment of this strip, Saturn is tied

with Isis.

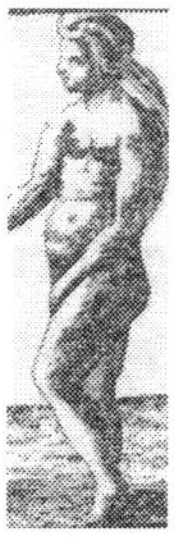

This Egyptian goddess is

> "the female counterpart of Osiris"[494]

and, as Saturn in Plate 5, Isis wears the moon on her forehead. Therefore, Saturn here identifies

with that Egyptian god of the dead. Furthermore, he holds a sword like a Chinese dadao.

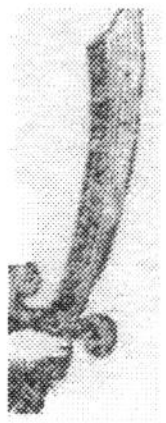

His nakedness represents his *warrior trance* and his sword alchemically symbolizes that, as Time, he has the double aspect of strength and ruler. Namely, he is the

> "destructor... and... constructor... [It is] the Athanor's fire... It is furthermore a ray of the sun."[495]

As such, Saturn equates with the Indian *Mṛtyu*-Hunger, the Creator, also called *Yama*-Restrainer, Death the destroyer.

> "*He* [Death] *desired a second and extended itself as a woman-wife* (*patnī*),[496] *as the object, and a man-husband, the subject, in a loving embrace*"[497]
>
> "*For as long as the space of time of a year, he parented his child. Thus, after that time, he projected him* [a babe]. *Once generated, Death opened his mouth to swallow him; he, the babe, made the sound 'Aa ahhh!' That, indeed, became speech.*"[498]
>
> *Mṛtyu-Death thought, 'Verily if I will kill him, I will consummate very small food.*'"[499]

Therefore, *Revelation* asserts,

> "*The dragon stood before the woman which was ready to be delivered, for to devour her child as soon as it was born.*"[500]

From that embrace, a new reality is produced: two pairs of stars, one for each subject-object, in both the waking and dreaming realms. As we have seen, the stars take the place of the triangular clouds that were obfuscating the star of pure I-consciousness. Now it is able to shine unclouded. They transformed and unified as the incorruptible and indestructible salt.

Isis, here, is portrayed naked representing her weakness as well as her paralyzing power upon viewing her mesmerizing, tempting and beautiful bareness.[501] More so, Isis, here, represents pure-objectivity, the *Mother-Word*, which confers sense to the object.

> "The symbol of Isis in the heavens was the star Sept, *, which was greatly beloved because its appearance marked... the beginning of a new year... renewed wealth and prosperity."[502]

In conclusion, Saturn and Isis portray the circularity of consciousness, which is the same circular flow of Time in the form of day or year. Breaking that circle would mean, not only to overcome Death, who is at the *end-of-time*, the all-eating-beast, but also to reach the final liberation in Awareness.

Barrel, detail of the *Voynich Manuscript*

PLATE 8: "THE NEW BEGINNING" (SECOND ASCENSION)

The ascent into the Realm of Transcendence

"STANDING FIRMLY IN THE SECRET SHADE OF THE HEART"

The new reality, produced up to this point, changes our waking and dreaming realms. In the new *room*,  the conscious unification  of the subject-object leads us to pure I-consciousness, now able to shine as unclouded 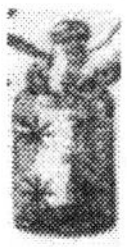 stars. This is the salt * of transformation, the beginning of a new reality, viz. the Transcendent one.

"*Having entered* [and] *standing firmly into the secret shade*  *of the*  *heart*,"[503]

then, this transformation takes place.

"*The All-knower, placed within both fire-sticks, like a fetus well borne by pregnant women,* [is] *the Fire-of-knowledge* (*agni*) *praised by the awakened persons offering oblations, day after day. Verily, this* [One, in the fourth state, is] *That* [Supreme Self]."[504]

The All-knower (*jātá-vedas*)[505] is Awareness-belonging-to-all. It is Agni, the fire of a three  level athanor at the center of the Subject-Object  circularity. There, rests the fetus, the embryo (*gharbha*),[506] the epistemic dewdrop, 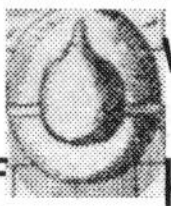 which rests within the two. It is ready to be born to the world of knowledge. The object points  to deliver it, through the shaft  of consciousness into the Transcendent world.

<<Like the manger, the feeder of Bethlehem, the House of food of knowledge, *Brahman*, the Self-existent is the Golden seed, the center (*gharbha*), the egg, the fetus (*hiraṇya-garbhá*) in the Primordial waters from which It

"*was born as Brahmā the Creator*."[507]

The pure potential enlightening Awareness in-itself without qualities is Transcendent. Different from the transcendental consciousness that is the source of the intentionality of consciousness in act. In fact, this last one is transcendental consciousness because is continuously turned towards the correlated object.>>[508]

"*Behold, a virgin shall be with child, and shall bring forth a son, and they shall call his name Emmanuel, which being interpreted is, God with us...*[509] *And she brought forth her firstborn son, and wrapped him in swaddling clothes, and laid him in a manger... And... the men-shepherds said one to another, Let us now go even unto Bethlehem, and see this thing which is come to pass, which the Lord hath made known unto us. And they came with haste, and found Mary, and Joseph, and the babe lying in a manger.*"[510]

A devotional Greek Orthodox icon, called *Our Lady of the Sign,* portrays the Virgin Mary as the Mother having the Creator in the secret of her womb.

ASCENSION TO HEAVEN

Two angelic messengers of the Transcendent transport that embryo to the

Heaven of Apodictic-Awareness towering, as the Sun, in the Supreme Sky. That fetus is the transformed reality of the consciousness-*of* this objective world into Pure-Mindful-Consciousness. The entire process is aided by

ten Sephiroth represented as ducks or seagulls or doves.[511]

Sephiroth

Like Aristotelian categories,[512] the Kabbalistic Sephiroth[513] are ten in number. They constitute the Tree of Life.[514] They are emanations, namely the procession that moves from the internal Intelligence of God-Head outwards to the external World.

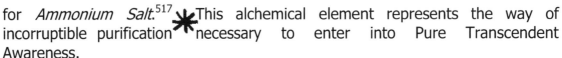

In this plate, they are represented as birds inverting their directions. In fact, from the external they are now reverting back to their source. In this plate, they are divided in two flocks.

The left one is led by

1) the Crown (כתר *kether*) or Pure-Consciousness. It is represented by a bird carrying in its beak a peaceful olive branch with the alchemic  symbol for *Sulfur*[515] of the Philosophers.  This alchemical element characterizes the Sun. It generates the male fiery light of individuation (*principium individuationis*) that serves as preparation and "transformation of the soul for the ascension"[516] into Pure Transcendent Awareness. Individuation, therefore, returns to its Universal Reality.

This Sefirah is followed by a flock of four other Sephiroth-birds:

2) Wisdom (חכמה *chochmah*) and Potentialities;
3) Understanding (בינה *binah*) and Intelligence;
4) Mercy (חסד *chesed*) and Spiritual Power; trailed by
5) Severity (גבורה *gevurah*) and Judgment.

The next flock, on the right, is led by the sixth Sefirah,

6) Beauty (תיפארת *tiphareth*) and Wholeness. It is represented by a bird carrying in its beak a peaceful olive branch with the alchemic symbol  for *Ammonium Salt*.[517]  This alchemical element represents the way of incorruptible purification necessary to enter into Pure Transcendent Awareness.

This Sefirah is followed by a flock of four more Sephiroth-birds:

7) Victory (נצח *netzach*) and Endurance;
8) Glory (הוד *hod*) and Majesty;
9) Foundation (יסוד *yesod*) and Pillar; trailed by
10) Kingdom (מלכות *malkhuth*) and Earth.

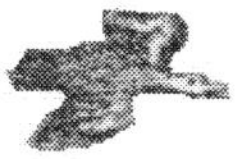

The return

Both the subject and object, alchemically transmuted into angels, are aided by those *birds'* return to their *nest*. Having fixed their unshaken concentration on the liberated embryo, they ascend through the shaft of consciousness into Transcendent Awareness.

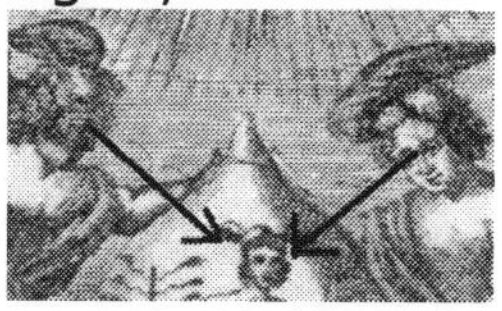

A new alchemic process takes place here. It is based on Paracelsus' three principles (*tria prima*), namely the combination of 1) the transforming spirit of sulfur (*spiritus sulphuris*), 2) the ascending spirit of mercury (*spiritus* ☿ *mercurii*) and 3) the purifying spirit of salt (*spiritus salis*).[518]

This embryo is the dewdrop, the cosmic egg.[519] It is the unified state of mind in deep sleep.

Enter dreamless sleep with awakened Awareness

In it, transformed by sulfur and purified by salt, the entire world is fused into the one path of escape from this transitory world. Portrayed as Mercury, he is the way of consciousness between the sun-subject and the moon-object unifying all the ten

Sephiroth into his

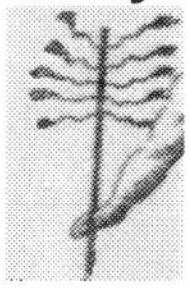

caduceus as snake-powers.[520]

However, this unification is not final. A deeper refinement of this Alchemic Art is necessary in order to reach a total transmutation into the Gold ☉ of Awareness. Our heavy-*lead* ♄ nature is still grounding and anchoring us to this

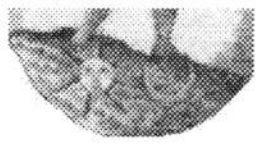

Earth 🜃 or mountain of representations. In fact, from the deep-sleep state (NREM) we return to the land of representation in the dream (REM) and waking states.

The Caduceus in the *Voynich Manuscript*[521]

PLATE 9: "RETURN OF THE SAGE"

Gilgamesh returns in the dream world

IN THE DREAM WORLD

In this strip, the subject returns on the road of the dream landscape. There, once again, the object presents herself with the offer of fluid events served from the circularity of experience. She pours it in the vial of the subject's consciousness. There, the epistemic synthesis takes place anew.

The first 1677 original print presents a different landscape with no boulders. There is only one rocky formation, which, nevertheless, does not change the overall metaphorical rock symbology, as we will describe.

In deep sleep without dreams, the subject reaches the state without perception and without representation from which the entire creation started.

> *"And the Lord God caused a deep sleep to fall upon Adam, and he slept."*[522]

Thus, from the level of deep sleep Adam comes back to find Eve, an alter ego. The process of generation starts once more. Eventually, both eat again of the fruit of the Tree of Knowledge. Similarly, Gilgamesh[523] misses Immortality because

> "a mist of sleep like soft wool teased from the fleece drifted over him."

However, this time, the realization of the subject-object synthesis, in the unity of the mercurial embryo depicted in the previous plate, has reached a new conscious enlightenment. The object, in fact, is not referred any longer to an external reality different from that synthesis. Rather, it is realized as being the product of that synthesis. In fact, it is Mercury himself, namely the embryonic synthesis of mindfulness reached in the awaken deep-sleep, that hands the vial of consciousness to the object herself.

The woman-object draws attention to the rocky formation of the ground below to indicate that the objective and rock solid world *out there* is testimony to the new alchemic transmutation. To prove it, she points to the soil. Similarly, the Buddha touched-the-ground (*bhūmi-sparśa*) to summon the Earth as witness of his enlightenment.[524]

Therefore, Mercury, the unity of reality, hands her the novel realization in a metaphorical vial. And the object points to herself as if to say – for me?–

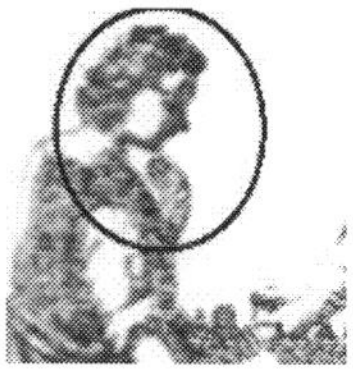

The flask represents the pre-epistemic synthesis of deep-sleep. Mercury hands it to her over that rocky formation.

> *"Upon this rock I will build my church; and the gates of hell shall not prevail against it…*
> *And I will give unto thee the keys of the kingdom of heaven."*[525]

In fact, the presence of the *solid* objective world confirms and witnesses the Pure-Aware-Certitude without which the objective *solidity* of the earth itself would and could not be.

CONCENTRATION

For the higher segment of this plate, refer to the upper part of Plate 4. The significant difference between this and that plate is the rendering of the five senses. In Plate 4, they are, figuratively, square hemp sheets in a rectangular formation and grounded on objectivity basking in the Light of Awareness. Their four-sided appearance indicates that all the senses are directed towards the four corners of the universe.

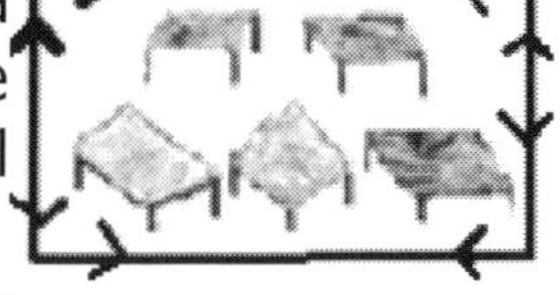

In this ninth plate, however, the senses are represented as round dishes containing the fluidity of experiences. There are six dishes, namely the mind followed by the five senses in formation.

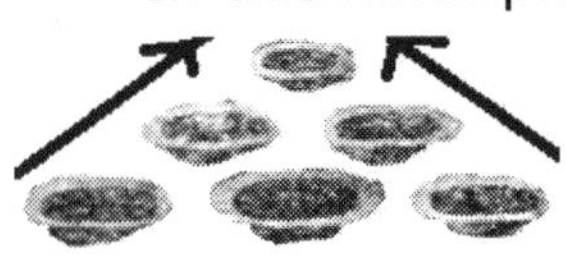

"And there were set there six waterpots of

stone, after the manner of the purifying of the Jews."[526]

Their triangular arrangement points up △ to the Light of Awareness shining on them. In addition, that light itself has a triangular shape. In fact, the equilateral triangle pointing up is the alchemical symbol △ for fire. In this case, it is the Fire of Awareness.

To explain the reason why the mind is listed with the five senses, we must turn to the Indian tradition. There, the mind (*mánas*) is conceived as yoked (√*yuj*), fused in a unity (*yoga*) with all the faculties of the senses[527] (*indriya*), which form the experiencer, the enjoyer of this world. This unification is evident when,

> "*as all the rays of the setting sun become united in this circle of light and as those rays radiate out when it rises again and again, so indeed all those* [senses] *become one in the higher shining entity of the I-think. Therefore, when a person does not hear, see, smell, taste, feel, speak, take, enjoy, evacuate or move, then they say s/he is sleeping."*[528]

On the level of the waking and dream states, we are whipped around, like Odysseus through the tempestuous oceans of life,[529] by all the psychological impulses, namely, the gods (*deva*), the demons (*asura*), the lustful hunger (*mṛtyu*) and the desires (*kāma*) of our own making.

> "*Thus* [for one] *who is ... with the faculty of the mind always un-concentrated, his faculties* [are] *un-submissive, like vicious horses for the driver./*
> *However,* [for one] *who has intuition* [and] *the faculty of the mind always yoked in concentration, his faculties* [are] *submissive, like good horses for the driver./*[530]
> *Also, whosoever is always impure, without intuition,* [and] *without intellect does not attain that goal* [and] *falls into the flow of worldly illusions."*[531]
>
> "*Verily, the vigilant knower should control her/his mind as s/he would with restive horses yoked to a chariot."*[532]

Trapped in the dream of oneiric illusions, the persons, who are without clear insight, can never reach liberation. They are dust, illusion seized by their desires and needs. Therefore, in that dust, they shall return. However, those who are of one-mind (*sa-manas-ka*), Self-aware and unanimous,[533] shall reach the final liberation.

> "*Blessed* [are] *the pure in heart: for they shall see God."*[534]

It is through *yoga* (√*yuj*), *i.e.* through the act of unifying the mind, that one *yokes* (*yukta* √*yuj*) through concentration (*dhāraṇa*) the faculties of the senses.

In Patañjali's eighth fold yoga steps (*ashṭā-ṅga*), the act of concentration (*dhāraṇa*) follows the inward withdrawal of the senses (*pratyāhāra*) and precedes meditation (*dhyāna*). In it, one reaches the complete identification of the subject with the object, which grasps, in a synthesis of knowledge (*prajñānaghana*), the unity of all multiplicity. In this synthesis, Being is seized as the Qualified Supreme Spirit (*saguṇabrahman*).[535] Then, all the five

> "*faculties of the mind* [are] *always yoked in concentration*."[536]

Then, the exterior merges with the interior. This, in yoga is called *dhāraṇa*, steadfast concentration. The beam of consciousness focuses on one pinpointed mark in total concentration by holding the mind firmly in one place and on one concept without wavering or being distracted by any other thought. Then, the mind and the five senses are centered in a steady pinpointed circularity of consciousness.

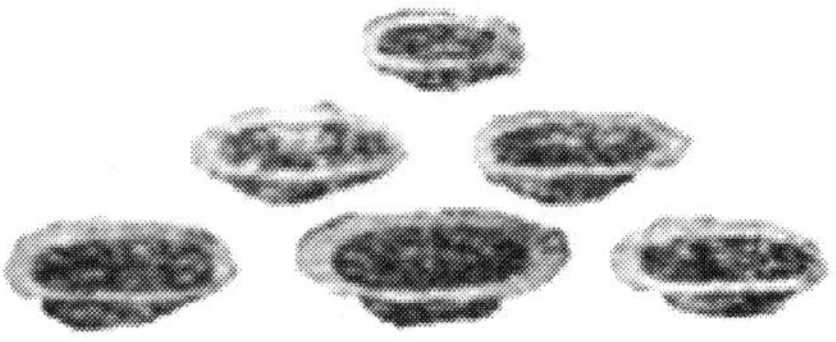

This is represented by the six round dishes. Each one contains the flowing-stillness of the experience pinpointed by *dhāraṇa*. This process will be detailed and depicted in the next plate.

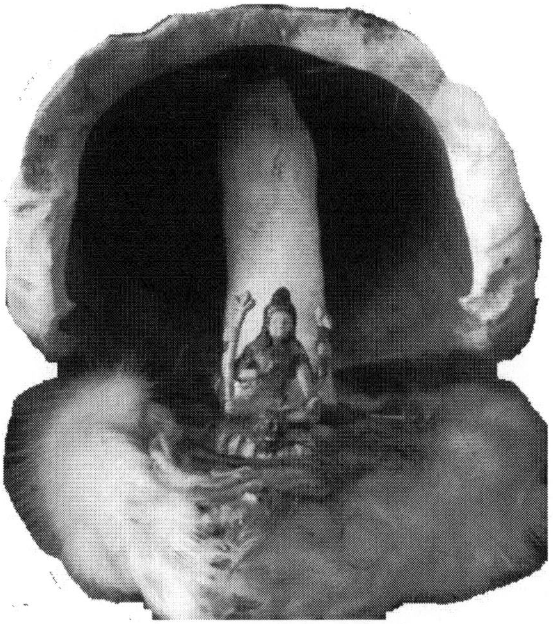

The cave of the heart

PLATE 10: "THE PINPOINTED DREAMING MIND"

Immovable concentration of the dreaming mind upon one mark

AWAKENING IN LUCID DREAMS

 **Enter dreams with awakened Awareness.** 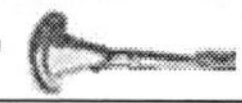

This open-ended strip instructs how to entertain a lucid dream.

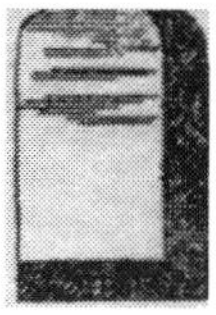

The semi-circular right-projected window indicates the oneiric world.

While in this state, bring the steadfast dreaming *dhā́raṇa*, viz. the "immovable concentration of the mind, upon"[537] the unity realized in the dreamless-sleep.

Dhā́raṇa means *to hold the thing*, to concentrate on one-thought-object only, with the total exclusion of all others. This concentration is done by weighing precisely the clear subject-object synthesis of consciousness, symbolizes by the grain of salt,  with pure detached enlightenment, as a blossomed lotus. 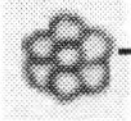 This means that the serene gaze of Certainty looks upon only one conceptual object and nothing else.

This entire process of pinpointed concentration is depicted as the subject pouring

the purified subject-object star-like consciousness-unity  on one dish of a scale and the pure-enlightened gaze on the other

dish, in order to reach the perfect pinpointed  balance.

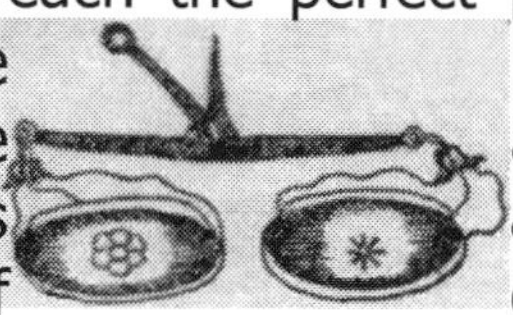

The average reader may regard the scale and the weighed substances portrayed here as a confirmation that the book is describing measurable substances of chemical experimentation with actual physical elements. Consequently, our interpretation of the scale may seem highly implausible. However, we should examine the symbology of the balance according to different traditions.

The Egyptian *Papyrus of Ani* describes a scale on which a heart is weighed against a plume. The heart, emblematic of consciousness and hieroglyphically represented by the Heart-Canopic-Jar (𓄣), is balanced with the goddess Ma'at's weightless plume (𓆄), emblematic of purity. The jackal-headed Anubis weighs the heart before the assembly of the gods.[538] Here no physical chemical experimentation is taking place. Therefore, we must understand it as a clear metaphor.

The Egyptian Great-Balance has on its top the god Thoth, the ape-headed dog representing equilibrium. At Anubis' side is the ibis–headed scribe, again as the god Thoth. It represents Truth.[539] Revelation says,

> "*I saw, and behold, a black horse, and its rider had a balance in his hand.*"[540]

Daniel declares,

> "*Thou art weighed in the balances, and art found wanting.*"[541]

The *Śatapatha Brāhmaṇa* states that the dead is weighted in order to receive its just reward.[542] In the Egyptian accounts, a metaphoric crocodile is said to drag the soul, whose heart weighs more than the feather, in the stream of life's torments where it gobbles it up. If the heart, however, is found to be *lighthearted*, namely weighing as the plumy pure consciousness, then the soul *Ka* (𓂓) gains immortality among the gods.[543]

Ramana Maharshi clarifies that

> "The meaning of the word Heart is the Self. As it is denoted by the terms existence, consciousness, bliss, eternal and plenum it has no differences such as exterior and interior or up and down. That tranquil state in which all thoughts come to an end is called the state of the Self. When it is realized as it is, there is no scope for discussions about its location inside the body or outside... Heart means the very core of one's being, the centre, without which there is nothing whatever... This spiritual Heart-center is quite different from the blood-propelling, muscular organ known by the same name. The spiritual Heart-center is not an organ of the body... [With a play on words he further explains] The undifferentiated consciousness of pure being is the Heart or *hṛdayam*, which is what you really are, as signified by the word itself (*hṛt* + *ayam* – Heart am I). From the heart arises the `I am'-ness as the primary datum of one's experience."[544]

Returning to our book, the entire process of concentration takes place on the table  of world manifestations. Nevertheless, *dhāraṇa* or concentration is not only 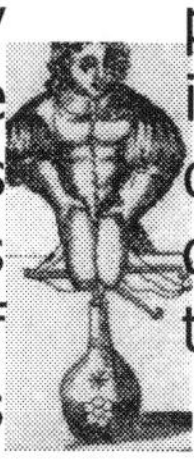 prerogative of the subject. The object takes an active role in it. She pours 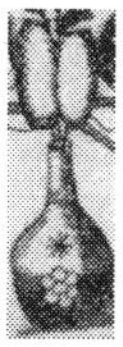 the content of the two plates of the scale in the flask of unity. Meanwhile, the subject concentrates on that flask. In fact, as depicted in the  second segment of this strip, in that vial, held by objectivity, he pours his consciousness.

BREATH SUSPENSION AS STILL CONSCIOUSNESS STARTS ITS ASCENSION

New changes take place, as the adept of the Hermetic Art proceeds on this solar path. At this level of awakening, the practice of concentration (*dhārạṇa*) requires to pin-focus on one and only one small object with the total exclusion of all others. The table of  the world of manifested representations is restricted. This 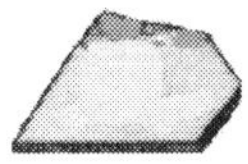 restriction, caused by concentration, affects not only the mind but also breath. Thought, excitement and/or tranquility affect the flow of breath. Experience, as in-breath flow, takes in the objective world and, as out-breath, projects it out. As the concentrated focus of *dhārạṇa* becomes more intense, also the physiological breath slows down, becoming almost imperceptible. In fact, when we fall asleep our breath slows down. *Dhārạṇa* withdraws the flickering senses and reaches the intense concentration of one-mindedness. Then, if

> "*thine eye* [] *be single* (ἁπλοῦς *aplous*), *thy whole body shall be full of light.*"[545]

Then, breath or the thought flow stops in its centrality, *viz.* in the Pure Self, the point of equilibrium between subject and object from which the entire epistemic circularity irradiates. Physical breath follows suit, it will slow down or have moments of prolonged quiescence.

What Altus depicts in the first segment of this strip is what in yoga is called *prāṇā-yāma*, breath-control. It is concentration on the suspension of breath. It is the disengaged focused  attention to the breathing stillness between the rhythmic flow of inhaling and exhaling.

The entire process, assisted by objectivity, is rendered as a glass blowing technique. Breath passes through a blowpipe at the end of which rests a *gather*,  namely, a lump of molten glass that must be blown into shape over an open fire source. The alchemist here, as a yogi

> "by his respiratory rhythm, repeats and, in a sense, relives Cosmic Great Time, the periodic creations and destructions of the universes. This exercise has a dual aim: on the one hand, the yogin is brought to identify his own respiratory moments with the rhythms of cosmic time, and in so doing realizes the unreality of time. But on the other hand, he obtains the reversibility of the flow of time (*sāra*) in the sense that he returns upon his tracks, he re-lives his previous lives and *burns up* (as the -*Kālacakra Tantra*- text puts it) the consequences of his previous actions – he annuls these action, and so escapes from their karmic consequences."[546]

In the vignette, the subject is cutting short the long 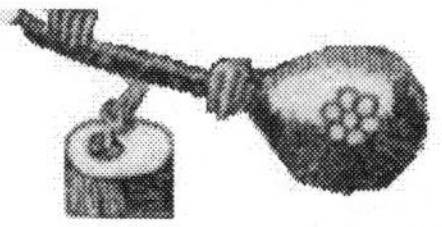 neck of the matrass, *viz.* the glass vessel with a round body and a long narrow neck containing the blossom flower of pure-enlightenment. The blowpipe  and the flask's neck symbolize the

 breath channels. The  gather represents the lungs. Breath, contained in the blowpipe and the gather is motionless and suspended. The stillness of breath, as described in *prāṇāyāma*, is metaphorically portrayed by those object being idle and displayed  resting on the table before 

objectivity. The gather itself represents  the stillness of the lump of breath contained in the symbolic glass- lungs and not inhaled or exhaled. The subject-blower has reached the *prāṇāyāma* breath suspension, as indicated by the gesture of the object-woman touching her lungs. 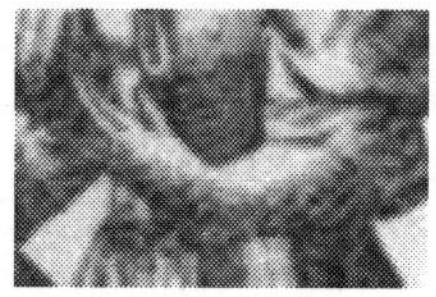

In the next 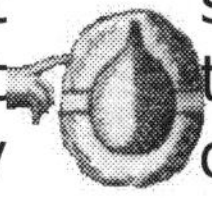 segment of the second strip, the subject points out that the new compound, obtained by concentration and breath suspension, is the dewdrop, the embryonic unity of realization. That *dewy* composite, that realization is placed in the three level athanor with the aid of the object that is now covering up the shaft of  consciousness. This action and gesture symbolizes that objectivity is only within. In fact, there is no objective world *out there* that is not necessarily contained within our own subjectivity. Then, the caduceus, the athanor, the pillar of the world leads to the heights of Transcendent Awareness.

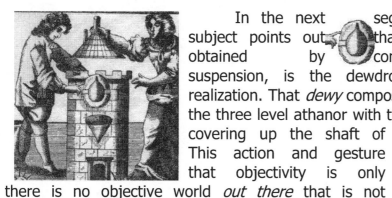

THE *DEWDROP* IN THE TRANSCENDENT REGAL UNITY

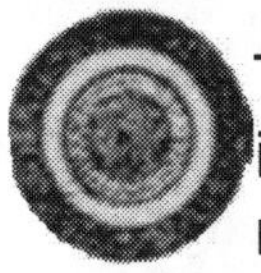

The discharged arrow of the Self has reached its target,[547] the journey completed, the quest achieved. This is the goal! Isis is the Moon, which now has transmuted in the true Nature-of-Things. Therefore, this time, it is not

the Sun (as in Plate 6), but it is she who holds the bow which shoots

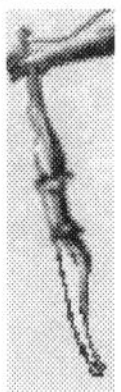

> *"the self as an arrow and the Supreme Spirit is the target which one should hit without any distraction and, as an arrow, one must become united with that.*"[548]

As Isis is pointing out, the arrow reaches its goal through the three level athanor.

Dressed in her robe, she declares,

> "I am all that has been, and is, and shall be, and my robe no mortal has yet uncovered."[549]

In the eighteenth century, Novalis wrote,

> "According to the inscription, no mortal can lift the veil, we must seek to become immortal; he who does not seek to lift it, is no true novice of Sais."[550]

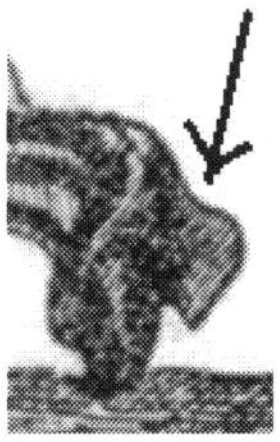

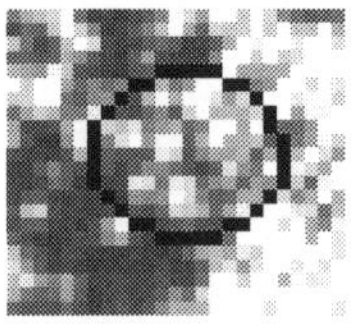

Embroidered on that robe and hardly visible is the lotus flower of enlightenment.

Symbolically, Isis' robe evokes the secret concealments of enlightenment. Therefore, who removes it reveals her light and, ultimately, oneself.[551]

Actually, the target is no other than the entire psychophysiological topography of

emanation. Except, now it is realized that the goal and its source are the same center of everything.

The Objective-Queen-Moon-Isis and the Subjective-King-Sun-Apollo, through the shaft of the Athanor-Conscience, have reached the union in the Hermetic royal wedding 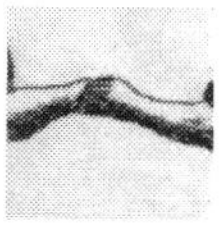 of the sublimated Subject and Object. In other words, it is the mesmerizing esthetic rapture of the Pure-Subjective-Mindfulness at the presence of the Pure-Objective-Consciousness.

The couple stands on this transient world. There, the demons of ravenous hunger, gorging appetites, illusory desires, hideous hatreds, teeth gnashing anguishes, nightmarish fears, depressing anxieties and excruciating sufferings, just to mention a few, lurk in the folds of dreams and are all trampled upon and vanquished by the Noble

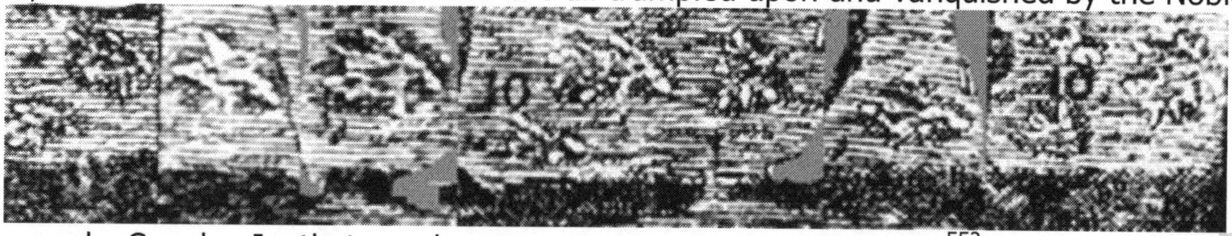

Heavenly Couple. In that murky swamp or rugged 10 terrain,[552] two number 10 stand out, one following Isis, the other Apollo. The number ten corresponds to the Kabalistic ten Sephiroth and the Pythagorean *tetractys* (τετρακτύς), the one triangle made of ten distinct ones. Furthermore, it is composed of the sum of 1+2+3+4, symbolizing the harmony of the four states of life, the four elements, the four directions of space, the fire, the phallus, the original couple and more. Over all, it symbolizes duality and unity.[553]

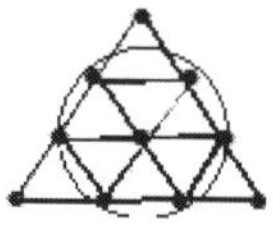

However, the ground on which the King and the Queen stand needs to be purified and leveled in the next state of enlightenment.

Mindfulness

PLATE 11: "VICTORY!" (THIRD ASCENSION)

The victorious achievement of the Hero

IN THE SILENCE OF INTERIORITY

"*But thou, when thou prayest, enter into thy closet, and when thou hast shut thy door, pray to thy Father which is in secret; and thy Father which seeth in secret shall reward thee openly.*"[554]

In the silent secret centrality of the heart, focus on the indivisible unity of the Divine King and Queen. That is the Pure Conscious Mindfulness.

"*Wherefore they are no more twain, but one flesh. What therefore God hath joined together, let not man put asunder.*"[555]

The presence of semicircular and especially of the round windows portray that center and  that secret heart. Expecially these circular ones represent the  pinpointed focus of the unified distilled essence of cognition present in the NREM state.

"*The state of deep-unconscious-sleep*[556] *alone, having become one compact knowledge, made of bliss.*"[557]

In this vignette, we are inside the waking, dreaming and dreamless reality at the same time. The realization obtained is present on all levels and not conceiled by any drapery, as depicted in the previous Plates (2 and 8). The unified realization travels along the three level Athanor of consciousness freely ascending to the Transcendent world of Awareness.

Let it be clear, the Consciousness realized here is not that of the consciousness-*of* an object, but is that of Mindfulness devoid of any objectivity. It is Fullness ready to disclose the door to the Apodictical Certitute following the Present-Sure-Awareness of the Ultimate-Perceiver, the One Who cannot be undersood while being the One Who understands.

"The first step in the practice of initiation is to *know* that *silence* and that *concentration* of which we discussed about...

The second step is to bring the sense of self from the head to the heart, that is, from the reflected conscience to the central organic consciousness... Then, the possibility to establish contact with the *subtle body* is open...

Sleep, the way it is lived by the common human type, is annihilation of consciousness, a sort of death barely illuminated by the mirage of dreams...

However, when a greater introversion is reached, when the internal life, fortified, becomes preponderant and the external world ceases to be felt as the only center of interest – one has vaguely the sense that the life of sleep is a continuation instead of a pause, an integration of the waking's life instead of a sudden, periodical and incomprehensible interruption...

The night, instead, is a cosmic awakening, a surfacing, a palpitation and a resonance of spiritual forces that the physical solar light subdues with its violence. It is a *spiritual sun* that rises and that our subtle body seeks out orienting itself towards it. One must cultivate a sense of expectation for an incommensurable form of life freer and more extended than the ordinary wakeful life...

From one state of consciousness to another, upon falling asleep, there is a moment of obfuscation and discontinuity that needs to be overcome... One must learn the *art of falling asleep* (1)...

(1) Its counterpart is the *art of dying* – *ars moriendi* – not less neglected than the first one and now lost. [Ur's Note]."[558]

With penetrating concentration, this art leads the up, through Athanor of conscience, to the Transcendent *Midnight Sun*.

THE MIDNIGHT SUN

The drawing of this Vignette is similar to the upper part of Plate 2 and 8. Therefore, we will not repeat the explanations for each part. Nevertheless, we will emphasize the differences.

First, left and right of the Awareness/Sun, we see two spheres, the moon and the sun.[559] They symbolize the final sublimation in the unity of Awareness of both Isis (Moon) and Apollo (Sun) of the previous Plate.

As in Plates 2 and 8, the towering Sun symbolizes the Transcendent. The entire vignette is different from the other two, in that it portrays the apotheosis of the Adept who ascends to the supreme Transcendent levels of Pure Apodictical Awareness.

The ascension in the previous plates was not complete since the dew-embryonic-drop had in itself residues of the objective world. In fact, Plate

2 shows Neptune in the dewdrop, synthesis of unity, seated on the world's rock with a dolphin, the fish that traverses the world of duality. On Plate 8, Mercury in the synthetic dewdrop is shown still grounded on the earth of dualism.

However, in this Plate, Mercury, the definite conscious synthesis of subject and object, is finally free from all earthly attachments and can identify with that Pure Awareness from which he derived.

"O abundant grace, by which I presumed
to fix my sight upon the eternal light,
so that therein I consumed the vision!
In its depth far down I saw that is placed
bound together with love in single volume,
what unfolds through the universe ...
The universal form of this knot

I think I saw...
the love that moves the sun and the other stars."[560]

PLATE 12: "THAT WHICH UNFOLDS THROUGH THE UNIVERSE"

The love that moves the sun and the other stars

The upper vignette of this design is similar to Plate 4 and identical to Plate 9. Previously, we have pointed out their differences and, therefore, we will not go over them. However, it is interesting to compare it with a much later illustration of the *Divine Comedy* by Doré. There, angels move along a staircase coming down from Dante's Paradise.[561]

We should keep in mind that in this Plate we are still in the concentration (*dhāraṇa*) stage of this alchemical art. In the previous Plate, this concentration was taking place in the dream world. Now, this Plate represents concentration in the wakeful state. In the state of wakeful concentration, the mind with

> "*all the faculties of the senses become one in their corresponding deities and the deeds and the intellectual self all* (become one) *in the Supreme Imperishable One.*"[562]

In fact, according to the *Bṛhadāraṇyaka Upanishad*, the mind resolves in the moon, the eye in the sun, hearing in heaven's quarters, body in earth, speech in fire, breath in wind and the hair in plants.[563]

The light of Awareness shines over the three states of life, namely, wakefulness, dream and dreamless sleep. The Adept should remain concentrated in that light.

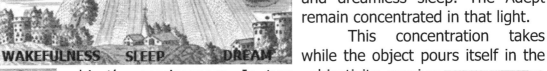

This concentration takes place while the object pours itself in the subject's consciousness. In turn, objectivity receives that conscious object from the hands of the Mercurial Unity.

This strip is similar to the one in Plate 9, however, without the presence of the boulders or rocky grounds, namely, the objective solid world.

PLATE 13: "BEYOND CONCENTRATION"

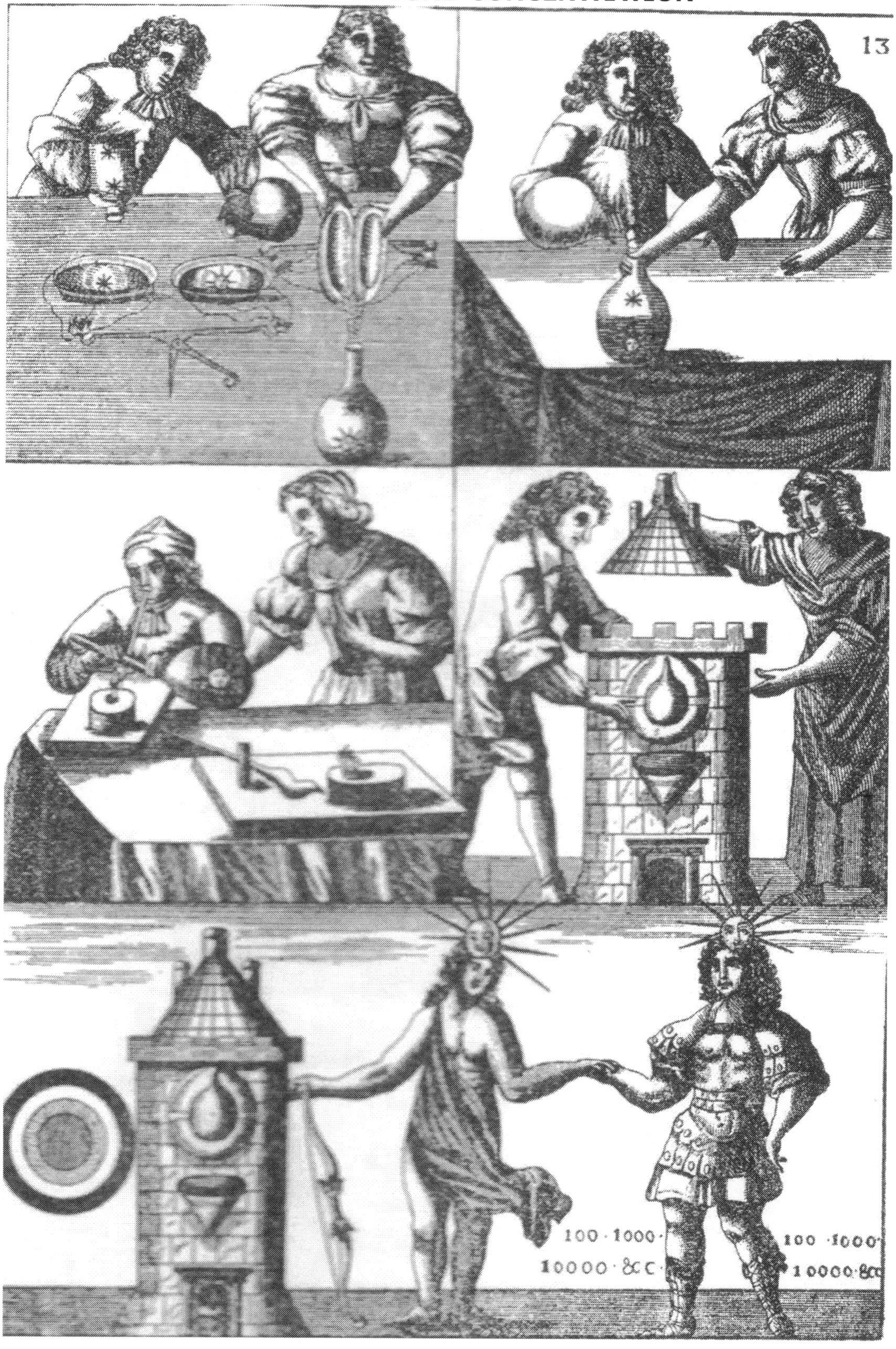

Going to the next step, having mastered concentration

THE CONCENTRATION OPUS IN THE ENTIRE WAKING STAGE

This plate is like Plate 10, but with some differences. All that we described for that Plate remains valid for this one too. However, we will analyze only the differences.

The first segment of the first strip is open-ended. There are no columns. Here, we are not in a *room*, meaning that this process continues in all stages of life. Like Plate 10, the subject pours  the purified subject-object star-like consciousness-unity on one dish of the scale and the pure-enlightenment on the other dish, in order to reach a perfect pinpointed balance.

However, the concentration does not lead to the blossomed flower  of enlightenment. It is now pure enlightenment as Pure Mindfulness. It is like a sun  on which the  subject pours its entire attentive consciousness. At the same time, the object 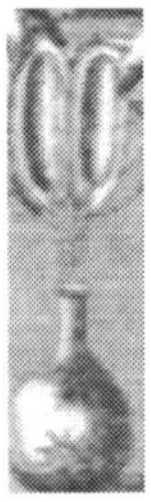 unifies  the salt of subject-object synthetic consciousness with the newly realized Mindfulness. 

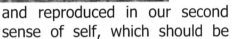

In the second segment of the first strip, the object hands  to the subject the new product. In return, the subject, to further distillate it with concentration, pours  on it its consciousness again.

A meaningful light, coming out from the subject's solar plexus, was  portrayed in the first 1677 edition and reproduced in our second  edition. It is the light of heart, the sense of self, which should be brought "from the head to the heart, namely, from the reflected conscience to the central organic consciousness."[564]

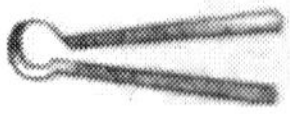

"*The Person the size of a thumb*  [is] *the Inner Self, always seated in the heart of the creature. From one's own body, one should draw him out with firmness like a stalk from the reed. One should realize Him* [as] *the Pure, the Immortal. Indeed, one should realize Him* [as] *the Pure, the Immortal.*"[565]

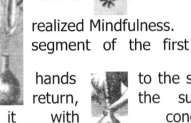

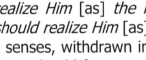

To be precise, all the senses, withdrawn inward and reabsorbed in the centrality of the Heart of Awareness, now should focus concentrated on the unity of Mindfulness. The *Chāndogya Upanishad* says,

"*This is my Self within the heart. Although smaller than a grain of rice or a barley-corn or a mustard seed or a grain of millet or a kernel of a grain of millet, this Self of mine residing within the heart is greater than the earth, greater than the sky, greater than heaven, and greater than all these universes.*"[566]

Jung defines the Self as

"smaller than small,"[567]

the foundation of this body.

"*Verily I say unto you, Whosoever shall not receive the kingdom of God as a little child shall in no wise enter therein.*"[568]

The Capuchin Padre Pio of Pietrelcina (1887–1968), writes, that while praying,

"Jesus' heart and mine, if you allow the expression, fused. They were not any longer two pulsating hearts, but only one. My heart disappeared, like a drop of water is lost in the sea."[569]

The heart, then, is the metaphorical seat of the Self-in-Itself, the Transcendent which

"to translate the meaning in words
is not possible, yet the example is sufficient."[570]

Ramana Maharshi clarifies that

"The meaning of the word Heart is the Self. As it is denoted by the terms existence, consciousness, bliss, eternal and plenum it has no differences such as exterior and interior or up and down. That tranquil state in which all thoughts come to an end is called the state of the Self. When it is realized as it is, there is no scope for discussions about its location inside the body or outside... Heart means the very core of one's being, the centre, without which there is nothing whatever... This spiritual Heart-center is quite different from the blood-propelling, muscular organ known by the same name. The spiritual Heart-center is not an organ of the body."[571]

"All the faculties of the senses become one in their corresponding deities, deeds and the intellectual self all in the Supreme Imperishable One."[572]

"Verily, the gods are the five channels of perception of this heart."[573]

"O Agni,[574] *Divine-flame, bring here the gods."*[575]

Agni-fire assimilates food as a 'Digestive-fire.'

"He eats food in all worlds, in all beings, in all Self."[576]

"This digestive fire common to all humans is, in other words, the Cosmic-being... rooted within the human being."[577]

The mind (*manas*) is considered a sixth organ of perception and the Moon presides over its mental expansion.

The second strip of this Plate does not need much explanation, in that it is similar to Plate 10 and has already been discussed there.

Be awake in the light of Awareness.

THE ROYAL WEDDING

The last strip, however, although similar to Plate 10, offers some meaningful differences. We invite the reader to refer to that plate for the similar parts, but we will explain the differences.

First, we must point out that the ground on which the Royal Couple is standing is not any longer the rocky or murky swamp of this transient world. Now, it is the purified

world of Mindfulness. Furthermore, there are new numbers inscribed here. The number 10 of Plate 10 has increased. We find **100•1000•** and **10000•&CC•** next to Isis and the same repeated for Apollo.

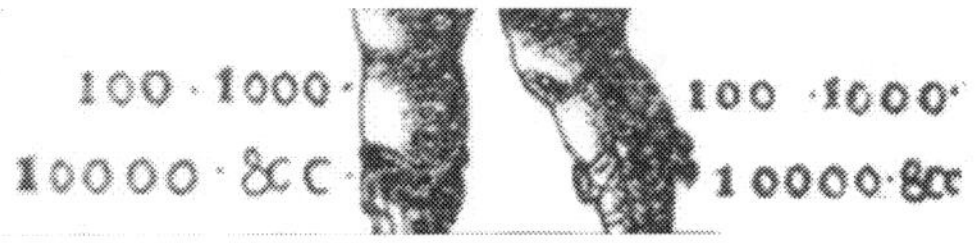

100 is the number indicating everything, namely,

"it is a part that forms a whole from the whole."[578]

1000 is the number of immortality, the return of the Savior and Paradise.[579] Moreover, 10000 is

"the number symbolizing completeness... a renovation of the earth."[580]

Therefore, the Royal Couple, viz. Isis and Apollo, individually and together, are realized now as the immortal totality of the earth's renovation, the Savior and the completeness in Paradise. In addition, their greatness grows with an exponentially geometrical progression, **&CC** etc. etc. Explicitly, the unity realized is the Alpha (A) and the Omega (Ω), the beginning and the end of everything.

GODS AND INFINITE NUMBERS

The great Renaissance astronomer, mathematician and philosopher Giordano Bruno[581] can clarify this unity of Isis and Apollo, their totality and, at the same time, their exponentially geometrical number progression. The Renaissance philosopher states that the infinite variety of beings, of their powers and of their acts is the perfect adequate manifestation of God. Along this infinity, Bruno recognizes different levels or degrees. On the lower levels, the natural laws, through love and civil virtues, govern the human society mediating among individualities. On higher grounds, the *furious* Eros directs the mind to God's endless confines. There is no contradiction between the two. The earthly love, as a shadow of the divine erotic frenzy, beyond its interests and political passions, must make way for the intellect to reach its sublime goal. It would be arrogant, for the individual human mind, with which the whole divinity is one, to consider itself divine. In fact, it would imply individualizing God.

> "The intellect, in whatever state it is found, does not receive the divinity in substance but in similitude, for then there would be as many gods as there are intelligences, thus, these are not formally gods, but are named divine, remaining the divinity and the divine beauty one and exalted above all things."[582]

Therefore, the intellect, in a heroic frenzy, an infinite tension, distances itself ever so much from the confines of its own individuality as it flies towards the unlimited

"divine object that is Truth."[583]

Again, we see a double act that pervades all Neoplatonic philosophies.[584] On a side, there is the One who,

> "realizing its wholeness, does not move locally, since it has nothing outside where to transport itself. Realizing its totality of being, does not generate itself; since there is no other being that it may desire or look for. Realizing its being everything, it is not corrupted, since there is nothing into which to change. Realizing its infinity, it cannot diminish or increase...
>
> [On the other hand] the world-soul is the constitutive formal principle of the universe and all that is contained in it... I understand it to be one in all things... It comes to produce diverse configurations, and to carry into effect different faculties... thus, only the exterior forms change... [This does not diminish the One, because] the soul is all in the whole world, and all in any one of its parts."[585]

It remains substantially and indissolubly One, without ever moving out of itself. In fact, Bruno reiterates that these are the dynamic psychological forces of the universal human being.

Giordano, almost as an *ante litteram* existentialist, declares that these are

> "the divinities who have set me here, I who find myself here, and those who have eyes and see me here."[586]

We must understand the faculties of the mind, of the intellect and of the senses, in Bruno's philosophy, as in the Indian tradition, correlated to divine mythological figures. In fact, they are numina, dynamic geniuses that are the internal luminous cognitive forces constituting the inwardness of the universal human being. Thus,

> "the divinity dwells in us by means of the reformed intellect and will...[587]
> These are not formally gods, but are named divine."[588]

Psychological paradigmatic forces, metaphorically equated to gods, determine destinies and regulate even the most menial of actions or events. However, each one of them is immersed in the always-shining present light of Awareness. Giordano Bruno, in the *Spaccio de la bestia trionfante*,[589] records that

> "Jupiter... [among his] acts of Providence...[590] has ordained that at that time the cuckoo should be heard singing from Starza.[591] In addition, that it must *cuckoo* neither more nor less than twelve times. Then, that it must depart to make its way to the ruins of Castle Cicala,[592] for eleven minutes of an hour, and thence fly away to Scarvaita[593]... As to what is to be done afterwards [Jupiter] shall provide later on... The worlds placed under Jupiter's Providence are infinite... [Every] grain of sand on earth,"[594]

regardless of how insignificant and minimal it may appear, is an axis of the whole containing innumerable focuses each projecting immense dimensions. Unity and infinite number, while being different, are, at the same time, one into the other. Unity is not an accident, but is the essence,

> "the end and goal of intelligence, and the abundance of all things... [The Divine Mind, in its Providence] is able to perform all things, not only in the universal but also in the particular."

Bruno lashed against fanatic dogmatists. There was no privileged revelation, there was only the natural religion based on the law of love, which maintains the universal freedom of philosophy with its pursuit of Truth. There is an infinite interconnection and order among all things. It operates from within, as the soul of each natural being. In our mind ideas gradually lead us to be accustomed and to discern the world. Thus, everything, as by magic, can be deducted from everything. In that totality, each thing can be known and all can be remembered by memory. All is in the ocean of *Awareness*.[595] Everything, is under that *Providential Sight*, in fact,

> "Jupiter, has ordained and disposed... that an institution or law, whether coming from heaven, or arising from earth, must not be approved or accepted if it does not deliver utility and comfort"[596]

to the human society.

Nevertheless, also the most unassuming and minute thing is present in It. And Bruno makes a point in describing that the Universal Mind is conscious of the "*red lace of Paolino*" Casoria, the Inn keeper, as well as of the gown of tailor Adanesio Biancolella, alias "*Master Danese.*" It takes care of Don "*Franzino's melon patch*" and each fruit "*from the jujube tree*" of Filippo's father. It moves the "*average size*" bug of the bed of his relative Costantino and each beetle, "*born out of the dung*" of the ox of his maternal uncle Albenzio. It is aware of the moles "*in Antonio Faivano's garden*" as well as each puppy of the bitch of his relative "*Antonio Savolino.*" It does not forget each hair of "*Vasta, the wife of Albenzio,*" and of the poor widow "*Laurenza,*" or of Paolo Alemanno, "*Martiniello's son.*" It is aware also of the molar of "*the old woman of Fiurulo*" and of Ambruoggio's semen, derived from "*his affair with his wife.*"[597]

> "Furthermore, I [says Bruno] with my divine object, that is Truth, for so long, as fugitive, hidden, depressed and submersed, have judged that term by order of fate as the beginning of my return, apparition, exaltation and magnificence so much greater as greater had been the opposite antitheses."[598]

The ancient land of Nola, its soil, air, fruits, animals and people, all become the very essence of Bruno's spirit, the hub of his cosmopolitanism that never made him lose his identity as *il Nolano*, the Nolan freethinker.

As a young boy, Filippo realized that, by shifting the center of observation, the circumference changes perspective.[599] This realization took place during his first trip to Mount Somma, the Eastern side of the Vesuvius. First, the young boy had observed the far away mountain from the green, fruitful hill of Cicala and the mountain appeared barren and desolate. However, when he was on the volcanic slopes, they looked green and lush with vegetation. While in turn, Cicala, from that distance, seemed barren and desolate.[600] Then, he must have also realized that this reflection was possible only if the first and opposite point of observation remained ideally vivid in his memory as if he had never left it.[601]

As in his diagram titled *Expansor*,[602] he looked at new horizons always from his subjective vantage point, from his home at the foot of Cicala's hill, in Nola. This was his center of observation. Thus, he called himself *il Nolano* (the Nolan). In the young mind the quest for certitude ensued. That quest took him around the world and beyond.

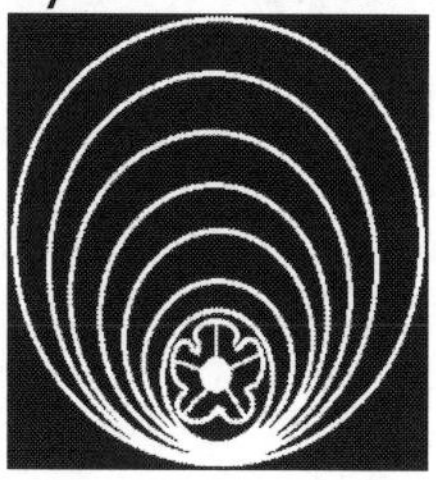

Bruno explains that he

> "who, from his elevated vantage point, looks and considers the life of other men subject to many mistakes, calamities, miseries, useless toils, is a Jupiter. He alone is blessed, he alone lives the heavenly life, when he contemplates his divinity in the mirror... While each is individually one, he alone is all."[603]

The Nolan went abroad to visit other European castles in order to satisfy his

> "great desire... to see customs, to know talents, to become aware... of some new truth of something that he may be missing."[604]

Breaking away from his native land must have given Bruno a new perspective, a sense of freedom and another vantage point from which to view the world. He started seeing himself as a

> "citizen and servant of the world, son of the father Sun and the mother Earth...[605] To the true philosopher every land is the motherland."[606]

The scope of life is the search for the

> "*coincidenza de' contrarii*,"[607]

as expressed by Cusanus.[608] Namely, the *coinciding of contraries* that leads to Truth, to the One, from Which nothing and no one, even if generated, never departed.

> "As the principle of being is one, so is the principle of conceiving the two contrary objects [and] we delight in... that, which comprehends in itself all sensible impression."[609]

In the fire of his *Heroic Frenzies, il Nolano* was now One and all (ἓν καὶ πᾶν *èn kaì pân*) with the Principle of Certain-Truth that Caused him in the first place.

> "For happiness in life, it is better to consider oneself Croesus and be poor, than to consider oneself poor and be Croesus.[610] We see that every pleasure consists only in a definite transit, journey and motion. Just as troublesome and sad is the state of hunger, so, displeasing and grave is the state of satiety: thus, that which gives delight is the motion from one place to another... There is no pleasure in rest."[611]

Giordano sang about infinity. Beyond the Copernican heliocentrism, he envisioned the infinite Cosmos as the live mirror of the infinite Deity.[612] *Bruno's Revolution* ventured far beyond the narrow confines of Copernicus' cosmology. However, while the Copernican theory took about sixty years to be proven by Galileo, Bruno's view required more than four centuries. In April 1999, with the discoveries of different planetary systems,[613] the scientific community confirmed Giordano's intuition of the Cosmos. Furthermore, in August 2013, NASA's probe, Voyager 1 left the solar system giving proof of

> "an infinite universe... and... besides this world another, and infinite others... There is an infinite number of particular worlds similar to this of the earth... other planets, and other stars, which are infinite; and that all these bodies are worlds, without number, which make up the infinite university in infinite space, and we call this the Infinite Universe, in which are numberless worlds."[614]

PART IV

THE SUBLIME BEGINNING

PLATE 14: "DEEP MEDITATION"

14
VI
II
X
Ora
Lege Lege Lege Relege labora
et Invenies.

The state of object dissolution into Certitude alone

THE ALCHEMICAL LABORATORY

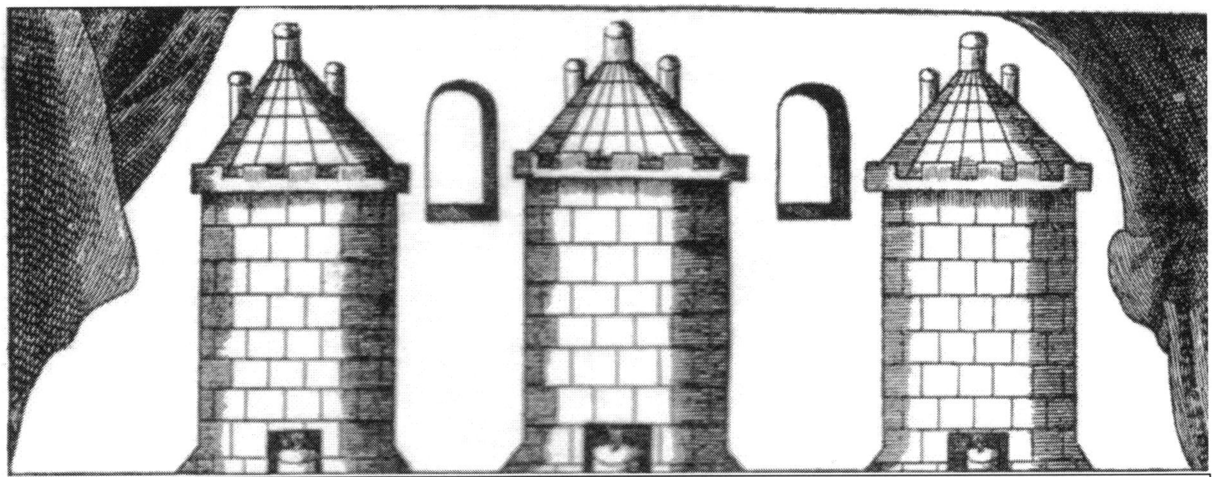

WAKING	NREM	REM

The Alchemical Laboratory is secluded within the drapery of our internal secrecy, our own epistemic loneliness. In fact,

"*there is no one with me in this world*!"[615]

The real Alchemical Laboratory is our whole life in all of its three circadian phases. Each phase has its own furnace.

The first one-level athanor is our waking stage with our own personal perspective window on the world seen as external. Note that this window is semicircular because the wakeful world starts from us and ends in us. Nothing can be truly external.

The second and central one-level athanor is our dreamless sleep (NREM) with no window. In fact, the other two start from this state.

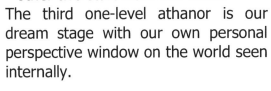

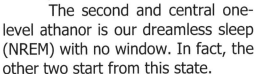

The third one-level athanor is our dream stage with our own personal perspective window on the world seen internally.

THE WORKERS IN THE ALCHEMICAL LABORATORY

Atropos-Morta **Clotho-Nona** **Lachesis-Decima**

Each of the above athanors has, in order, its own worker. Thus, there are three workers in the Alchemical Laboratory. They are the three Greek Moirai, Latin Parcae or Fates sisters. They weave controlling all destinies with their distaffs  or rods for unspun threads. Their spinning is the beginning and end of time/consciousness poured in the flame of Awareness.

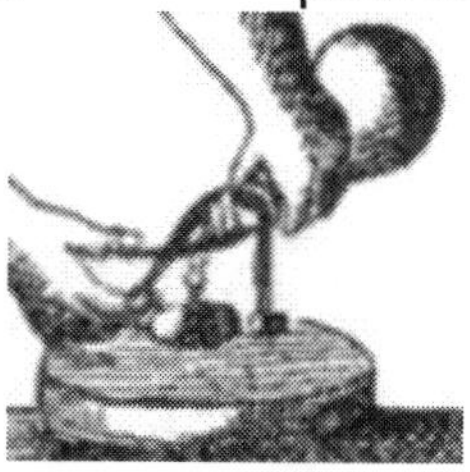

1) Clotho, Latin Nona, knits the cord of consciousness, existence and birth.

2) Lachesis, Latin Decima, measures the consciousness' lifespan.

3) Atropos, Latin Morta, cuts the lifetime thread.[616] Namely, she cuts the flow of consciousness.

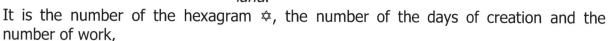

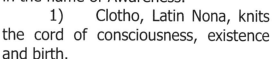

The first worker is Atropos, death itself (*morta*, *mrtyu*). She operates weaving the waking stage of life and cutting its thread. Her number is **VI** VI. It is the number of Jesus' crucifixion when, at

"*the sixth hour there was darkness over all the land.*"[617]

It is the number of the hexagram ✡, the number of the days of creation and the number of work,

"Six *days thou shalt work.*"[618]

"Some exegetes went so far as to read the opening of the Hebrew book of Genesis... "*in the beginning*" differently in order to obtain the phrase... *He created the Six.*"[619]

Six is the distinction between God and creatures and the heart-center of the circle of consciousness.[620]

"*Let him that hath understanding count the number of the beast: for it is the number of a man; and his number* [is] *Six hundred threescore* [and] *six.*"[621]

The second worker is Clotho, here represented as a toddler or a dwarf cutting the string of life and consciousness. He is the dwarf (*vāmana*),

"*the dwarf seated in the middle.*"[622]

"*The person the size of a thumb is the inner self who dwells always in the heart of creatures. It is Wisdom in accordance with the mind and the heart.*"[623]

He

"*stands firmly in the middle of the self.*"[624]

In the Indian tradition, the dwarf is the fifth descent (*avatāra*) of Vishṇu. He is the Dwarf (*vāmana*) who controls over the three worlds. Jung, in his *Phenomenology of the Spirit in Fairy Tales*, recognizes that the metaphor of the dwarf highlights

"a connection with the unconscious."[625]

However, as a child, he is still interested in recreation. He is the child that Saturn did not eat. He is the II

"*second self... born from... Death or Hunger... the year... Death opened his mouth to swallow him.*"[626]

Nevertheless, since the babe would have been a

"*very small food,*"[627]

Death/Saturn did not eat him. That is because he is the wholeness of dreamless sleep without objects, *i.e.* food. He is what Jung called the

"self... the Unknown... [Its symbol is] a living body, *corpus et anima*; hence the 'child' is such an apt formula for the symbol."[628]

The infant represents the Auto-transparency, the sphere of unified Unconsciousness. He is number **II** II, *viz.* the principle of dualism. From him, in fact, the world of duality, life, birth, existence, wakefulness and dream find their beginning.[629]

The items of the child have two different, but both pertinent, interpretations, which, we believe, were intentionally left indefinite by Altus. They can be either toys or utensils for chemistry. In both cases they have symbolic meanings.

I) As toys, namely, a tennis racquet and ball represent the boy's play. In fact, as Self, he starts the play of life. The mortal comes to understand life as an eternal play.[630] It is a play that hurts, but it is a play nevertheless. Life and death, knower and known, *yin* and *yang* ☯,[631] all flow into each other as cosmic play. On the physical plain, this play is the sexual union, on the logical level, it is the synthesis *a-priori*[632] in which the subject-knower can never be separated by the known-object. On all levels of life, physical, logical, psychological or pragmatic, this union has the specific aspect of interactive desire, viz. of play. It is the lure, the fascination, the bondage generated by Death-Mṛtyu's hunger. That hunger subjugates the mortal's mind to the game of the object.

II) As tools for chemical experiments, they are a strainer and a sphere. The colander represents the sifting process to reach a compound, which, in this case, is indicated by a sphere. In the Vedic tradition, the strainer was used to produce Soma, the inebriating juice of immortality

 "*where the filter pours its stream.*"[633]

As we have stated, the child/dwarf in the vignette represents the unity in dreamless sleep. He sifts all duality in a unified  sphere. In fact, sleep without dreams

> "*having become one-compact-knowledge...* [stands] *alone...*[634] [In effect] *in that state, there is no otherness and nothing else that he may know.*"[635]

The third worker is Lachesis. She operates measuring the life's span, weaving the dream state and cutting life's thread. Her Latin name is *decima* (= tenth), which is also her number **X** X, symbolizing that she is the principle of all things and the totality in movement.[636] It is also the number of the Sephiroth, of

"completeness and perfection."[637]

It is interesting to note that Atropos, the first one on this row, is she who ends life, while Lachesis, the last one, is she who weaves the process of life. However, the strip is open ended. This creates a circularity by which life begins from the same nothingness that characterizes the state of death, viz. Mṛtyu. As well as, life ends in the middle of its flow, reducing it to a dream.

The generative procession

TOTAL SILENCE IN MEDITATION

The central part of this strip is very revealing. Let us examine it in all its details.

Here, the *Mutus Liber* depicts with alchemical metaphors the process of Meditation. Usually, meditation is referred to as *thinking with intensity*. However, true meditation has nothing to do at all with thought. It is *Muteness*, Pure Silence.

At this point, if we followed with attention Altus' alchemical process, we know that we have left thought behind. We left it at the moment of the pinpointed balanced  concentration of our alchemical experiment. The last thought we had in our mind was the one we focused upon with steadfast concentration. In addition, the ladle,  with which objectivity nurtures, tastes and articulates the objects of experience, was suspended. Furthermore, the life-ending scissors  of the three Fates are idly resting in the two experience-measuring cups  at the side of the mortar.  What remains in the laboratory 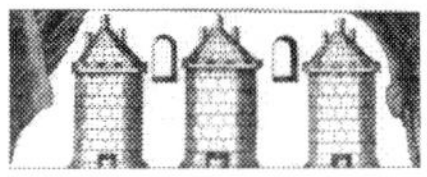 of our mind when the pestle  in the mortar of our brain crushes even that last thought?

What remains is *dhyāna*, profound meditation.

"Meditating is entering truth without discovering [viz. taking the robe off] it, without seeing it from outside, without opening it into words,"[638]

i.e. the *Mutus Liber*.

Meditation is the state in which, the subject, having shed the senses and the objects, dissolves into Certitude.

 **Certitude is the Alchemic-Philosopher's Stone** 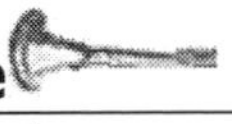

That, Certain-*faith* is the cohesive central point, which holds the two subject-object spinning together along the orbit of its circumference.

– What perseveres when Atlas sheds the world from his shoulders? Only pure strength remains. –

If we could lift from the subject the burden of the object, it would not *subject* the 'I' to its weight. We can think of a knower without a known. However, that would be only a contradictory thought. In fact, we can never experience or *know* it. Atlas must endure, bearing the vault of the sky.[639] Indeed, even when the subject knows itself, it becomes an object for-itself, while the knower, as such, remains unknown, Transcendent. – What persists when the seer sheds the seen, when the hearer sheds the heard, when the thinker sheds the thought and when the understander sheds the understood? Only the Unknown Pure Aware Certitude remains. It was, is and will be there from the very beginning. –[640]

"*This is your Shining Self, the Apodictic Transcendent that is in everything.*"[641]

"*I am That Supreme Swan Spirit dwelling in the light clear waters.* [I am] *the beneficent dwelling in the intermediate region, the sacrificer sitting on the wheel-shaped-altar-of-knowledge.* [I am] *the guest residing in the house, dwelling in the human being, sitting in the circle.* [I am] *the truth dwelling in the order of truth, born in truth's order.* [I am] *the wide dwelling in the air, born in water, the soul produced from the friction of Stones* [and] *born in the earth's-milky-rays-of-knowledge.*"[642]

The mortar  subjugates and conquers the objective world. In it, thoughts are crushed to produce the divine elixir of meditation. The *Ṛg Veda* declares,

"*There where the broad-based stone raised on high to press the juices out... drink... the droppings which the mortar sheds/....*
where the woman marks and leans the pestle's constant rise and fall/...
o Mortar thou art set for work... give thou forth thy clearest sound, loud as the drum of conquerors."[643]

The mortar, which takes the central part of this strip, is decorated with a ten-groove shell flanked by two snakes coming out of it, like the decoration on an Egyptian Pharaoh's head. The shell represents the fecundity of the waters from which Venus was born. It is a symbol of cosmological prosperity, birth, death and rebirth.[644] It is death to the lead-weight of this world of duality and rebirth into the gold-of-Awareness. The ten grooves are the ten Sephiroth and the ten snakes on the caduceus.

Summarizing, the mortar represents the activity within the

Hermetic Caduceus. Therefore, whatever takes place in the mortar happens on the caduceus. The grinding beat of the pestle in it, is the sound of the conquering meditative ascension of the Alchemist along the central axis of Mercury's staff.

At the sides of the mortar/caduceus are two athanors 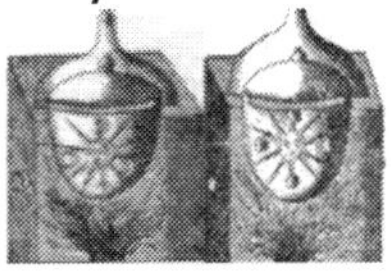 with no levels. One belongs to the moon/ object and the other to the sun/ subject. However, at the presence of the transmuting light of sulfur, the moon sublimates  in a new compound. Through meditation, the Moon does not represent any longer the world of objectivity with its subject-object duality, but it is the totality of space. It is transformed now, by the power of salt, into the incorruptible unification of meditation.

Similarly, at the presence of the transmuting light of sulfur, the sun

sublimates in a new compound. Through meditation, the Sun does not represent any longer the world of subjectivity with its subject-object duality, but it is the totality of space. It is transformed now, by the power of salt, into the incorruptible unification of meditation.

The mortar, between them, has crushed any duality in the distinct stillness of subject-less and object-less meditation.

The drum-sound of the conquering meditative ascension

THE INSTRUCTION

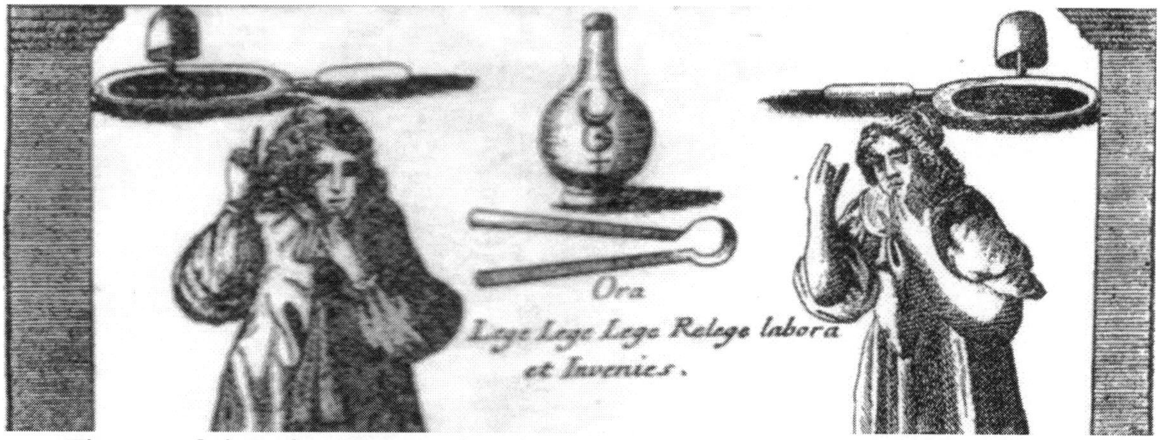

The proof that the *Mutus Liber* does not want to be a simple book of chemistry, in the physical sense of the term, is given by its first word of instruction: **Ora**, Pray or Meditate. The book refers, yes, to chemistry, but it is a Total-Chemistry in all its meta-physical and psycho-physiological aspects. In one word, it is Alchemy. Therefore, MEDITATE.

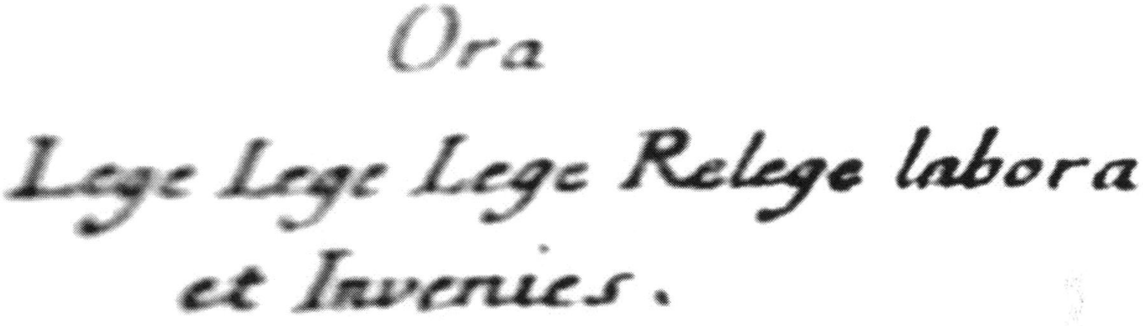

Ora
Pray
Lege Lege Lege Relege labora
Read, Read, Read, Re-read, practice
et Invenies.
and ye shall Dis-cover.

By meditating, by reading, by reading over again, and by practicing in the *labora*-tory of the Art, as depicted in the plates, one will un-cover the arcane mystery of life. The teaching is imparted in silence  and in secrecy,  not only because it is expressed in images, but mainly because that mystery is ineffable. Therefore, practice the Art in the secret 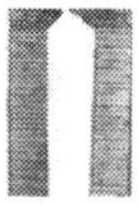 chamber of your *labora*tory.

Like Yoga, this Art has only a pragmatic validity. It is not true because it is based on a dogma imparted by the *Magister*, the Master or the *Guru*. It is TRUE when proven TRUE by the results that one must un-cover or Dis-cover.

In fact,

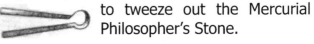

I) First, look up  to the results you obtained when you poured your consciousness  in the concentrated unification of your thoughts.
The left index pointing to Heaven indicates your "penetration into knowledge."[645]

II) Second, look up 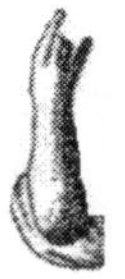 to the results you obtained when you dissolved the objects of your thoughts  in the meditative synthesis of silence.
The woman's hand, with index and pinky extended, points to Heaven. The *horn*-gesture symbolizes the bull of fertility and Isis, viz. the goddess head crowned by *moon-horns*. Thus, that dual objectivity now realizes her divine origin.

Then, you will be able to use the tongs 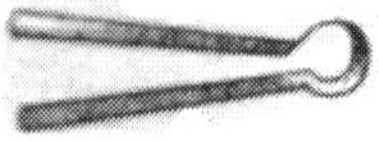 to tweeze out the Mercurial Essence of Unity, namely, the Philosopher's Stone.

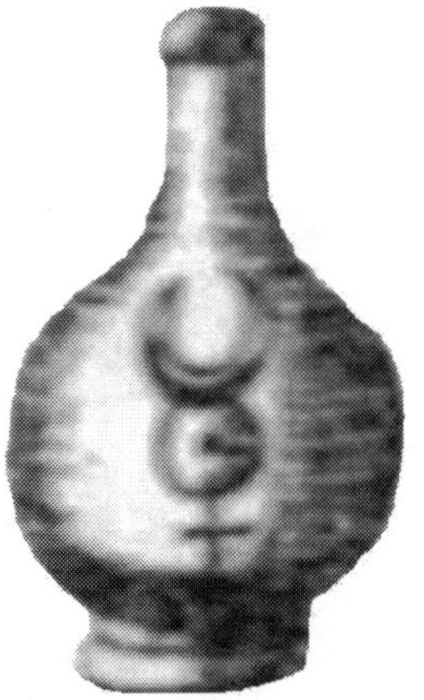

PLATE 15: "ECSTATIC APOTHEOSIS" (FOURTH AND FINAL ASCENSION)

Final liberation

SUBLIMATIONS OF THE VORTEXES ON THE CADUCEUS' CENTRAL STAFF

We reached the last Plate representing the completed ascension. Therefore, any analysis of this print must follow its rising process. Thus, our comment will start from the bottom and reach the sunny top.

At the foot of the plate, we find a coat of arm encircled by a wreath, symbolizing victory.

> "Studies devoted to hermetic symbolism seldom touch upon its connections with heraldry though it seems that they should be obvious even to someone with quite limited knowledge of both systems of symbolism...
>
> HERMETIC HERALDRY ... includes ... the conscious use of hermetic symbols and emblems in later heraldic designs in order to show the owner's interests or make the arms '*speak.*'"[646]

One of the heraldic designs on the *Mutus Liber* coat of arm is the  chevron^, an inverted V pointing  to the top and dividing the shield in two parts. On the lower part, below the chevron^, there are three mountain peaks 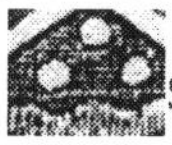 surmounted by three circles. On the upper part, above the chevron^, there are three shells  reminiscent of those on the *Merez*'s coat of Arms. 

To understand the symbolism on our book's shield, we must refer to the function the heart has on the hermetic  caduceus. The heart is the pivotal middle of the world axis. It is the center of the epistemic circumference on which the subject and the object travel chasing each other, like Ouroboros 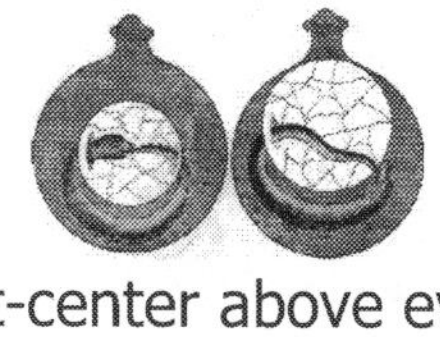 biting its own tail.[647] The chevron, therefore, symbolizes the inversion of direction. The usual direction, from the head to the heart, is inverted. It puts the heart-center above everything  else.[648] Like in the Muslim prostrating prayer-posture, when the head touches the ground, it recognizes its  submission to the heart that stands above it. Al-Ghazali declared,

> "Bowing and prostration are accompanied by a renewed affirmation of the supreme greatness of God... [With] submissiveness [*i.e. Islam*] and humility ... [there is] a fresh awareness

of… impotence and insignificance before the might and grandeur of your Lord Almighty."[649]

The three mountain peaks in the shield represent the three stages of life with the consequent mind-states circles of wakefulness, dream and dreamless sleep. The chevron points to their inversion and sublimation. In fact, the shells represent their rebirth.

<<The new birth reverts on itself, returns to the 'I' and relates to the unconscious state of deep sleep with no representations. From this life of struggle (*jihad*),[650] the holy man (*sādhu*), as an unerring arrow (*sādhu*) aimed directly to the very heart of Auto-transparency, attacks the Transcendent world and seizes it. Thus, s/he reaches the pure uncontaminated state of bliss. There, the 'I' is at the point when Mṛtyu produced the self-for-itself. This is the state of blissful tranquility, where we go from the self to the transparency of the self yet unknown as such.

Previously we have seen the vorticose forces of 1) Life, 2) Libido and 3) Power forming the very beginning of the caduceus as life's journey. Traveling through that shaft, we reach the seat of the Self, the Unknown Transcendent, the babe who Saturn/Death/Mṛtyu was unable to eat at the beginning of his creation. That babe is the Person,[651] the dwarf the size of a thumb seated in the Center of the Heart.

4) THE VORTEX IN THE HEART, in the Indian tradition represented by the vortex-

cakra anāhata, is symbolically located in the heart. Again, we must keep in mind that this heart is not the physical organ, which is only a metaphor referring to the centrality of the Transcendent Real Aware Bliss In-Itself, in the middle of the subject-object correlation. The irruption into the realm of the Heart modifies the entire world, which becomes intuited synthetic comprehension, as signified by the hexagram (✡). In fact, the name *an-āhata* means intact, not multiplied, not (*an*) struck (*āhata*) by something else. It is the sound AUM in its totality. It is the reverting of the objective world towards its source. During that reversal, the previous three *cakra*s are sublimated in their spiritual counterpart. The presence of an inverted triangle (▽), in the circular area (*maṇḍala*) of this *cakra*, indicates a new womb from which the second birth (*dvija*), the virgin birth, takes place. Dante describes this new life (*vita nova*) as,

"I felt myself *awakening* in the heart
a loving spirit that was *sleeping*:
and then I saw Love coming from far."[652]

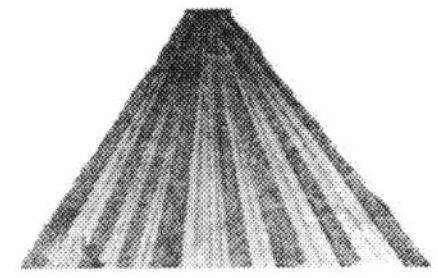

At this level, the individual finds reconciliation with the universal archetypes, as described by Jung, for whom the unconscious becomes transpersonal (*uberpersonliche*).[653] This vortex corresponds to the (M) NREM dreamless sleep. Once the serpent-coiled power of the caduceus reaches the heart it goes back over its steps. From the Heart-*vortex*, it retraces back to the vortex of power (*maṇi-pūra cakra*) to lift that vortex in the spiritual dimension. Power is sublimated becoming, therefore, truly-purified spirit (*vi-śuddha*) in the next *cakra.*

Those same qualities that were characteristic of the first three *cakras* are now reverting

to receive a new identification in the heart. This is the virgin birth at the entrance of the Transcendent spiritual level:

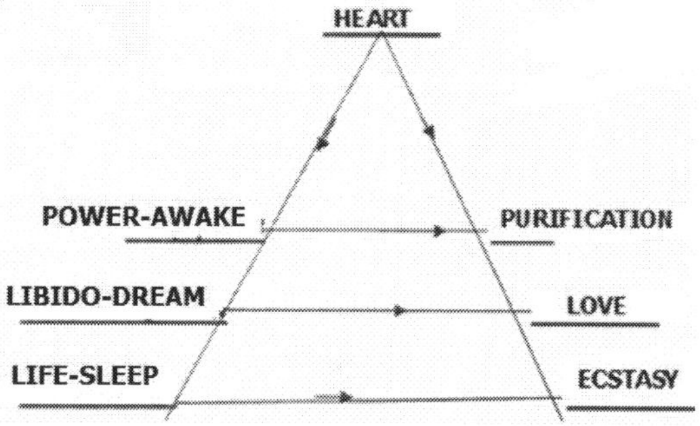

5) THE VORTEX OF <u>PURIFICATION</u>, represented by the *viśuddha*

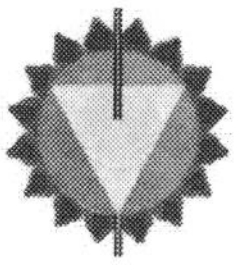

cakra, is symbolically located in the throat. This vortex corresponds to the (U) REM dream sleep. The entire world of will and representation, purged from its objective combative power and conquest, reverts from the exteriority to conquer its own true spiritual interiority. Life itself is *jihād*, a struggle.

> "*O ye who believe! Be mindful of your duty to Allah, and seek the way of approach unto Him, and strive in His way in order that ye may succeed.*"[654]

Based on a well-known traditional (*hadith*) saying of the Prophet Muhammad, upon his return from a war,

> "*We return from the little jihād to the greater jihād,*"

the Muslim tradition distinguishes two holy struggles or wars,
the great one (*el-jihādul-akbar*), conducted by the personal intention (*niyyah*) to submit (*islam*) oneself to the Will of Allah (هللا *Allh*) and the small one (*el-jihādul-açghar*), conducted to spread to others

> "*the law of God*' (*dar al-islām*).[655]

At this stage, the struggle of political power becomes <u>Gandhi</u>'s non-violent respect-for-life (*a-himsā*) and beholding-of-the-truth (*satyā-graha*).[656]

From this level, the force of the coiled serpent (*Kuṇḍalinī*) lifts up, along the caduceus, the second *cakra, svā-dhishṭhāna*, to the level of Love.

6) THE VORTEX OF <u>LOVE</u>, represented by the *ājñā cakra*, commonly

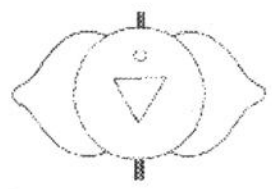

called the third eye, is symbolically located

> "*between the eyebrows.*"[657]

This vortex corresponds to the (A) wakeful state.

During rabbinical Jewish prayers, the worshiper straps the  tefillin or phylactery box, containing Biblical verses, on the forehead. Between the eyebrows is the perception center of command and knowledge (*ā-√jñā*). Here, the mere Libido sublimates into pure Transcendent spiritual love. Dante, the Faithful of Love, calls Beatrice,

"that Lady who was leading me to God"

and he described her as

"something that came
from heaven to earth to show a miracle.
She shows herself so pleasant to the admirer,
that she gives through the eyes a sweetness to the heart,
that cannot be understood by him who does not feel it."[658]

Again, from this level the serpentine power lifts the first vortex of Life to the realm of Ecstasy in the Pure Transcendent.

7) THE SEAT OF ECSTASY, represented by the *sahasrāra cakra*, the thousand-spoked lotus, is symbolically located on the crown of the head; it is *the Interior Castle* of Saint Teresa of Avila.[659] It corresponds to the (•) Transcendent forth state. Here, Life sublimates and identifies with the real internal source of Life itself.

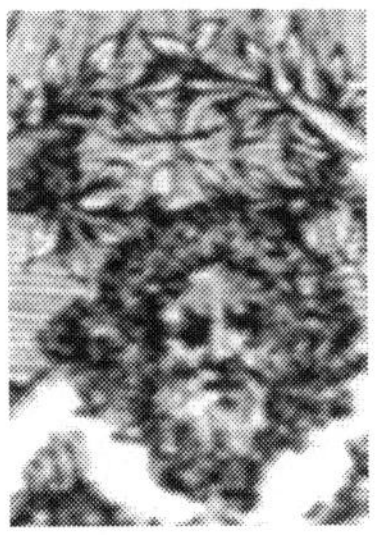

"*A hundred and one* [are] *the vein-channels of the heart and one of them goes out towards the crown of the head. Going up through that, one achieves immortality, the different others are for going astray*."[660]

The previous *Upanishadic* stanza said that one achieves immortality "*going up through*" (*niḥsṛta*) the *sushumnā* channel of intentionality. Since *niḥsṛta*, going up (√*sṛ*), has also the meaning of "*unsheathed*," as in the blade dance

"in which a sword is drawn out of a person's hands,"[661]

therefore the Self is drawn from the body like a sword from its sheath. Similarly, King Arthur, in the saga of Camelot,

"handled the sword by the handles, and lightly and fiercely pulled it out of the stone... without any pain."[662]

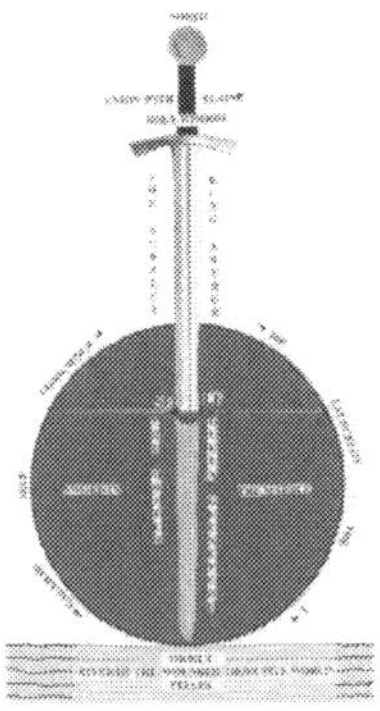

Kendo and Iaijutsu, the Japanese Zen martial arts (*kenzen itchi*), developed techniques for unsheathing the sword (*katana*), during which the *katana* itself becomes a life giver. In fact, the instantaneous drawing of the sword, accompanied by a very deep mind concentration, is recognized to induce a state of pure enlightenment (*satori*).[663] The same concept is expressed by the image of the tongs in Plate 14. With that, one should draw the Self out of the body with courage and intellectual firmness, "like a stalk from the reed," echoing the Biblical separation of tares or rush grass[664] from the blade of wheat.[665]>>

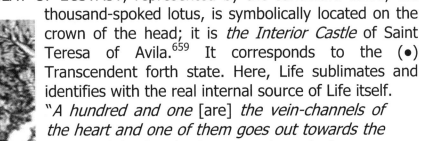

"*From one's own body, one should draw him out with firmness like a stalk from the reed. The*

> *Person the size of a thumb* [is] *the Inner Self, always seated in the heart of the creature. One should realize Him* [as] *the Pure, the Immortal. Indeed, one should realize Him* [as] *the Pure, the Immortal."*[666]

There is an equivalency between the drawing of the self from the central caduceus axis, the symbology of the samurai sword[667] and Altus' tongs. Thus, the two angels, like tongs, draw out the Self of Pure Apodictical Awareness from the dead body.

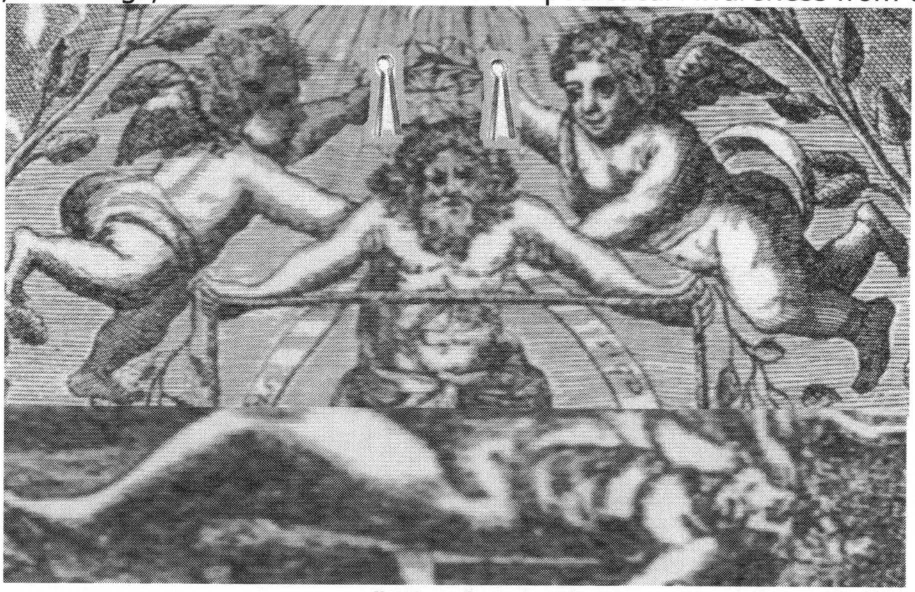

> *"The far reaching narrow ancient path has been traveled by me and verily has been realized by me. Through it, the sages, knowers of the Supreme Reality, having reached liberation, go to the heavenly world."*[668]

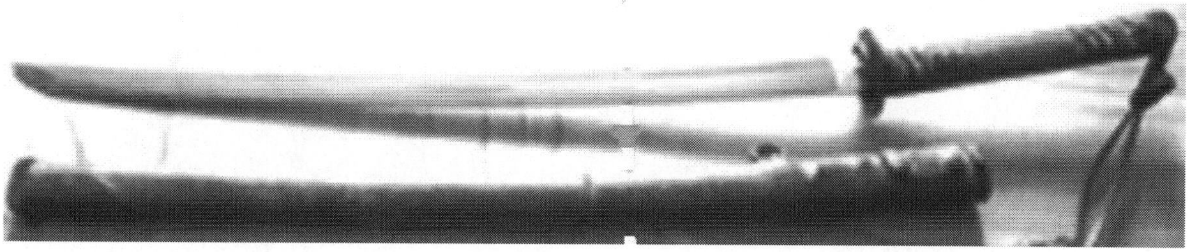

UNTYING THE KNOT

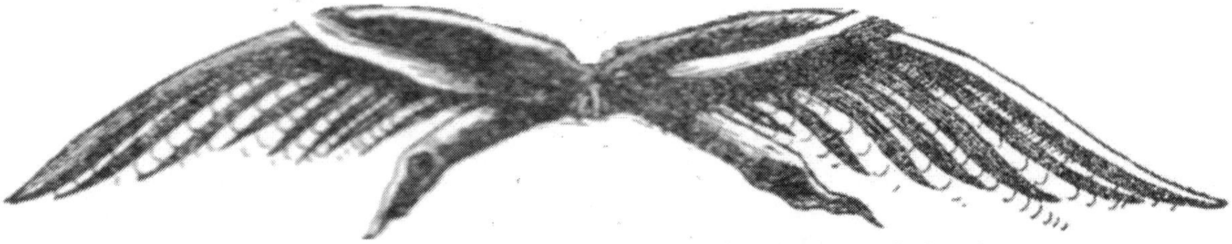

"*When here all the knots of the heart are cut, then the mortal becomes immortal.*"[669]

The knot that we saw in Plate 1 is now unfastened, it *flies* away. It becomes the sphere or truck on the top of caduceus' staff.  It is the vortex of love, represented by the *ājñā cakra*, commonly called the third eye, symbolically located "*between the eyebrows.*" The wings on 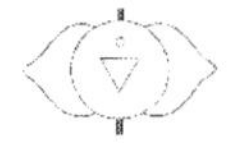 it prove its flight towards its final liberation.

Finally, the circadian wreath shows no pains, no thorns  and, having been severed, it becomes a symbol of victory. Its branches are those of the  *Rosa rubiginosa*, a rosy pink or white rose with long stems and fragrant leaves. Its buds and leaves are  symbols of the new blossoming, namely, the transmutation into a new life. In fact, its berries are in the shape of the symbol of the transmuting light of sulfur.  The subject-object circularity is interrupted. The binding ring is broken. Ouroboros does not bite 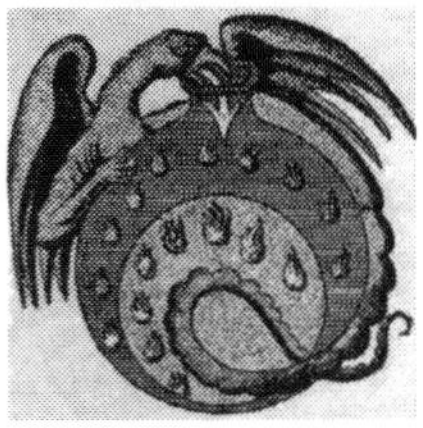 its own tail[670] any longer. Actually, the ring is open to the rays of the Sun of Awareness.

Now we understand the metaphor of the tongs. They are the symbol of the extraction of the most internal Self, the 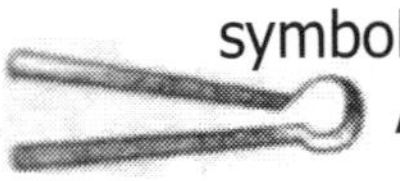 Apodictical Awareness, the Philosopher's Stone from the bodily sheath.

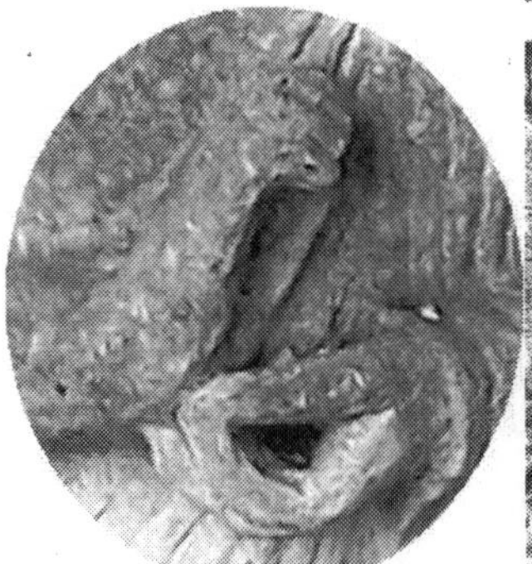

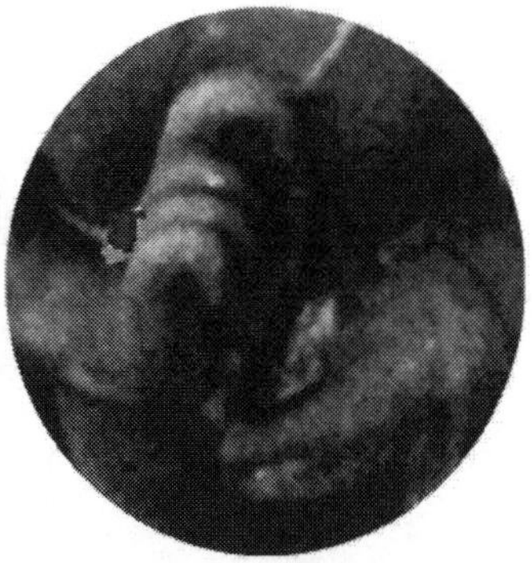

Thus, the Buddha unfastens the bondage, which prevented the final liberation.[671] We arrived at the fundamental differences between the first and last plate.

Plate 1 is the state of ignorant-obliviousness in the darkness of the immanent sleepy obfuscation.

Plate 15, instead, is the splendor of enlightenment in the Transcendent Awareness.

> *"Then Jesus said unto them, Yet a little while is the light with you. Walk while ye have the light, lest darkness come upon you: for he that walketh in darkness knoweth not whither he goeth. While ye have light, be certain in the light, that ye may be the children of light."*[672]

However, how is this Herculean labor possible?

THE HERCULEAN FATIGUE IS ACCOMPLISHED

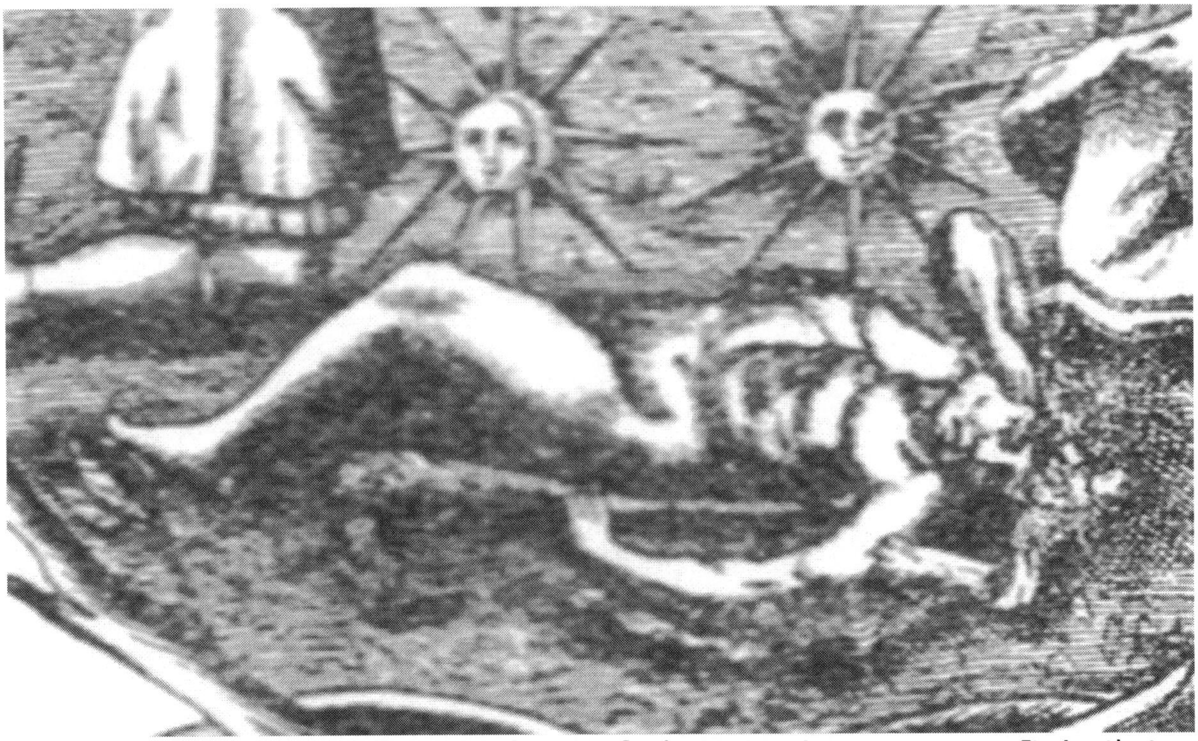

At the bottom of the wreath, we find an inanimate corpse. It is that of Death/Mṛtyu, the body of Saturn. The second edition of the book portrays the babe attached to him,  whom he is about to devour. However, the first edition does not show the child.  However, the corpse is also the body of Jacob, who was portrayed sleeping in Plate 1.  In this plate, the lifeless body is not only that of Death, Jacob and/or Saturn, but also that of Hercules/Heracles.[673] He is recognizable by the club and lion-skin wrapping him. In fact, the demigod was traditionally represented[674] wearing the skin  of the Nemean lion he had killed in his first fatigue. Furthermore, he is shown here holding also the club  with which he killed the nine-headed Lernaean Hydra in his second labor.

At this point, the question arises: - What is the meaning of Hercules in this contest? - To answer the question we must visit Heracles' eleventh fatigue. In that Mythological event, the demigod convinced Atlas to fetch for him three Golden Apples from the tree of Gaia and Hera in the Garden of the Hesperides.[675] While Atlas went to procure the fruits, Hercules held for him the world on his own shoulders.

This myth, chosen by Altus, is meaningful on five accounts.

1) The Garden of the Hesperides corresponds to the Garden of Eden.
2) The tree of Gaia and Hera suggests the tree of knowledge (viz. thought) of everything,

"*good and evil* (רע *ra'*)."[676]

3) The apple is a metaphor for evil, *malum*. In Latin this word means also apple or fruit, thus, the word-play that makes Adam and Eve sin eating the *evil*-apple.
4) The three apples signify the three stages of life, namely, waking, dreaming and sleeping with no dreams.
5) Atlas, relinquishing the World's weight on Hercules, signifies the final liberation. Moreover, it is on this last metaphor that we will focus our attention.

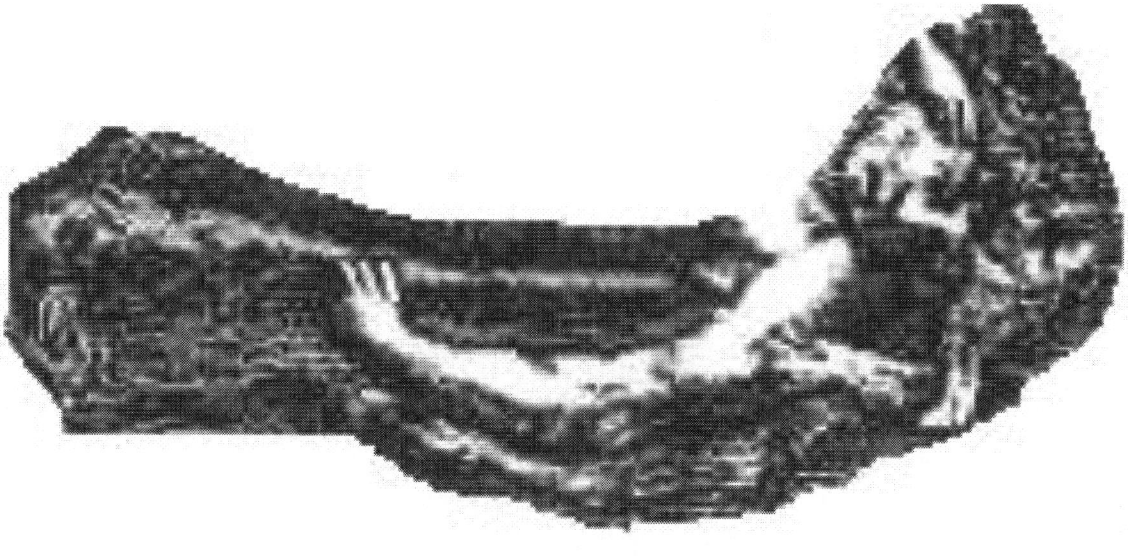

THE ENTIRE WORLD IS WAKING, DREAMING AND DREAMLESS SLEEP

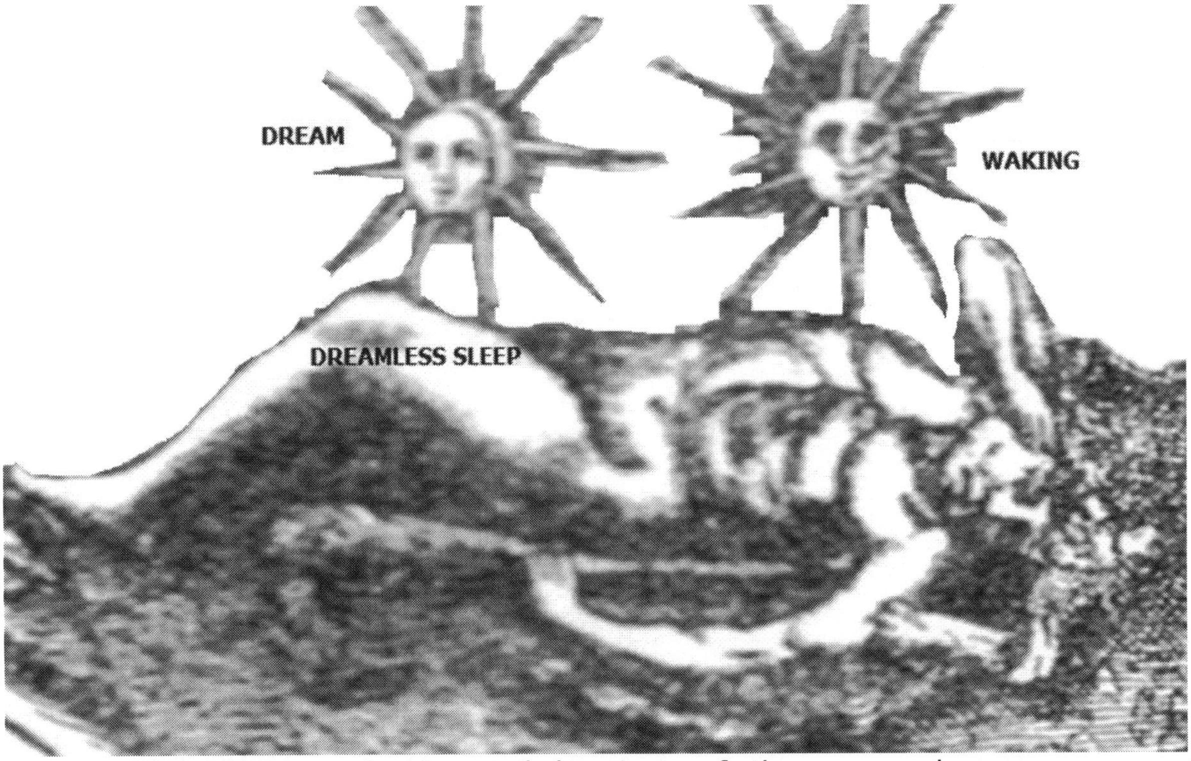

In this vignette, the inverted locations of the sun and moon represent metaphorically the dreaming and waking states and not the usual subject object distinction. In fact, the moon is near the man-subject and the sun is near the woman-object.

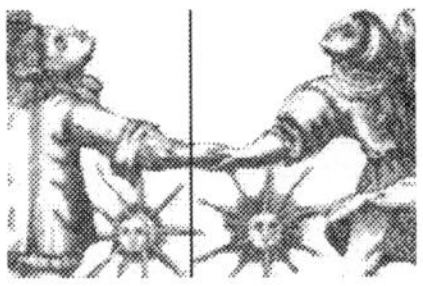

Outside wakefulness, dreams (REM) and dreamless sleep (NREM), there is nothing. At best, there is the thought-*of-nothing*, which is still the thought-*of-something* being outside. WAKEFULNESS, REM and NREM are the Entire Known-World. Nothing can be said to exist if it is not experienced or imagined. Existence belongs only to that, which is known or perceived in some way,

1) when awake, as *external*-experience, or as thought, or as belief, or as imagination or as hallucination,

and,

2) when asleep, as *internal*-experience or as dream.

An object can be said to exists only

a. if it is known through *external*-experience, viz. its subject-object correlation,
b. if it is thought, then, it exists only as an object of thought,
c. if it is believed, then, it exists only as an object of belief,
d. if it is imagined, then, it exists only as an object of imagination,
e. if it is hallucinated, then, it exists only as an object of hallucination,
f. if it is known through *internal*-experience, viz. its subject-object correlation,
g. if it is dreamt, then, it exists only as an object of dream.

Metaphorically, Atlas represents the existential condition of the subject continuously *sub-jected*, *below-jetted* or thrown-under the leaden (♄) weight of the object, viz. the burden of the world. In this vignette that load is symbolized by the sun, as wakefulness, and the moon, as the dream state. Both stand on Saturn, the dreamless stage. This is the Entire World, which Hercules is now bearing, having lifted it from Atlas' shoulders. The entire weight of the World now presses on Heracles. Crushed by it, he literally dies under its burden. Hercules, here, can be equated with the Indian iconographic representation of the god Śiva. He is depicted dead and crushed by the weight of the objective world, while the goddess Kālī triumphantly stands on him.[677]

<<The sexual union is what, on the logical level, is the synthesis *a-priori*[678] in which the subject-knower can never be separated from the known-object. On all levels of life, physical, logical, psychological or pragmatic, this union has the specific aspect of interactive desire or drive. This is the lure, the fascination, the bondage generated by Death/Mṛtyu's hunger. That hunger subjugates the mortal's mind to the object, which is represented as the corpse of the god Śiva, who is *sub-ject*, namely thrown or placed under the *ob-ject*, represented as the goddess Kālī that subdues being placed opposite or above Śiva's corpse. Thus, the intercourse is an event of cosmic proportions on all planes and all levels of life. The union of Śiva-Kālī represents the subject-object in their synthesis of knowledge. Moreover, the search for

the Self in-itself is exactly the reason for Death's objectifying process of creation, with the difference that Mṛtyu's search was *mis-directed.*>>[679]

In other words, we conceptualize Awareness, which becomes an object declared existent, while forgetting the silent Certitude that sustains existence. This is the original sin. This is the *fruit*, which should not have been eaten. Nothing can be said of Awareness, not even that it exists. However, during the process of return to Awareness, once the miseries of life are evident,[680] then the first *glimpse* of the Imperishable-Awareness, the Immortal Self-in-Itself is realized. The knower transpires to itself as Certitude and the death-wish of *pro*creation starts vanishing.

The Gospel of Thomas states that

> "*whosoever has come to understand the world has found* (only) *a corpse, and whosoever has found a corpse is superior to the world.*"[681]

This is the eternal life-death, knower-known, wakefulness-dream vicissitude. This is the hungry bondage that subjugates the mortal's mind. And, in our vignette, Hercules/Saturn points to the mind. This indicates the location where waking, dreaming and dreamless sleep take place. Concomitantly, the lion's mouth that covers his head gnaws it. The mind is the beast eating greedily the skull and impeding the realization of our True Nature. The metaphor here is that the beast to defeat is the mind itself. The lion-mind is the devourer of our liberty. This subjugating burden is taken up by Heracles upon himself, while, at the same time, he is freeing Atlas from his load.

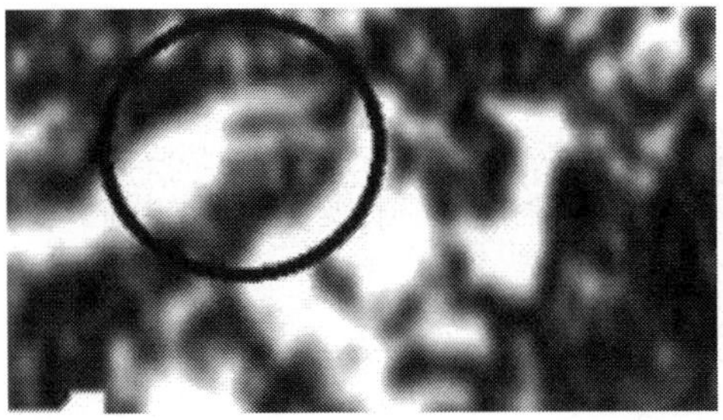

The *Mutus Liber* initiates us to thoughtlessness while identifying with Apodictical Awareness. It teaches us to give up *wordy-thoughts* that drive us away from Pure Awareness. Thoughts distract us from the Apodictical Awareness. Ramana Maharshi states,

> "*The one obstacle is the mind; it must be got over whether in the home or in the forest.*[682] [In fact] *when the mind comes out of the Self, the world appears. Therefore, when the world appears* [to be real]*, the Self does not appear.*"[683]

ATLAS ASCENSION IN THE FOURTH STATE

When Saturn/Hercules takes upon himself the weight of the world, it means, metaphorically, that Atlas is finally liberated. The ladder leading to heaven is obsolete.

It is not vertical any longer. Instead, it lies horizontally on the ground. Then, both roses of enlightenment, one for the subject and the other for the object, bloom in the awaken realization of Awareness. Therefore, the *Ṛg Veda* declares,

"the seers searching with reflection in the heart, found the connection of being in non-being...
The seers had found their measuring cord (raśmí), which, as beam of consciousness, eventually spread across the spectrum of reality.

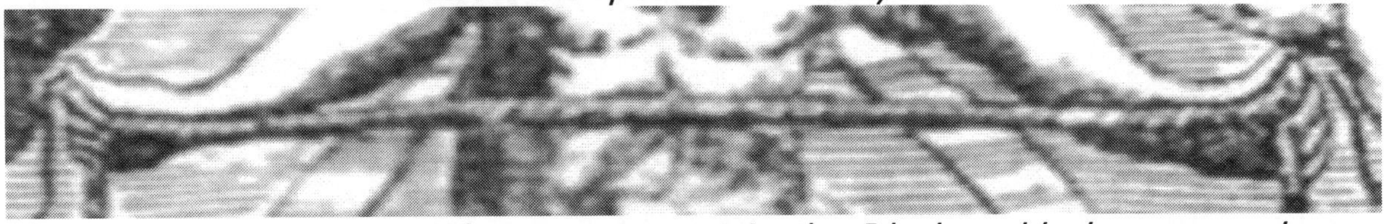

What was present in the Ideal world above was also present in the Natural world below."[684]

Below the cord is the immanent world of manifestations in which Saturn/Hercules is dead and where

"the dead bury their dead."[685]

Above the cord rules the Pure Transcendent Apodictical Awareness.
That same cord, that same beam of consciousness pulls up the sublimated subject-object unity into the silent stillness of Awareness.

Ramana Maharshi says,

"When the world which is what-is-seen has been removed, there will be realization of the Self which is the seer... That [is] *Awareness which alone remains ... The Self is that where there is absolutely no 'I-thought'... The world should be considered like a dream."*[686]

"Watch ye and pray [*i.e.* meditate], *lest ye enter into temptation-of-object-experimentation: the spirit indeed* [is] *willing, but the flesh* [is] *weak."*[687]

Temptation, then, is synonym of the loss of the Aware-Certitude, the true source of everything. That is what the *Bible* calls *temptation-of-object-experimentation.*[688] This is exactly the same injunction not to eat from the tree of knowledge.

"Pay attention and pray that ye enter not into the temptation"[689]

Therefore, one

"*should always pray* [*i.e.* meditate], *and not to be utterly spiritless.*"[690]

Oculatus abis[691] –Aware (*oculatus*) you go away (*abis*)*!* – Blissfully, declares the subject.

Oculatus abis – *You depart being Vigilant!* –

"***AWARE ye DEPART!***"

AWAKE BEING AWARE.

Ecstatic, announces the object.

Both the subject and the object speak out and say,

– Now that you have seen these pictures... depart ... from the images and realize the Art. BE AWARE.–

The Latin word *oculatus* derives from *ocŭlus* meaning eye. From it, comes the verb *ocŭlāre*, as in the English *ocular* meaning visual, to be furnished with sight or to furnish sight, to be illuminated or to illuminate. From it derives also the Latin adjective *oculatus*. Consequently, it means eyed, having eyesight, being furnished with eyes, also being circumspect, wise and watchful. Finally, it is the

Consenting Eye of Awareness,[692] the Egyptian *Eye of Horus* (𓂀),the Latin *uraeus*, the *risen one* represented as a hawk[693] wearing on the head the disk of the Sun god Rā with the snake *khut*.

"*O Eye of Horus, go forth from the god, and shine outside his mouth... Let Rā live, and let the poison die! Let the poison die, and let Rā live! These are the words of Isis,* [your mother].

[The Sun is] the right eye [subject], and the Moon the left [object]; a well known title of the Face is *Horus of the two Eyes* [𓂀𓂀], and when neither Eye is visible it is called *Horus dwelling without Eyes*,"[694]

namely the *Third Eye*, the silent ineffable one.

HE is the Ultimate Perceiver, the One Who Sees. He is the Illuminated Awareness. In that state of awareness, you go away (*abis*) from the *poison* of this immanent world into the Kingdom of the Sun god Rā, the Transcendent Awareness. *Abis*, Latin from the verb *ab-īre* to go-away, means "you depart." Thus, it signifies that the Ultimate Perceiver is the One who is vigilant in tracing her steps. Here, the Indian name *Akshapāda* would be appropriate. In fact, *aksha*, in Sanskrit, means eye, and *pāda* translates as foot, step or wheel, viz. *eye-foot*.[695] Consequently, that name gives the sense of being vigilant, aware of the steps leading away, ergo, *oculatus abis*.

Atlas is a metaphor for the subject, the one always *subjected* under the world of objectivity. However, once Hercules relieves him from the burden, he is neither Atlas nor subject. He is now Pure Consciousness that identifies with the Wonder-of-Awareness. We can call him Akshapāda. He *transcends* above and beyond the rope which measures (*raśmi*) and separates the Real from the immanent world of duality. He is the crowned victorious Hero and his crown corresponds to the *seat of ecstasy*, the thousand-spoked lotus. He is Jupiter who resides over the entire Creation. He is the Alchemical Gold, which transmuted from the heavy-led corpse of Saturn/Hercules. This transmutation started by being awake while the senses withdrew when entering sleep. The transmutation continued by being awake while concentrating into the pinpointed dream. When also that single dream was gone in the wakeful stillness of the dreamless sleep, then the Opus was concluded. Then, the doors of the Luminous Gold of Pure Awareness were open.

"And they heard a great voice from heaven saying unto them, Come up hither. And they ascended up to heaven in a cloud."[696]

HISTORICAL PERSONALITIES RELIEVED FROM THE WORLD'S BURDEN

Al-Husayn ibn Mansur al-Hallaj (858-922) proclaimed,

> "*I am God* (*Ana 'I Haqq*)."[697]

Jesus stated,

> "*I and* [my] *Father are one* [and] *ye shall know that I* [am] *in my Father, and ye in me, and I in you...*
> *All may be one; as thou, Father,* [art] *in me, and I in thee that they also may be one in us: that the world may believe that thou hast sent me.*"[698]

Ramana Maharshi echoes,

> "*To see God is to be God ... He alone is real and all the three states are equally unreal.*"[699]

Jung writes that, regarding

> "the identification of the Self with God, as expressed in Śrī Ramana's utterances, Psychology cannot contribute anything further."[700]

However, affirmations as "*I am God*" or "*I know that I am not God*" are both erroneous.[701]

A synonym for God is Ineffable-Transcendence, and nothing can be said about Transcendence without making it describable and immanent, thus not-god.

> "*Therefore the best course is to remain silent,*"

affirms Ramana Maharshi.[702]

Whoever states, –*I am*– implies *being* and her/his *being* does not require another being in order to be. S/he is because s/he is. Even postulating a creative intervention, the Creator becomes, by definition, that constant certain-centrality of her/his being, without which s/he would not be. Whatever is stated: Being, Creator, or non-Being (where being becomes un-known in-itself), it must necessarily be the core centrality of existence. Thus, the Certainty of the stated –*I am*– is the true Self-of-self, as distinguished from the mental concepts of I-think, subjective consciousness or Ego.

Jelal-ud-din Rumi in his poems writes,

> "*God slept in the mineral kingdom,*
> *dreamed in the vegetable kingdom,*
> *awakened to consciousness in the animal kingdom,*
> *and became manifest in His own image in the human being.*"[703]

<<Figuratively speaking, consciousness searching in its infinite scanning possibility, for its own Awareness, entered among the waking moments, passed through the dream stages and reached the deep sleep state, only to recognize Itself as never having left Its own Conscious-Awareness in the All-pervading Fourth State (*turīya*), the Transcendent from which we come. This is not a dogmatic affirmation. It does not matter if one defines itself theist, atheist or agnostic, in each of these cases one envisions and defines its prenatal condition as being beyond thought, which is inevitably a tacit silent declaration of Transcendence. If, at the question

–Where were you before you were born?– one does not answer, that is an affirmation of Transcendent, namely, that which rests beyond the subject-object correlation, which, once thought, is not Transcendent.>>[704]

On his deathbed, Ramana Maharshi declared,

"*They say that I am dying, but I am not going away. Where could I go? I am here.*"[705] Then, absorbed in the heart, the Yogi goes beyond life and beyond death.[706]

"*Where your treasure is, there will your heart be also.*"[707]

CONCLUSION

THE MUTE BOOK HAS SPOKEN!

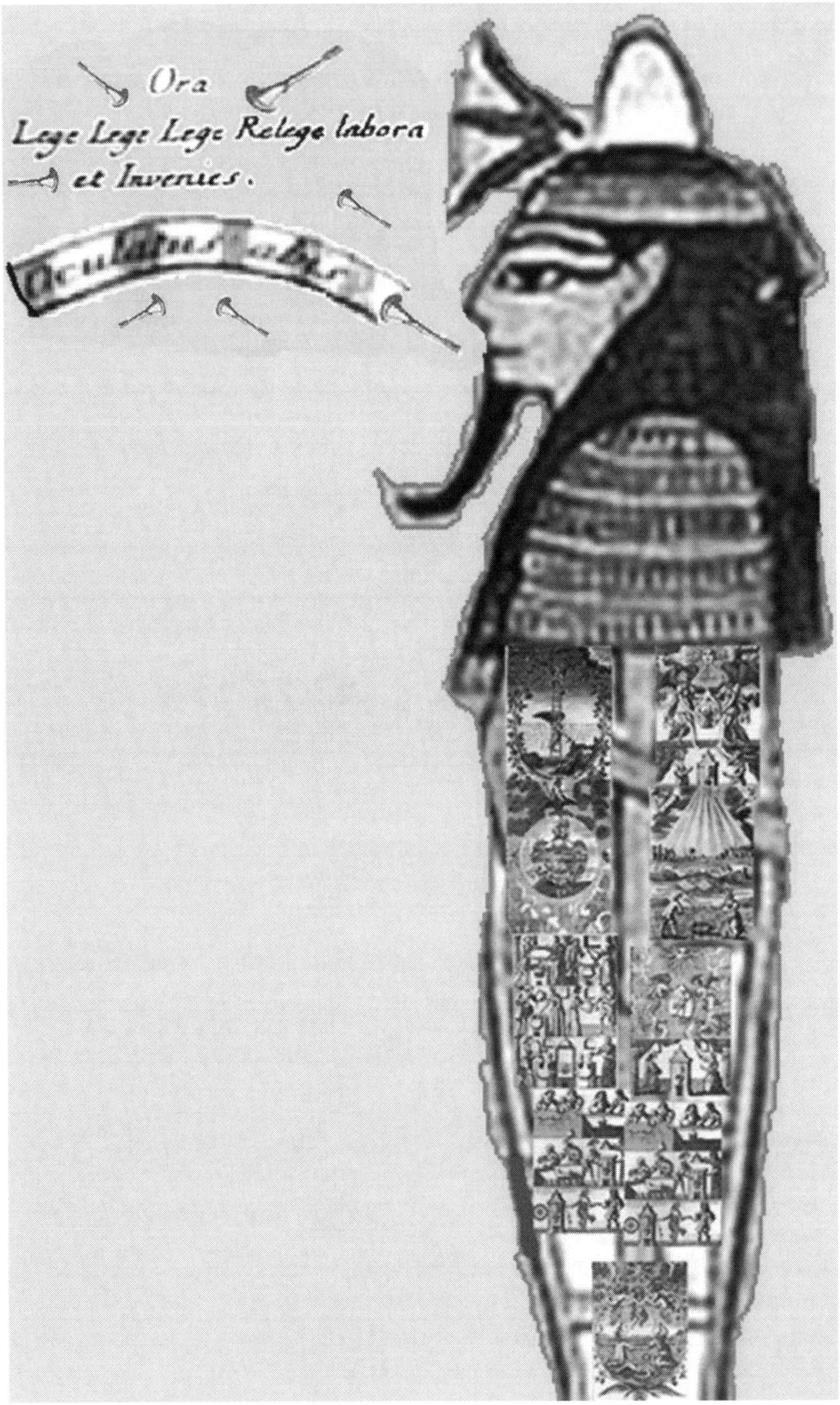
Ora
Lege Lege Lege Relege labora
et Invenies.

LEGE RELEGE

The *Mutus Liber* orders us,

Lege

–Read!– And we did.

The *Mutus Liber* orders us,

Lege

– Read! – And we did.

The *Mutus Liber* orders us,

Lege

– Read! – And we did.

The *Mutus Liber* orders us,

Relege

– Reread! – And we did it again.

Up to this point, as directed by the book, we read and reread. We understood it conceptually, namely we did not realize it. We did not *labor*. We did not practice, or meditate. We did not identify with the Mute, Non-Conceptual-Awareness. Hence, we did not discover. Therefore, we shall start to put it into practice following the book.

Time

"In the beginning there was nothing.
All was concealed by Death and death is hunger."[708]

Hunger is desire to know. To know is to reach knowledge. Knowledge is comprehension of the objective-world. The objective-world is the totality of all possible objects. Objects are measures of space-and-time. Space and time are conceived as elements different from the knower. In fact, the knower lapses through space and time. The perceiver travels between objects considered achievements outside and other than the subject. They are known as different from oneself. What we define as now or here, is never really NOW or HERE. Space is the circular time-distance from the observer. How long does it take an object to reach the perceiver?

If we look at Proxima Centauri, the closest star to the Sun, the brightness we see comes from a distant-past of about 4.24 light years ago.[709] That means that its light we see is not there anymore. We may also ask, -How far are we from this book we are reading here and now?- No matter how short is the distance or the time it takes for this book's image to enter our visual cortex, nevertheless there is a laps of space-time. That means that the book is located outside and in the past. It is not now, thus it is not here. When it reaches our visual cortex, it is already departed from *there*. It is already bygone, dead.

That is where knowledge leads us. It leads us to that which is dead. Therefore, inevitably, we follow suit. We may be with this book for one hundred years, but eventually it will crumble and we will die.

"Thou shalt not eat of the tree of the knowledge... for
in the day that thou eatest... thou shalt surely die."[710]

LABORA

in the *labora*tory of the *Amphitheatre of Eternal Wisdom*[711]

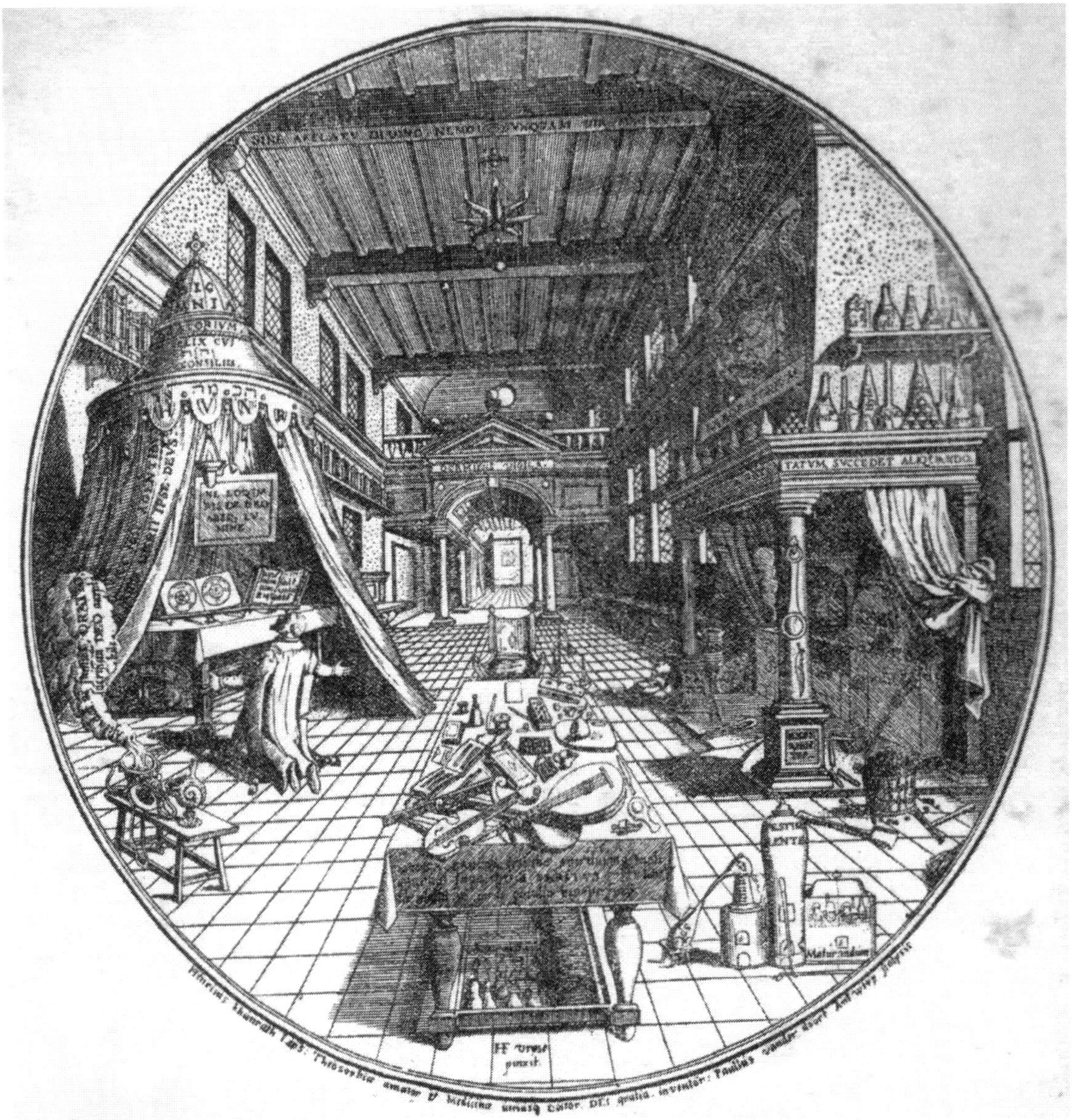

The *Mutus Liber* orders us,

labora

– practice! – And we will do that.

However, how does one put into practice and operate according to Altus' teaching? The question is, – How can we reproduce his alchemical opus and put it to work in our life? –

In general, the laboratory is the location in which we experiment, work and *labor*. However, the real alchemist, as such, should not build a stone laboratory with athanors, alembics and vials containing physical chemical substances. It would be a squander of money. In fact,

"the obsession of the alchemist leads to his impoverishment."[712]

The stereotype of the alchemist is

> "one of those men that dig in chimera to rush in misery. Stubbornly persisting in the search for their philosopher's stone, they have enough science to be ruined, and do not have enough to discern the limits of the human spirit that will never reach the transmutation of base metals."[713]

The sincere alchemist should not start collecting material morning dew and process it with physical elements like salt, sulfur, mercury and other elaborate ingredients to obtain gold. It would be a waste of time, with possible health consequences. It is true that, during historical pseudo-alchemical experiments, some alchemists stumbled upon true chemical reactions. However, those were discoveries that opened the road to the science of chemistry, which has nothing to do with true Alchemy itself. The popular acceptance of the alchemist is of a person lusting for gold and lost in the self-deluding vain search to produce it *magically*.

On the contrary, Dr. Henricus Khunrath,[714] in his laboratory of the *Amphitheatre of Eternal Wisdom*, reminds us that the real Alchemist strives for universal spiritual unity, leaving behind all myths, dogmas, sophisms and unsupported preconceived ideas. Mimma Benvenuti, an Italian spiritual anthroposophist, stated, that the spiritual exercises are a science.

> "The Science of the Spirit is not a theory, as it is a practice... To those who... criticize and blame us, we owe great gratitude, because they are in that moment our teachers... Many things of collective and human value depend from us... not from the international communities."[715]

Therefore, enter the *Door of the Amphitheatre of the True Eternal Wisdom*

PORTA AMPHITHEATRI SAPIENTIAE AETERNAE... VERAE[716]

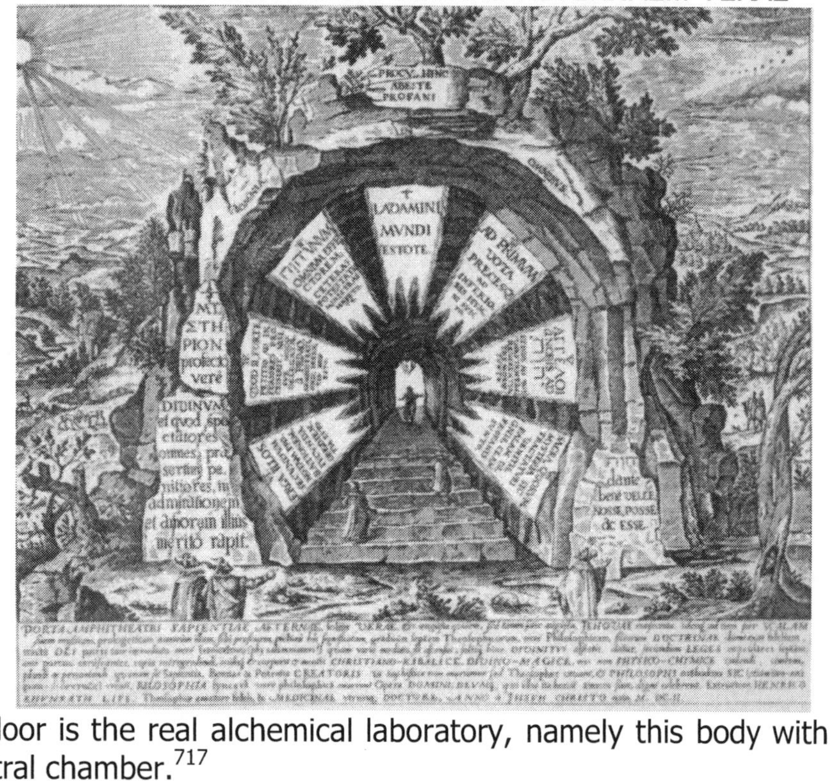

Beyond this door is the real alchemical laboratory, namely this body with this heart as its secret central chamber.[717]

All practices, experiments and *labor* start and take place in the centrality of this heart and only <u>here</u> and <u>now</u>. Therefore,

> "*If one watches whence the notion of I arises, the mind is absorbed into that,*"[718]

viz. in the heart. This absorption is the first step of the *Opera*.

<u>Labora absorbing the senses</u>

<<Resting on your back, enter a state of complete relaxation, with your legs slightly separated and your arms, palms down, parallel to your body. Visualize your entire body. Next, tense your feet for a few seconds and then relax them. In sequence, do the same for your legs. Continue with your thighs, then your arms. Perform the same with your abdomen. Follow up reaching your chest and then your throat. Finally tense your head and relax. Now revert the process, from your head, go down to your feet, from there all the way back to your head again. Repeat this three times, as waves of energy from head to toes and back to the head again. As you do these relaxation exercises, send your wakeful attention through your entire body. Visit all your limbs as if you were performing a ritual pilgrimage.

> "*Carry out the pilgrimages within your own body as from one 'ritual pilgrimage to sacred rivers' to another!*"[719]

Now tense your entire body, keep the tension for a few seconds and let go completely. Feel you are sinking deeply in a cloud of softness. Then, be immersed in your body awareness.

Gradually withdraw inward the consciousness-*of* the objects deriving from the senses' activities. Look, hear, taste, smell and feel objects without paying attention to them. It is like those comforting moments when we enter in a suspension of perception while fully perceiving. These moments were more frequent in our infancy, when we were staring at something in an intense stillness. You may remember those instants and the surprising annoyance when somebody snapped us out of that intense state. However, now we willfully seek to recreate that state. It is similar to the aesthetic moment described by Kandinsky,

> "Lend your ears to music, open your eyes to painting, and... stop thinking! Just ask yourself if the work has enabled you to 'walk about' into a hitherto unknown world. If the answer is yes, what more do you want?"[720]

Focus on the constant presence of the five-faculties-of-the-senses (*indriya*) and the mind as a sixth organ. These are the powerful gods, the resplendent beings belonging to the 'I,' which bring the world into existence. However, in themselves, the senses are independent and indifferent to any form of pleasure, apathy or aversion towards their objects. Pleasure, apathy and aversion are the demons, which color the world's reality and of which they are conscious-*of* but with *felt* participation.

A) On the level of the six organs of perception,
   1) Engaging your ears, hear any delightful harmony. Then, listen at any sound that bores you. Next, listen at any screeching sound. In each event, realize that the act of hearing is always the same, independent from its feelings.
   2) Engaging your eyes, look at any object that is agreeable to you. Then, look at any object that leaves you apathetic. Next, look at any object that is unappealing to you. In each event, realize that the act of seeing is always the same, independent from its feelings.
   3) Engaging your nose, smell any aroma. Then, smell any odor that leaves you uninterested. Next, smell something offensive for you. In each event, realize that the act of smelling is always the same, independent from its feelings.
   4) Engaging your skin, feel any pleasurable object. Then, feel any object that leaves you undisturbed. Next, feel any object that hurts you. In each event, realize that the act of feeling is always the same, independent from its feelings.
   5) Engaging your tongue, taste any delicacy. Then, taste any food that you consider bland. Next, taste any food that you find unappetizing. In each event, realize that the act of tasting is always the same, independent from its feelings.
   6) Engaging your mind, think of any enjoyable thought. Then, think of anything that leaves you uninterested. Next, think of a disturbing thought.

In each event, realize that the act of thinking is always the same, independent from its feelings.

B) On the level of the five organs of action,

7) Forget the sound heard or emitted by the larynx and focus concentrating only on the act of hearing or sounding, unaffected by attraction, indifference or dislike.

8) Forget the object of sight or the direction covered by the feet and focus concentrating only on the act of seeing or walking with your spine straight, like

"Farinata who straighten up...
as if he held hell in great contempt,"[721]

unaffected by attraction, indifference or dislike.

9) Forget the scent smelled or the pleasure of the generative act and focus concentrating only on the act of smelling and generating, unaffected by attraction, indifference or dislike.

10) Forget the object felt or touched and focus concentrating only on the act of feeling or touching, unaffected by attraction, indifference or dislike.

11) Forget the food tasted or evacuated and focus concentrating only on the act of tasting or evacuating, unaffected by attraction, indifference or dislike.>>[722]

Labora absorbing the mind

Once your senses are completely withdrawn, focus on your thoughts. Look at them as if they pass by, floating on an incessant flowing river.[723]

Do not be disturbed or attracted by them.

"*Be still, and know that I am God.*"[724]
"*Be ye stedfast, unmoveable, always abounding in the work of the Lord.*"[725]

"Be carefree,"

says Herodotus,[726] followed by Dante's verses,

"be firm as a tower, which does not ruin
ever the top due to blowing winds"[727] and
"let us not discuss about them, but look and pass."[728]

Paul is more specific, be as

"*those who mourn, as if they did not; those who are happy, as if they were not.*"[729]
"*Therefore,* [says Jesus] *take no thought for your life, what ye shall eat, or what ye shall drink; nor yet for your body, what ye shall put on... But seek ye first the kingdom of God, and*

his righteousness; and all these things shall be added unto you."[730]

Once you have reached that stage of disengaged look towards your thoughts, choose only one object of those detached thoughts and focus on it with the exclusion of all others. Do not drift with your mind. Remember your senses are withdrawn and your mind is concentrated only on one object. Repeat this exercise as you go to sleep.

<<On the onset of sleep, under the auspices of the Moon, immediately preceding slumber, the mind enters a state of total, immovable concentration, in Sanskrit called *dhāraṇa*. Be awake, be attentive, be *oculatus*. Then, focus on that state of consciousness, where the mind forgets its own objects of thought together with its own Ego-consciousness. Concentrate only on that act of thinking unaffected by attraction, indifference or dislike. From this juncture, a new internal organ takes over. Thought, the Imperishable thinking process, takes over with renewed vengeance, so strong that it creates a new world, namely the realm of dreams. If, during the waking state, you successfully centered your attention on the faculties of the senses alone and not on their objects, then that focus has become your second nature. Therefore, it will be possible for you to focus also on those same faculties, as they operate in the dream state, and be unaffected by attraction, indifference or dislike for the objects experienced during the nighttime visions. Then, you will be *awake* in your dreams. If you should fall asleep, do not worry,

"*the spirit indeed* [is] *willing, but the flesh* [is] *weak."*[731]

You will succeed next time.

Then, the I-consciousness, presided by the I-think ruler, awakens and arises in this dreaming juncture. With an immovable concentration, become conscious-of the Dreaming One as the pinpointed object of concentration.

Practice, practice, practice and practice this over again. In a way, this entire work is at this stage. It leads consciousness to become here and now conscious-of Awareness, to recognize the I-aware as the building block, as the founding keystone of this entire waking and dreaming world and draw attention only on it.>>[732]

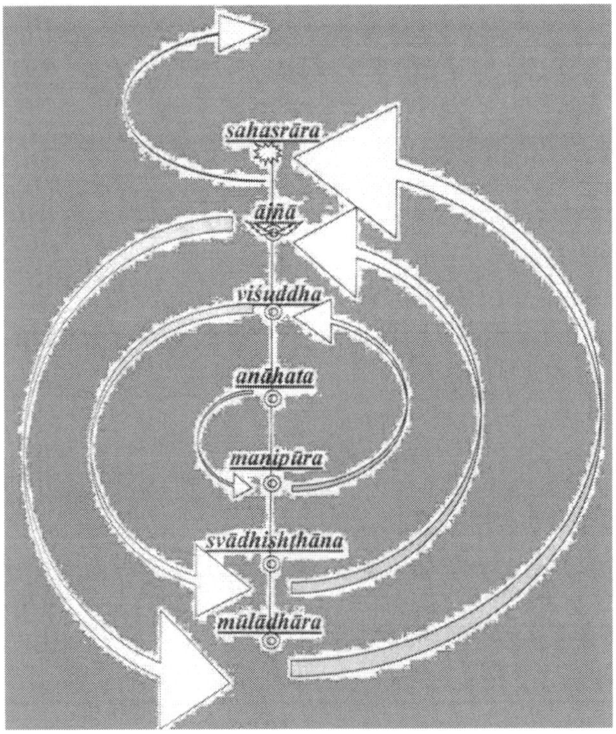

Ora

The *Mutus Liber* orders us,

Ora

– Pray, Meditate! – And we will do that.

However, how does one Meditate according to Altus' teaching?

If you succeeded to concentrate on a pinpointed thought without diverging from it and to control your dream, then you make the transition in the dreamless sleep. Realize that we do this naturally, but the effort here is to bring consciousness to identify with the Awakened Awareness while this natural process takes place.

<<In the deepest sleep without dreams, in the presence of a unified cognitive mind, having gone through all the previous concentration steps and without any object of the senses, you will enter in a Zen (*dhyāna*) like meditation state. In that is the comprehensive realization of Awareness. There, the consciousness-of Awareness disappears to leave only the shining presence of Awareness-in-Itself, the Sun of Apodictical Certitude and the ultimate Blissful Absolute Reality that makes the world come into existence.>>[733]

Invenies

The *Mutus Liber* assures us,

et Invenies

– and Discover thy shall! – And we will.

However, what shall we Discover and Realize? We realize that Awareness is the Only One which determines the certitude of the universe. In fact, without Awareness nothing, nothing, nothing can be stated. Nonetheless, Awareness Itself is ineffable. The kingdom of Heaven is the realization of Truth Foundation of Awareness. Therefore,

> "*the kingdom of heaven is like unto treasure hid in a field; the which when a man hath found, he hideth, and for joy thereof goeth and selleth all that he hath, and buyeth that field.*"[734]

Having withdrawn the senses, having concentrated on one thought, having erased also that one thought in meditation, now <<we realize that the unification (*yoga*) of the individual self with the Universal-Self, with that Awareness, takes place in the deepest introspection. There, in ecstasy (*samādhi*), individuality unifies fusing and identifying with Pure-Aware-Certitude, like the extinguishing (*nirvāṇa*) of a fire consuming its fuel while not burning itself out as Fire. *Samādhi*, the final ecstasy (*i.e. out staying*) or, better, *enstasy* (*i.e. in-staying*), is the final union, yoke or yoga with the Supreme Reality, when all-is-put-together (*sam-ādhi*), joined, united, completed and concluded. In that state, when,

> "*all things were now accomplished,*"[735]

is the last stage of yoga. It is the stage that brings everything into harmony and the intense absorption into silence. It is the awakening of the serpentine power of *kuṇḍalinī* that, having traveled through six centers along the spinal cord [viz. the caduceus], reaches the seventh on the crown of the head.

However, so long as an effort is made to discover that state... that state is not really reached.

"*There is no reaching the Self... You are the Self; you are already That.*"[736]

The state of Being-in-itself does not necessitate an effort to be-in-itself. Focusing on Awareness alone, then the whole world will be discovered in its true essence. Whereas, not having recognized that Awareness, then even that necessary fundamental Awareness will be unrealized for us. This is the meaning of the Biblical injunction,

"*For to everyone who has, more will be given, and he will have abundance; but from him who does not have, even what he has will be taken away.*"[737]

In fact, when that Awareness is discovered as consciousness-*of*-something, then it is lost, but when consciousness-*of*-something is set aside, then that Awareness shines of its own nature.

"*Whoever finds his life will lose it, and whoever loses his life for my sake will find it.*"[738]

Remember you are the immortal. BE AWARE.>>[739]

Mṛtyu-Death is now resurrected from the dead. Like Osiris, his body has been completely *reassembled* and in it

"*are all the gods.*"[740]

OCULATUS ABIS

Twice the *Mutus Liber* states,

Oculatus

– Aware – And we are.

Twice the *Mutus Liber* says,

abis

– go ahead – And we do.

<<Like a tiger in the wild, walk aware of your surroundings. Feel the breeze and the wind on your skin, in your hair. Look ahead while looking behind and at your sides. Feel the other persons' consciousness. Feel their pains. Feel their sadness. Feel it in compassion without attachment.

Like a horse, gallop aware in your dreams. Cover your interior fields aware of your designing and changing landscapes. Remember you are the dreamer.

Like an eagle, soar aware in the sky of still silence in your dreamless sleep. Be aware in that thoughtless sky without dreams. Remember you are that serenity.

In the shining midnight black sun of silence, be aware in the instant of death. You are *oculatus*, namely you are furnished with eyes. Of all the sense organs, the one that actively goes out towards the world is the eye. Beyond metaphor, it represents the intentionality as consciousness-*of*. In fact, the eyes are projections  and windows  to the world, with which one identifies by means of desires; thus, the recurrent return to it. The heart, on the other hand, represents, beyond metaphor, the centrality of Apodictic-Certain-Awareness.

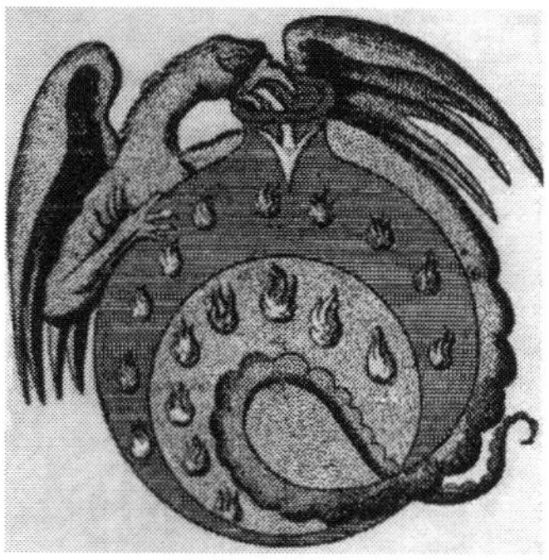

"*Thus, verily, used to say Śāṇḍilya, the revered seer Śāṇḍilya, 'This Self of mine, the source of every action, of every desire, of every scent, and of every flavor, residing within the heart, encompassing all this, but indifferent, without conferring meaning or sense to the objects, this is the Supreme Transcendent Spirit. Thus, upon dying, I shall reach This One. Certainly, there is no doubt for the one who should tend towards This One.'*"[741]

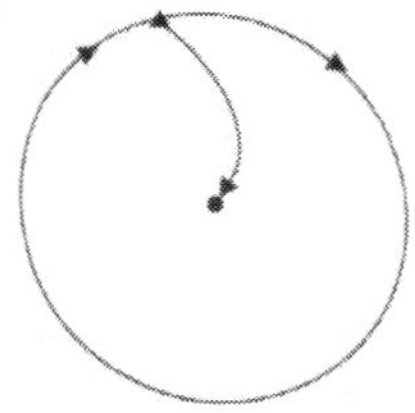

This One is the Absolute-Aware-collapse of the subject-object-circumference in its Self-dimensionless-center.[742] This is our real nature, in that whatever we do, even when we think we are being selfish, we are in reality seeking for It, for the Pure Self in It-Self, for the Transcendent, *beyond the world*, beyond Ego-consciousness, beyond I-consciousness, beyond Auto-transparency,

> "*beyond bliss... A yogi who is in this state is inactive even while engaged in activity.*"[743]

This is the natural state of absorption in oneself without concepts, the collapse of the life and death circle disappearing in its own center.

Beyond the world, beyond the object, beyond your identification with it, there stands the ever present foundation of Awareness. Focus on It. You do not need to abandon life to do this. On the contrary, live life to its full extent. However, constantly and incessantly identify with This Awareness here and now. Let this identification become your real nature. From the outside, no one will notice the difference. No one will notice that you became an Alchemist. Except that, you will become the innermost essence of everyone, because the entire world is established on your Awareness that belongs to everyone. This meditative training will not inhibit your life productivity, on the contrary, it will let it escalate, surge and increase. Your action will border perfection and its outcome will be most favorable for you.

***OCULATUS ABIS*, AWARE CARRY-ON**

Actively fully participate and live your life completely. Nevertheless, look at the world Aware, without seeing it. Listen to the world Aware, without hearing it. Savor the world Aware, without tasting it. Inhale the world Aware, without smelling it. Sense the world Aware, without feeling it. Conceptualize the world Aware, without thinking of it. What is most important, keep practicing your identification with the Christ-Consciousness in you, with the Buddhahood in you. In you is the Kingdom of God, identify with it. Constantly

> "*watch ye and pray, lest ye enter into temptation.*"[744]

The temptation is the identification with the impermanent object conceived as real-in-itself. The *Mutus Liber* declares,

Pray, Read, Read, Read, Reread, labor and Ye Shall Discover

Namely, you shall *un*veil the Hidden One. That veil impedes immortality, tempts, distracts and lures away from it. Therefore,

> "*provide yourselves bags which wax not old, a treasure in the heavens that faileth not, where no thief approacheth, neither moth corrupteth.*"[745]

Therefore, the emphasis is on a vigilant and constant attention on the Truth, which is the inherent apodicticity of Awareness. During your entire life, your entire effort should be to enhance and to train being constantly in the Presence of Awareness. Perhaps, at the fatidic moment upon entering the state of death, at that very juncture where the consciousness-*of* the world will leave you, then, your meditative-alchemical training on Awareness will be present to usher you into immortality. Try not to think in terms of what you may have experienced during meditation and definitely do not tell others. The thought of it will reduce to an object what you may have realized, thus destroy its spiritual achievement.>>[746]

Therefore,

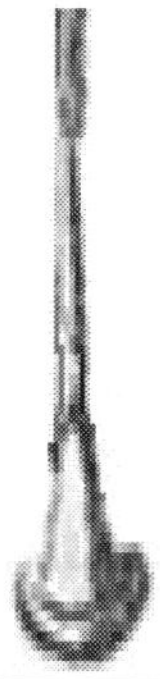

Breathing, be *OCULATUS* 𓂀, identify with the breathing One
Feeling, be *OCULATUS* 𓂀, identify with the feeling One
Hearing, be *OCULATUS* 𓂀, identify with the hearing One
Seeing, be *OCULATUS* 𓂀, identify with the seeing One
Sniffing, be *OCULATUS* 𓂀, identify with the sniffing One
Tasting, be *OCULATUS* 𓂀, identify with the tasting One
Thinking, be *OCULATUS* 𓂀, identify with the thinking One
Living, be *OCULATUS* 𓂀, identify with the living One

This shall be your constant prayer. It is the realization of the center that puts the circumference into existence, without which there would be no circumference of any size.

A All starts from *Ω*
APODICTICAL WONDROUS AWARENESS
all transmutes in
Ω **ALCHEMICAL GOLD** *A*

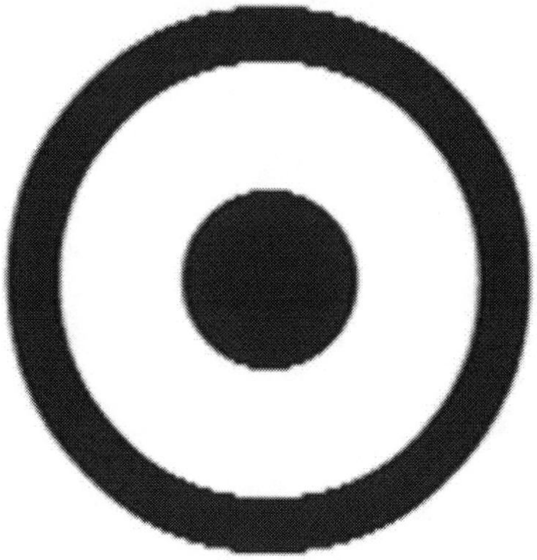

"We search for Him here and there
while looking right at Him.
Sitting by His side we ask,
'O Beloved, where is the Beloved?'
....
Let silence take you to the core of life."[747]

The circularity has disappeared, only the center duedrop remains.

During a total eclipse, the sun's corona is visible, namely, that star, obfuscated by a non-reflecting moon, shows its own contours. However, only the corona is visible, the sun itself remains invisible. Metaphorically, Awareness In-Itself is like an eclipse in which the sun is *seen* throughout without being *eclipsed* by the moon.[748]

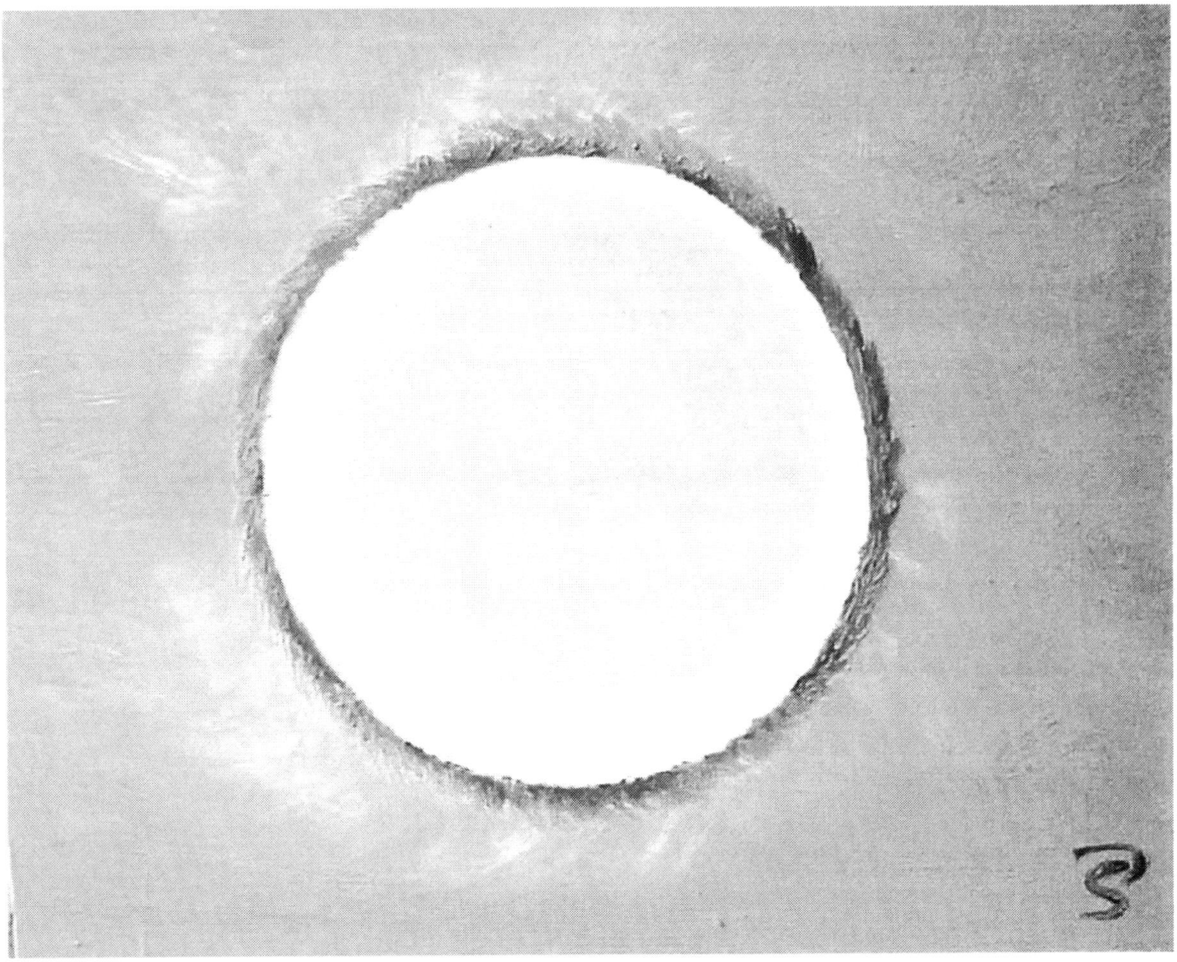

INDEX

NOTES

[1] Tagore, Rabindranath, *Gitanjali: Song Offerings*, 49 p. 42.
[2] *Bible*, Psalm 51:15.
[3] Budge, *The Egyptian Book of the Dead*, [Chapter XXIII]: *THE CHAPTER OF OPENING THE MOUTH OF THE OSIRIS ANI*, p. 306, *cf.* pp. 264-270. The *iron knife* was an "instrument... made of a sinuous piece of wood, one end of which is in the form of a ram's head surmounted by a *uræus*" (264, n.1). Modified image from the Public domain File:Opening of the mouth ceremony.jpg, http://en.wikipedia.org/wiki/File:Opening_of_the_mouth_ceremony.jpg.
[4] *Bible*, Deuteronomy 32:20.
[5] Carrington Bolton, *Chemical Literature*, in *The Chemical News*, p. 147. Cf. also Stanley Redgrove, *Bygone Beliefs*.
[6] *Bible*, Mark 14:38.
[7] Tolle, *A New Earth*, p. 7.
[8] *Cf. Voynich Manuscript* (XV century) p. 92-166.
[9] *Bible*, John 12:25.
[10] Plato, *The Republic*, VII, 514-521.
[11] *Odyssey*, 11, 489-491.
[12] Jealous (קַנָּא *qanna'*), *Bible*, Exodus 20:5 also *cf.* 34:14; Deuteronomy 4:24 & 5:9 & 6:15; *cf.* Joshua 24:19.
[13] Anonimo - *Recensione al Mutus Liber* (Italian translation).
[14] *Bible,* Matthew 11:15.
[15] Simonelli, 2009 and 2013.
[16] Adolf Bastian (1826-1905), *Ethnische Elementargedanken...*, p. IX.
[17] Austin, *Zen and the Brain*, p. 7.
[18] Boas, *The Mind of Primitive Men*, p. 228.
[19] Jung (1875-1961), *Psyche and Symbol*, p. 86.
[20] The plates are so called because they are made utilizing a metal (copper in this case) sheet or *plate* completely and smoothly layered with an acid resistant resinous paste. On this gummy surface, the artist carves the design with a burin or spike-pen, plowing the resin until the laminate below is exposed. Once the illustration is completed, the drawer carefully covers with an acid solution the entire design on the resinous side. The acid, repelled by the resin, corrodes only the copper exposed by the carved lines. Then, upon removing the resinous cover, only the clean sheet remains with the design permanently and precisely engraved on it by the acid. That etched metal is now ready to be inked. Another possible way is by etching and carving the design on a smooth wood block. The woodcut process is called also xylography. Either way, metal or wood, the ink is repeatedly rolled over the surface so that it finds housing only within the lines of the design. At this point, this completed work is ready to be pressed on paper and printed.
[21] Dr. Marc Haven, *Collection D'Albums Ésotériques*, 1914 re-edition by Paul Derain of the 1702 second edition and recut of the engravings by Mangeti, *Bibliotheca Chemica Curiosa*, II.
[22] The third edition, drawings and/or recuts of these 15 Plates (with two more additional plates?), was published in Paris in 1725 (?) and said to be in the library (?) of St Andrews University, College of Saint-Salvator and Saint-Leonard, Scotland [Read, *Prelude to Chemistry*, pp. 155 fol. (*cf.* also Canseliet)]. Also see Laplace, J. (Ed.) *Altus, Mutus Liber, reproduction des 15 planches en couleur d'un manuscrit di XVIII siècle. Introduction et commentaire par Jean Laplace*
[23] The most significant difference between the first and second edition is the addition, in the second one, of the sea in Plate 1. Since both water and land refer to the world as the establishment of objectivity, therefore the symbology does not change at all.
[24] See Title in Plate 1, "*tota philosophia hermetica.*"
[25] *Sieur* (*seigneur* = sir, lord) *des* (of) *Marez* (Old French *mareis* = marsh).
[26] *Cf.* Allan, *A catalogue of the books...*, p. 6 entry 71 and Haven, *Collection...*, fifth page. *Cf.* Canseliet, *L'alchimie et son livre muet (Mutus liber)*, p. 10.

[27] *Cf.*, among others, Rivière, *Fulcanelli...*, p. 21.

[28] Altus, Baulot, Isaac. (2013). *Mutus liber La Rochelle's Edition, Privilége du Roy*, King's concession: "*Nostre bien amé Jacob Saulat, Sieur des Marez, Nous a fait remontrer qu'il luy est tombé entre les mains un Livre de la haute Chimie d'Hermes, intitulé: Mutus Liber... authore cuius nomen est Altus... A CES CAUSES,... Nous luy avons permis & accordé, permettons & accordons... de faire imprimer le dit Livre*" (underlining is ours).

[29] *Cf.* Flouret, *À propos de l'auteur du Mutus Liber*, n. 1619. Pharmacist *pharmăkeús* (φαρμăκεύς), in ancient Greek, meant also alchemist.

[30] Altus, *Mutus liber La Rochelle's Edition.*

[31] La Rochelle is a French seaport founded in the X century on the Bay of Biscay. The city had a long history of heresy. In 1139, it became the most important port of the Knights Templar on the Atlantic Ocean. During the French Wars of Religion (1562–1598), the population of La Rochelle became Protestant of Calvinist denomination. The members of that Reformed Church were called Huguenots. King Henry IV with his Edict of Nantes in 1598 granted the city freedom of cult. However, King Louis XIV, in 1685, revoked the Edict forcing many noble protestant families to flee the city and emigrate.

[32] *Cf.* Martyn, *A History of the Huguenots.*

[33] *Cf.* Marra, *Altus (Isaac Baulot) - Mutus Liber (1677) - Con una nota bio-bibliografica introduttiva. Cf.* Jourdan, *Les émigrés de La Rochelle*, pp. 424-428.

[34] In 1678, *cf. Locke's travels in France, 1675-1679. Cf.* Flouret, *À propos de l'auteur du Mutus Liber*, pp. 206-211. See *Journal de voyage de Locke*, fol. 281 a 286, in Locke Manuscripts, at Bodleian Library, University of Oxfordd.

[35] Arcère, *Histoire de la ville de La Rochelle*, p. 384.

[36] Haven, in Derain's *Collection...*, (fifth page).

[37] See Title in Plate 1 (*solisque filiis artis dedicatus*).

[38] See Plate 15 (*Oculatus abis*).

[39] In *Historia Deorum Fatidicorum, Hermes Mercurius Trismegistus*, p.37. Also a United States public domain; in:Image:HermesTrismegistusCauc.jpg; File:HermesTrismegistusCauc.jpg. http://commons.wikimedia.org/wiki/File:HermesTrismegistusCauc.jpg.

[40] *Cf. UK* in Simonelli, *Beyond Immortality.*

[41] *UK* V.2 (II.2.2) *haṃsaḥ* (I am that Supreme Swan Spirit) *śucishat* (dwelling in the light clear waters) *vasur-* (the beneficent) *antarikshasat* (dwelling in the intermediate region) *hotā* (the sacrificer) *vedishat-*(on wheel-shaped-altar-of-knowledge sitting) *atithir-*(the guest) *duroṇasat* (residing in the house)/ *nṛshat* (dwelling in the human being) *varasat-* (sitting in the circle) *ṛtasat* (dwelling in the order of truth) *vyomasat-* (dwelling in the air) *abjā* (born in water) *gojā* (born in the earth's-milky-rays-of-knowledge) *ṛtajā* (born in truth's order) *adrijā* (the soul produced from the friction of stones) *ṛtaṃ*(the truth) *bṛhat* (the wide)/ *Cf.* also *in VṚ* IV.40.5.

[42] *Cf. Vamana Purana*. See Plate 14.

[43] *Cf.* Simonelli, *Beyond Immortality*, pp. 189, 191.

[44] Ἑρμῆς (*Ermēs* = Hermes) ὁ (*o* = the) Τρισ-μέγιστος (*Tris-megistos*).

[45] E.3038; also Adler, Ada, *Lexicographi*, II, pp. 4134-4 & Copenhaver, *Hermetica*, p. xli.

[46] *Cf.* Copenhaver, *Hermetica.*

[47] *Cf.* Yates, *Giordano Bruno...*, pp. 27-8, 181-2, 196-7, ff.

[48] Shaikh Abd al- Qadir al Jilani, *Kitab Sirr al-Asrar.*

[49] *Secretum Secretorum*: *Secrets' Secret*). *Tabula smaragdina* text in Chrysogonus Polydorus, *De Alchimia*, and Khunrath, *Amphiteatrum...*, figure. 8.

[50] "*Quod est inferius, est sicut quod est superius. Et quod est superius, est sicut quod est inferius, ad perpetranda miracula rei unius... Ascendit a terra in coelum, iterumque descendit in terram, et recipit vim superiorum et inferiorum. Sic habebis gloriam totius mundi. Ideo fugiet a te omnis obscuritas... Sic mundus creatus est. Itaque vocatus sum Hermes Trismegistus, habens tres partes philosophiae totius mundi. Completum est, quod dixi de operatione Solis.*"
Adaptation from File:RWS Tarot 01 Magician.jpg

http://en.wikipedia.org/wiki/File:RWS_Tarot_01_Magician.jpg
image in the public domain Tarot card from the Arthur Edward Rider-Waite tarot deck, also known as the Rider-Waite-Smith deck. |Source = a 1909 card scanned by Holly Voley (http://home.comcast.net/~vilex/) for the public domain, and retrieved from http://www.sacr

[51] *Bible*, Psalm 18:35, מגן *magen* shield (of דָּוִד David).

[52] *UB* IV.4.19.

[53] *Bible*, Luke 11:52; "οὐαὶ ὑμῖν τοῖς νομικοῖς ὅτι ἤρατε τὴν κλεῖδα τῆς γνώσεως αὐτοὶ οὐκ εἰσήλθετε, καὶ τοὺς εἰσερχομένους ἐκωλύσατε;" νομικός (*nomikos*) lawyer, interpreter and teacher of the Mosaic Law; τὴν κλεῖδα τῆς γνώσεως (*tēn cleida tēs gvōseōs*) the key of knowledge.

[54] *The Power of Myth*, p. 49.

[55] Dante, *La Vita Nova*, chapter XXVI, "*Tanto gentile ...*" *una dolcezza al core, /*10 *che intender non la può chi non la prova*" /11.

56 Hellesøe tr., *MUTUS LIBER,* Translator's Note.

[57] Tolle, *Stillness Speaks*, p. 4.

[58] Stein, *The Language That Rises: 1923-1934*, p. 147.

59 Dylan, *18 Poems*: *The force that through the green fuse drives the flower.*

[60] In *AU LECTEUR* (To the Reader), Altus, Baulot, *Mutus liber*, 1677 first edition. "*Livre Muĕt, néanmoins toutes les Nations du monde... peuvent le lire & l'entendre. Aussi est-ce le plus beu Livre qui ait esté imprimé sur ce sujet, à ce que disent les Savans, y ayant-là des choses qui n'ont jamais esté dites par personne. Il ne faut qu'estre un veritable Enfant de l'Art, pour le connoître d'abord*" (underlining is ours).

[61] *The Power of Myth*, p. 5-6. In the image, Thai Prah Mae Kuan Eim (?) holding flower. (Wood block print on rice paper).

[62] *Bible*, Exodus, 2:10.

[63] Budge, *An Egyptian Hieroglyphic Dictionary*, p. 335b. Greek: hiero-glyphic = sacred-(ἱερός *ierós*)-engraving (γλύφω *glýphō*).

[64] Different from the *Demotic*, the popular documents' writing (*sekh shat*).

[65] *Bible,* Matthew 7:6.

[66] *Bible*, Job 4:16; דממה *dĕmamah* silence.

[67] Bhagavan, Sri Ramana Maharshi, Venerable Lovable Great-Seer (December 30, 1879 – April 14, 1950). Sri Ramanasramam, Tiruvannamalai, Tamil Nadu, 606 603 India 91-4175-237200, ashram@sriramanamaharshi.org, http://www.sriramanamaharshi.org/index.html. Ramana Maharshi with Mt. Arunachala in the background (1998 Indian Rs 2.^{00} stamp).

[68] Ramana Maharshi, *The Spiritual teaching...*p, 48 and 80.

[69] Margulis, *Silences in Music Are Musical Not Silent*. "You don't need courses and lectures to understand music; it's meant to naturally speak to you."

[70] "*Silenzio cantatore,*" words by Bovio music by Lama (1922), (Venci, *La Canzone Napolitana...*, p. 133).

[71] Dante Alighieri, *La divina commedia, Inferno* IX, 61-63 "*O voi ch'avete li'ntelletti sani / mirate la dottrina che s'asconde / sotto il velame de li versi strani.*"

[72] Painted vessel (*skyphos*), III c. BC. warrior's tomb, Saviano, Via vicinale 5 vie, Nola, Naples, Italy.

[73] *Bible*, Psalm 82:6.

[74] *Bible*, John, 10:34-35.

[75] *Bible*, Luke 17:21.

[76] *Bible*, 1 Corinthians 3:16.

[77] √*div* to shine (English: div-inity). *Cf. W* p.478b.

[78] *UMu.* III.2.7. *devāś-* (senses) *ca* (and) *sarve* (all) *prati-* (in corresponding) *devatāsu* (deities) *karmāṇi* (the deeds) *vijñānamayaś-* (intellectual) *ca* (and) *ātmā* (self) *pare'* (the Supreme) *vyaye* (Imperishable One) *sarva* (all) *ekī-* (one) *bhavanti* (they become).

[79] *UC.* III.13.1. *tasya* (of this) *ha vā-* (verily) *etasya* (here) *hṛdayasya* (heart) *pañca* (five) *deva-* (gods) *sushayaḥ* (channels).

[80] Latin *ignis* fire.

[81] *VṚ* I.12.3. *agne* (o Divine-flame) *devāṅ* (the gods) *ihā* (here) *vaha* (bring).

[82] *Vedānta-Sūtras*, I. 2. 25; vol. I. p. 145.

[83] *VṚ* V.3.1. *tve* (in you) *viśve* (all) *sahasas* (of Power) *putra* (son) *devās* (gods).

[84] Bruno, *Opere italiane*, *Eroici furori*, II, 4, Minutolo.

[85] *Ibid.* pt. I, IV, Cicada.

[86] *Cf.* Homer, *The Odyssey*.

[87] González-Wippler Migene, p. 13.

[88] *Cf.* Cabrera, *ANAGÓ Vocabulario Lucumi...*, p. 272.

[89] Epistemo-logy, Greek ἐπιστήμη *epistēmē* {[ἐπί *epi* (before) + στῆμα *stēma* (external support)] = knowledge} + λόγος *logos* (= understanding); gnoseo-logy, γνῶσις *gnōsis* (= knowledge) + λόγος *logos* (= understanding).

[90] See Plate 2.

[91] *Bible*, Genesis 1:27. Man אדם *'adam*, male זכר *zakar*, female נקבה *nĕqebah*.

[92] *Bible*, Genesis 3:3.

[93] *Bible*, Genesis 3:7.

[94] *Bible*, Matthew 19:6.

[95] *Bible*, Genesis 3:24.

[96] *Cf.* Byzantine alchemical manuscript (*Codex Parisinus graecus* 2327, Fol. 196, Pelekanos of Corfu – Khandak, Iraklio, Crete, 1478), Synesius of Cyrene (d. 412), text: Stephanus of Alexandria (7th cent).

[97] *Cf.* Aristotle, *The Basic Works of Aristotle, De Generatione et Corruptione.* In fact, and here we are being sarcastic, according to Aristotle's keen surveillance, the Earth must be the basic foundation where all stones return to when they sink in water. The second tier must be Water, since it sits on land. Third is Air because it rests on water and it bubbles to the surface when placed in it. Fire is the fourth, because its flames burn directed towards its *obvious* abode the sky. There the Sun shines with the heavenly spheres in Ether, the fifth element.

[98] *Cf.* Davies, *The Thought of Thomas Aquinas*, p. 9.

[99] Term used by Chögyam Trungpan, *Cutting Through Spiritual Materialism*, p. 3.

[100] See Socrates, Jesus, al-Hallaj, Bruno, Gandhi, King, just to mention a few.

[101] Chögyam Trungpan, *Cutting Through Spiritual Materialism*, p. 15 & 119.

[102] *Bible*, Matthew 24:5; *cf.* Mark 13:6; Luke 21:8.

[103] *Bible*, Matthew 24:24-26; *cf.* Mark 13:22.

[104] *Bible*, Mark 13:22.

[105] *UAb* *Amṛta*-(immortal-nectar)-*bindu* (point-drop) *Upanishad*, mantra 18.

[106] Eckhart, *Meister Eckhart: A Modern translation*, p. 130.

[107] Ramana Maharshi, *The Spiritual teaching ...*, p. 36.

[108] *Cf.* Kant, *Prolegomena* § 45.

[109] When atheists *think* in order to oppose theists, they *think* to contrast what they *think* theists *think* when they *think of god*. They do not *think* that they are *thinking* of differing from that *thinking of god* with another *thinking* of their own. Namely, they are *thinking* of a *supreme-world* in which there is not the *god* they *think* the theists *think-of*.
(P.S. the repetition of the word: "*think*" is clearly intentional; we want to emphasize that on both sides there is only brain activity and nothing rests outside of it).

[110] *Bible*, Matthew 24:29-30... & 18:20... & 6:26-34.

[111] *Bible*, Mark 13:35-36 & *cf.* 24-25; *cf.* Matthew 24:36.

[112] *Bible*, Revelation 8:6, *cf.* 7, 8, 10, 12, 13 & 9:1, 13, & 10:7.

[113] *Bible*, Matthew 26:41 and Mark 14:38, pay attention (γρηγορέω *grēgoreō*), from ἐγείρω *egeirō* = to arouse from the sleep of death; experience

(πειρασμός *peirasmos*), from πειράζω *peirazō* = to experiment. Experimentation = πειρασμός *peirasmos* (commonly translated as temptation).

[114] *Bible*, Luke 18:1.

[115] *Gilgamesh,* 6 The return, p. 114, "a mist of sleep like soft wool teased from the fleece drifted over him."

[116] The maenads were ravaging worshipers of the Greek wine god Dionysus, equivalent to the Roman Bacchus. Under the influence of that god's mind altering substance, they performed all types of atrocities. *Cf.* Euripides, *The Bacchae*. See the 2008 murder case of Jodi Arias. She, with sadistic frenzy, killed her lover shooting him in the face, after having repeatedly stabbed him multiple times and having sliced opened his throat, almost cutting his head off (*cf.* Santos, *Mistrial...*).

[117] *Bible*, Exodus 3:14 אֶהְיֶה אֲשֶׁר אֶהְיֶה (היה *hayah* to be אֲשֶׁר *'ashér that*).

[118] *Bible*, John 12:46, (our translation) ἐγὼ φῶς εἰς τὸν κόσμον ἐλήλυθα ἵνα πᾶς ὁ πιστεύων εἰς ἐμὲ ἐν τῇ σκοτίᾳ μὴ μείνῃ, (πιστεύων *pisteúōn*, credit)*ego lux in mundum veni ut omnis qui credit in me in tenebris non maneat.*

[119] Overbye, *Peering...*

[120] Wheeler (1911-2008), *Bhor ...*, p. 18. *Cf.* Simonelli, *Beyond Immortality*, pp. 99 fol.

[121] Isaac (יִצְחָק *Yitschaq*) = he laughs. Abraham laughed at the news that a child "be born unto him that is an hundred years old? and shall Sarah, that is ninety years old, bear?" (Genesis 17:17). Rebekah (רִבְקָה *Ribqah*) = The ensnarer.

[122] גוי *gowy* nations, gentiles, other animal, race.

[123] לאם *lĕom* people, race.

[124] פרד *parad* separated.

[125] אמץ *'amats* stronger, brave, bold, secure, assuring, alert and superior to.

[126] עבד *`abad* to serve, to be subject.

[127] Genesis 25:23.

[128] Evola, *Sintesi di dottrina della razza*, p. 116 (translation and underlining is ours). "*Nella realtà si danno fin troppi casi di persone, che sono esattamente della stessa razza del corpo, dello stesso ceppo, talvolta perfino – come fratelli o padri e figli – dello stesso sangue nel senso piú reale, ma che purtuttavia non riescono a comprendersi. Una frontiera separa le loro anime, il loro modo di sentire e di vedere è diverso e contro di ciò la comune razza del corpo e il comune sangue nulla possono. Esiste una possibilità di comprensione, e quindi di vera solidarietà, di unità profonda, solo dove esiste una comune 'razza dell'anima*.'"

[129] Genesis 25:25.

[130] *Bible*, Genesis 27:11. Hairy שָׂעִיר *sa`iyr* he-goat, buck hairy, as sacrificial animal.

[131] Genesis 25:30. אדם *'Edom* from אָדֹם *'adom* = red.

[132] *`Esav* (עֵשָׂו) from the past participle of *`asah* (עָשָׂה) = handling.

[133] See Plate 2.

[134] *Bible*, Genesis 25:26.

[135] *Bible*, Genesis 27:11. חָלָק *chalaq* flattering, smooth from חָלַק *chalaq* to divide, share, plunder, allot, apportion, assign.

[136] *Ya`aqob* (יַעֲקֹב) from עָקַב *aqab*, take by the heel, follow at the heel, to supplant, circumvent, assail insidiously, overreach.

[137] *Bible*, Genesis 25:28; *the mouth* פה *peh*; *hunt* ציד *tsayid.*

[138] *Bible*, Genesis 27:3-4; savoury מַטְעַם *mat`am* from to perceive טָעַם *ta`am.*

[139] ידע *yada`* to know by experience, to perceive, to discriminate, to distinguish.

[140] *Bible*, Genesis 25:27.

[141] See Plate 2.

[142] תם *tam* perfect, complete, who lacks nothing, innocent, pure.

[143] Bible, Genesis 25:27. אהל *'ohel* the sacred tent of Jehovah (the tabernacle).

[144] *Cf.* Adam and Eve eating from the *tree of knowledge.*

[145] Metaphoric color of activity (*cf.* the expression: *red-hot*).

[146] *Bible*, Genesis 25:29-30-31-32-33-34.

[147] V.1.6. *atha ha* (now once) *prāṇā* (the spirit of the senses) *ahaṃ-śreyasi* (I superiority) *vyūdire* (disputed) *ahaṃ* (I) *śreyān* (superior) *asmi* (am) *ahaṃ* (I) *śreyān* (superior) *asmīti* (am therefore)
8. *vāg* (speech) *uccakrāma* (departed) ... *paryetyovāca* (came back asked) *katham* (how) *aśakata* (have you been able) *ṛte* (without) *maj* (me) *jīvitum* (to live) *iti* (thus) *yathā* (like) *kalā* (dumb) ... *prāṇantaḥ* (living) *prāṇena* (with breath).
9. *cakshur* (the eye) *hoccakrāma* (departed) ... *paryetyovāca* (came back asked) *katham* (how) *aśakata* (have you been able) *ṛte* (without) *maj* (me) *jīvitum* (to live) *iti* (thus) *yathā* (like) *andhā* (blind) ... *prāṇantaḥ* (living) *prāṇena* (with breath).
10. *śrotraṃ* (the ear) *hoccakrāma* (departed) ... *paryetyovāca* (came back asked) *katham* (how) *aśakata* (have you been able) *ṛte* (without) *maj* (me) *jīvitum* (to live) *iti* (thus) *yathā* (like) *badhirā* (deaf) ... *prāṇantaḥ* (living) *prāṇena* (with breath).
11. *mano* (the mind) *hoccakrāma* (departed) ... *paryetyovāca* (came back asked) *katham* (how) *aśakata* (have you been able) *ṛte* (without) *maj* (me) *jīvitum* (to live) *iti* (thus) *yathā* (like) *bālā* (infant) ... *prāṇantaḥ* (living) *prāṇena* (with breath).
12. *atha ha* (then) *prāṇa* (vital breath) *uccikramishan* (was about to depart) *sa* (that) ... *itarān* (the other) *prāṇān* (senses) *samakhidat* (were uprooted) *taṃ* (to it) *hābhisametyocuḥ* (came said) ... *tvaṃ* (you) *naḥ* (among us) *śreshṭho* (the best) *si* (are).

[148] *Ayāsya Āṅgirasa* Agile Angel-limb. *UB* I.3.19. *so'* (he) *yāsya* (Agile) *āṅgirasaḥ* [of <*aṅgiras* Greek ἄγγελος = angel (Rocci 7)> angel-metrical-limb] *aṅgānāṃ* (of the metrical-limbs) *hi* (because) *rasaḥ* (the essence).

[149] *UC* III.14.2. *mano-* (mind) *-mayaḥ* (made of) *prāṇa-* (vital breath) *-śarīro* (as body) *bhā-* (light) – *rūpaḥ* (form) *satya-* (truth) *-saṃkalpa* (conceptual determination) *ākāś-* (space) *-ātmā* (self) *sarva-* (all) *-karmā* (actions) *sarva-* (all) *-kāmaḥ* (desires) *sarva-* (all) *-gandhaḥ* (scents) *sarva-* (all) *-rasaḥ* (flavors) *sarvam* (all) *idam* (this) *abhyātto'* (encompassing) *vāky* (not speaking) *anādaraḥ* (indifferent).

[150] *UB* IV.4.5. *sa* (that) *vā* (verily) *ayam* (this) *ātmā* (Self) *brahma* (the Supreme Transcendent Spirit) *vijñāna-mayo* (of knowledge-composed) *mano-mayaḥ* (of mind-composed) *prāṇa-mayaś* (of vital breath-composed) *cakshur-mayaḥ* (of sight-composed) *śrotra-mayaḥ* (of hearing-composed) *pṛthivī-maya* (of earth-composed) *āpo-mayo* (of water-composed) *vāyu-maya* (of wind-composed) *ākāśa-mayas* (of space-composed) *tejo-mayo* (of light-composed) *tejo-mayaḥ* (of darkness-composed) *kāma-mayo* (of desire-composed) *kāmo-mayaḥ* (of detachment-composed) *krodha-mayo* (of anger-composed) *krodha-mayo* (of tranquility-composed) *dharma-mayo* (of justice-composed) *dharma-mayaḥ* (of injustice-composed) *sarva-mayaḥ* (of everything-composed) *tad* (that) *yad* (which) *etat* (this) *idam-* (this) *-mayaḥ* (composed of) *adomaya* (of that composed) *iti* (thus) *yathākārī-* (as one acts) *-yathācārī* (as one behaves) *tathā* (the same) *bhavati* (becomes) *sādhukārī* (who good does) *sādhur* (good) *bhavati* (becomes) *pāpakārī* (who evil does) *pāpo* (evil) *bhavati* (becomes) *puṇyaḥ* (virtuous) *puṇyena* (by virtuous) *karmaṇā* (action) *bhavati* (becomes) *pāpaḥ* (evil) *pāpena* (by evil) *athau* (still) *khalv* (verily) *āhuḥ* (say) *kāmamaya* (of desire-composed) *evāyam* (indeed this) *purusha* (person) *iti* (thus) *sa* (he) *yathākāmo* (as the desire) *bhavati* (is) *tat* (then) *kratur* (will) *bhavati* (becomes) *yat* (which) *kratur* (will) *bhavati* (is) *tat* (then) *karma* (deed) *kurute* (performs) *yat* (whatever) *karma* (deed) *kurute* (performs) *tat* (then) *abhisampadyate* (achieves).

[151] He was the "*very froward generation... without Certitude*" (*Bible*, Deuteronomy 32:20).

[152] *Bible*, Genesis 27:1, 3-4, 6, 9, 10-12, 14-27.

[153] From Latin *cum-* (= with) - *scio* (= I know), *cf.* science.

[154] Ἡ βασιλεία ἡ ἐμὴ οὐκ ἔστιν ἐκ τοῦ κόσμου τούτου, *Bible*, John 18:36.

[155] From Latin *lux-* (= light) – *fero* (=I carry).

[156] *UK* I.10 (I.I.10) *prasṛshṭaṃ* (let loose by) *mā'-* (me) *pratīta* (recognizing)/. *Cf.* Simonelli, *Beyond Immortality*, pp. 114, 132, 178.

[157] *Bible*, Genesis 27:29.

[158] Ramana Maharshi, *Gems From Bhagavan*, p. 14.

[159] *Bible*, Genesis 27:30.
[160] *Cf. Bible*, Genesis 25:23.
[161] *Bible*, Matthews 11:12.
[162] *Bible*, Genesis 32:24-25, 28. יִשְׂרָאֵל *Yisra'el* = God prevails; from שָׂרָה *sarah* = persevering power, אֵל *'el* = god-like
[163] *Cf.* Salaman, *The Way of Hermes.*
[164] *Cf.* Newton, *Decoding Newton 's Notebooks.*
[165] *Cf.* Yates, *Giordano Bruno e la tradizione ermetica.*
[166] See Title.
[167] *Cf.* Budge, *An Egyptian Hieroglyphic Dictionary*, p. 787b.
[168] *Cf. Bible,* Job 38:36 New International Version (NIV). "*Who gives the ibis wisdom...?*" Reproduction of the statue of Thoth as an ibis.
[169] Attic red-figure, middle of 5th century BC. from Agrigento, Sicilia. File:Winged goddess Cdm Paris 392.jp, public domain in http://en.wikipedia.org/wiki/File:Winged_goddess_Cdm_Paris_392.jpg
[170] Head of Turms, on AR 5 Asses coin from Populonia, Etruria, 3rd century BC. File:Populonia 5 asses Turms 77000007.jpg, Classical Numismatic Group, Inc.http://www.cngcoins.com, GNU Free Documentation License, http://en.wikipedia.org/wiki/File:Populonia_5_asses_Turms_77000007.jpg
[171] Budge, *The Gods...*, I, pp. 401 and 415.
[172] *Cf.* Genesis 5.18–24.
[173] *Cf.* 19.57; 21.85.
[174] *Cf.* Faivre, *Eternal Hermes*, pp. 9, 20, 97, 102, 131,
[175] V century B.C. inv. n. 250162.
[176] *Cf. W.* p. 869c.
[177] Chögyam Trungpa, *Cutting Through Spiritual Materialism*, p. 17.
[178] Giordano Bruno in Prague dedicated his latest work, *Articuli adversus mathematicos,* (*Opera Latine*, I, 3, pp. 1 ff.) to the Emperor Rudolf II. The "*Divo... Augusto*," as he addressed the phil-alchemist Emperor, failed to understand Bruno's work or his intriguing diagrams to be used by the intellect as a map for operating and contemplating. Thus, Giordano did not find employment, but received only a meager sum of money for his dedication.
[179] *W.* p. 222b.
[180] *Cf. W.* p. 164b (*iḍā* - cow) and p. 624c (*piṅgalā* – fire).
[181] Wikimedia Commons, Attribution-Share Alike 3.0 Unported license, GNU Free Documentation License, Version 1.2, Zephyris, copyright holder, File:DNA orbit animated static thumb.png (http://en.wikipedia.org/wiki/File:DNA_orbit_animated_static_thumb.png).
[182] One of the Italian ancient cities buried in 79 AD by the Vesuvius' volcanic eruption.
[183] *Cf. UMaitrī* VI.21 and *UC* VIII.6.1 *fol.*
[184] *kuṇḍalinī* covering *yoni-liṅga* (XX century brass-work from India).
[185] (XX dynasty, 1145-1137 BC; fresco at the entrance of his tomb, *Wadi Biban el-Muluk,* Gates–Valley of the King, Luxor, Egypt).
[186] From the Arabic *al-tannūr* = the-furnace with a constant controllable temperature.
[187] *UB* V.9.1. *agnir* (the Divine-flame) *vaiśvānaro* (Digestive-fire) *yo* (who) *yam* (this) *antaḥ* (within) *purushe* (a person) *yenedam* (by whom this) *annam* (food) *pacyate* (is cooked) *yad* (which) *idam* (this) *adyate* (is eaten). *Cf. Maitrī* (friendship) *Upanishad.* II.6.
[188] <<Simonelli, *Beyond Immortality*, p. 211.>>
[189] For a deeper analysis of the *cakras* and their relations with Skinner, Freud, Adler Alfred, Jung, Gandhi, Dante and Saint Teresa of Avila see Simonelli, *Beyond Immortality*, pp. 211-13.
[190] *Bible*, Genesis 2:2; rested = שבת *shabath.*
[191] *The Collected Works of Sri Ramana Maharshi*, p. 23 (27, 8) and *cf. W.* pp 1159c and 138b.
[192] We added and translated *solar* to emphasize the Latin and cabalistic word-play: *solis-que* (*que*=and),
1) *solis* = of the sun (genitive singular of *sol, solis* = sun) = *to the sons of the sun and* of *the art*
2) *solis* = to only (dative plural m. of adjective *solus, a, um* = alone) = *to the only sons of the art.*

[193] *Macaca fuscata* or *Nihon-zaru* Japan's-monkey is a macaque, called the *snow monkey*. It is the only Primate, besides humans, to inhabit frigid snowy alpine localities and can be easily visited in the Jigokudani Monkey Park of Japan. One evolutionary trait of this primate is its swimming ability in hot springs, *cf.* Angel, *Snow Monkeys*.

[194] *Bible,* Genesis 27:28, 39.

[195] *Cf.* Chevalier, *dictionnaire des Symboles*, Rose p. 112 fol.

[196] Dante, *La Divina Commedia*, *Paradise* 33.145 "*l'amor che move il sole e l'altre stelle.*"

[197] "*Jacob went out from Beersheba,*" states the preceding verse, n. 10.

[198] חלם *chalam* dreamed.

[199] ראשׁ *ro'sh* top, head, beginning.

[200] יהוה *Yĕhovah* Lord.

[201] יקץ *yaqats* awaked. שׁוֹא *shehah* sleep. ידע *yada`* knew.

[202] *Bible*, Genesis 28:13, 14, 15, 16, 17, 18, 22.

[203] See Plate 11.

[204] Time Square, New York City, NY, USA.

[205] Dante, *La Divina Commedia*, *Purgatorio*, X,3, "*perché fa parer dritta la via torta*".

[206] (עץ החיים *etz hachayim*), Riccius, *Portae Lucis*, Cover.

[207] *Cf.* Simonelli, *Beyond Immortality*, (*UK* V.3) & *cf. W.*, p. 913a. Oil on canvas 1995.

[208] *Cf.* Halberg, (Dr. Franz, founder of the Chronobiology Laboratories at the University of Minnesota), *Phase relations of 24-hour.* From Latin *circa* (around) *diem* (the day).

[209] *UB.* IV. 3.15-16-17 *punaḥ* (again) *pratinyāyam* (in inverted order) *pratiyony* (to source of origin) *ādravati* (hastens towards).

[210] *Cf.* Ramana Maharshi, *The Spiritual Teaching ...*, p. 24 (12) & Chevalier, *dictionnaire des symboles*, III, p.267.

[211] *Cf.* *Śūraṅgama Sūtra* 4:237 and 5:1 fol.

[212] *Cf.* Simonelli, *Beyond Immortality*, *Māṇḍūkya Upanishad*, pp. 58-86.

[213] For present oneiric (Greek ὄνειρος *oneiros* = dream) studies see Dement, *Some Must Watch.*

[214] *VṚ* X.129.4. *pratíshyā* (searching) *hṛdí* (in the heart) *manīshā* (with introspection).

[215] See Plate 2.

[216] *Cf. W.* p. 731b.

[217] *Cf.* Jagadguru, *Vedic Mathematics*, p. 196. *Cf.* Tibetan *tongpa-nyi* (empty).

[218] Borbély, *Secrets of Sleep*, p. 57.

[219] *UB.* IV.3.11. *asuptaḥ* (not asleep) *suptān* (the sleeping ones) *abhicākaśīti* (casts a look upon).

[220] *Bible*, Genesis 27:27.

[221] *Bible*, Genesis 27:22 "*Jacob went near unto Isaac his father; and he... said.*"

[222] *Bible,* Genesis 27:31, 32, 33

[223] *Bible,* Genesis 27:37, 38.

[224] *Bible*, Deuteronomy 33:1.

[225] זבולון *Zĕbuwluwn*, from זָבַל *zabal to exalt.*

[226] From נָשָׂא *nasa'* (to endure) and שָׂכָר *sakar* (reward).

[227] אהל *'ohel.*

[228] *Bible*, Deuteronomy 33:27.

[229] From בָּטַח *batach* to trust and to secure.

[230] From דָּגָה *dagah* to increase.

[231] From יָרַשׁ *yarash* to take possession.

[232] From טָלַל *talal roof cover.*

[233] *Bible*, Deuteronomy 33:29.

[234] Ramana Maharshi, *The Spiritual Teaching ...*, p. 76 and 82.

[235] *UK* III.14 (I.3.14) *uttishṭhata* (arise) *jāgrata* (awake) *prāpya* (having obtained) *varān-* (boons) *nibodhata* (learn) / *kshurasya* (of a razor) *dhārā* (edge) *niśitā* (sharp) *duratyayā* (difficult to cross) *durgam* (of difficult access) *pathas-* (path) *tat-* (that) *kavayo* (sages) *vadanti* (declare).

[236] *Theogony*, 212.

[237] <<Simonelli, *Beyond Immortality*, p. 178.>> See Plate 15.
[238] Plato, *Charmides*, 164.
[239] Plato, *Apology*, 38a.
[240] *Bible*, Ephesians 5:14. *Cf.* Psalm 121:4-5 and Proverbs 20:13.
[241] Tolle, *The Power of Now*, p. 9.
[242] *UĪśa* 17 *krato* (intelligence) *smara* (remember) *kṛtaṃ* (the deed) *smara* (remember) *krato* (intention-will) *smara* (remember) *kṛtaṃ* (the magic-results) *smara* (remember).
[243] <<Simonelli, *Beyond Immortality*, p. 108.>>
[244] Scaligero, *Graal ...*, p. 143-4 and 150.
[245] Word = λόγος – *logos*, Rocci, p. 1156b, II, reason... fundament... proof.
[246] *Bible*, John 1:1, 3.
[247] Not present in the 1677 first edition.
[248] *Bṛhad-āraṇyaka* (vast-forest), one of the oldest sacred *Upanishads* (I millennia B.C.?). *UB* IV.3.1. *tam̐* (him) *ha* (indeed) *samrāḍ* (the supreme ruler) *eva* (verily) *pūrvaḥ* (with formal speech accompanied by smiles) *papraccha* (asked). 2. *yājñavalkya* (o Sacrifice-Speaker) *kim̐-* (what) *jyotir* (light) *ayam* (this) *purusha* (person) *iti* (truly) *āditya-* (of the sun) *jyotih* (light) *samrāṭ* (supreme king) *iti* (truly) *hovāca* (said) *ādityenaivāyam̐* (with the sun verily this) *jyotish-* (light) *āste* (one stays) *palyayate* (moves) *karma* (work) *kurute* (performs) *vipalyet* - (returns back) *īti* (thus) *evam* (so) *evaitat* (verity this) *yājñavalkya* (Sacrifice-Speaker). 3. *astam* (has set) *ita* (when) *āditye* (the sun) *yājñavalkya* (o Sacrifice-Speaker) *kim̐-* (what) *jyotir* (light) *evāyam* (verily this) *purusha* (person) *iti* (truly) *candramā* (the moon) *evāsya* (verily his) *jyotir* (light) *bhavati* (is) *candramasaivāyam̐* (with the moon verily this) *jyotish-* (light) *āste* (one stays) *palyayate* (moves) *karma* (work) *kurute* (performs) *vipalyet* (returns back) *īti* (thus) *evam* (so) *evaitat* (verity this) *yājñavalkya* (Sacrifice-Speaker). 4. *astam* (has set) *ita* (when) *āditye* (the sun) *yājñavalkya* (o Sacrifice-Speaker) *candramasy* (the moon) *astam* (has set) *ite* (thus) *kim̐-* (what) *jyotir* (light) *evāyam* (verily this) *purusha* (person) *iti* (truly) *agnir* (fire) *evāsya* (verily his) *jyotir* (light) *bhavati* (is) *agnin-* (with fire) *aivāyam* (verily this) *jyotish-* (light) *āste* (one stays) *palyayate* (moves) *karma* (work) *kurute* (performs) *vipalyet-* (returns back) *īti* (thus) *evam* (so) *evaitat* (verity this) *yājñavalkya* (Sacrifice-Speaker). 5. *astam* (has set) *ita* (when) *āditye* (the sun) *yājñavalkya* (o Sacrifice-Speaker) *candramasi* (the moon) *astam* (has set) *ite* (thus) *śānte* (extinguished) *agnau* (the fire) *kim̐-* (what) *jyotir* (light) *evāyam* (verily this) *purusha* (person) *iti* (truly) *vāg* (the word-idea) *evāsya* (verily his) *jyotir* (light) *bhavati* (is) *vāc-* (with the word-idea) *aivāyam̐* (verily this) *jyotish-* (light) *āste* (one stays) *palyayate* (moves) *karma* (work) *kurute* (performs) *vipalyeti* (returns back) *tasmād* (therefore) *vai* (verily) *samrāḍ* (supreme king) *api* (also) *yatra* (where) *pāṇir* (the hand) *na* (not) *vinirjñāyate* (is discerned) *atha* (then) *yatra* (when) *vāg* (the word-idea) *uccarati* (is uttered) *upaiva* (therefore truly) *tatra* (there) *nyet-* (leads towards) *īti* (thus) *evam* (so) *evaitat* (verity this) *yājñavalkya* (o Sacrifice-Speaker). 6. *astam* (has set) *ita* (when) *āditye* (the sun) *yājñavalkya* (o Sacrifice-Speaker) *candramasy* (the moon) *astam* (has set) *ite* (thus) *śānte* (extinguished) *agnau* (the fire) *śāntāyām̊* (has quieted) *vāci* (the word) *kim̊-* (what) *jyotir* (light) *evāyam* (indeed this) *purusha* (person) *iti* (thus) *ātmaivāsya* (the Self his) *jyotir* (light) *bhavati* (is) *ātmanaivāyam* (due to the Self indeed this) *jyotish-* (the light of intelligence which is placed in the heart – *Cf. jyotir hṛdaya āhitam yat Vṛ* VI.9.6-) *āste* (exists) *palyayate* (moves perceiving - *Cf. W.* p. 605b "*parī*... to perceive, ponder,... to move round or in a circle."-) *karma* (work) *kurute* (performs) *vipalyeti* (returns back - *Cf. W.* p. 974a "*vi-parī...* to turn around or back, return."-) *iti* (thus). 7. *katama* (which one) *ātmeti* (the self then) *yo* (who) *yam̊* (this) *vijñānamayaḥ* (composed of knowledge) *prāṇeshu* (among the vital senses) *hṛdy* (heart) *antarjyotiḥ* (the light within) *purushaḥ* (person) *sa* (he) *samānaḥ* (serenely centered in itself) *sann* (being) *ubhau* (both) *lokāv* (worlds) *anusañcarati* (penetrates) *dhyāyatīva* (thinking as if) *lelāyatīva* (moving to and fro as if) *sa* (he) *hi* (upon) *svapno* (dream state) *bhūtvā* - (becoming) *imam̊* (this) *lokam* (dimension) *atikrāmati* (beyond goes) *mṛtyo* (death) *rūpāṇi* (the forms). 9. *svena* (by his own) *bhāsā* (light) *svena* (by his own) *jyotishā* (brightness) *prasvapiti* (he sleeps dreaming) *atrāyam* (in this state)

purushaḥ (person) *svayam̐* (self-) *jyotir* (illuminated) *bhavati* (becomes).... 4,6 *Brahma-* (Being Supreme Awareness*) iva* (verily) *san* (obtains) *brahmā-* (to Brahman-Awareness) *payeti* (goes)... 7 *yadā* (when) *sarve* (all) *pramucyante* (are shed) *kāmā* (desires) *ye'* (which) *sya* (one's) *hṛdi* (in heart) *śritāḥ* (fastened)/ *atha* (then) *martyo'* (the mortal) *mṛto* (immortal) *bhavaty-* (becomes) *atra* (in this manner) *brahma* (Supreme Spirit) *samaśnute* (one reaches) [identical verse in *UK* VI.14 (II.3.14)].

[249] *Bible*, John 8:12.

[250] *Bible*, John 1:5, 9. In the photos: a solar halo on the New Jersey Shore, USA (5/14/2013).

[251] In the Latin sense of fire.

[252] *Cf.* Simonelli, *Awareness*, p. 58 fol.

[253] *Cf. Bible*, Genesis 1:4. *Cf.* Greek etymology: *sees* (*eidov* εἶδον), idea (*eidos* εἶδος), *idol* [*eidōlon* εἴδωλον (from *eidos* εἶδος)].

[254] *Cf.* Bible, Luke 20:17 & Mark 12:10.

[255] *Cf.* Ovid, *Metamorphoses*, III:402-436. See Caravaggio, Narcissus beholding his own reflected image (Galleria Nazionale d'Arte Antica, Rome, Italy. Wikimedia Commons, public domain reproduction by The Yorck Project, Zenodot Verlagsgesellschaft mbH, GNU Free Documentation License, File:Michelangelo Caravaggio 065.jpg. http://en.wikipedia.org/wiki/File:Michelangelo_Caravaggio_065.jpg).

[256] Campbell, *Mythos I...*, "*On Being Human. Cf.* also *UC* VIII.8.1.

[257] Hebrew: אמון *'emuwn*, from אָמַן *'aman* to support, be sure. Greek: πίστις *pistis* certitude.

[258] *Bible*, Deuteronomy 32:20.

[259] *Bible*, Matthew 17:20.

[260] *Bible*, John 1:18 θεὸν οὐδεὶς ἑώρακεν πώποτε.

[261] Lao Tzu, *Tao Te Ching*, Chapter 1.

[262] Pierce *The Intuitive Way*, p. 130-1.

[263] *Bible*, Genesis 1:3.

[264] *Bible*, Genesis 1:16.

[265] Chevalier, *dictionnaire des Symboles*, I, p. 21. "*Symbole de la perception directe de la lumière intellective.*"

[266] *Cf.* Sanskrit *gahana* and the deep (תהום - *tehowm*) in *Bible*, Genesis 1:2.

[267] *Cf.* Sanskrit *ámbhas* and the waters (מים - *mayim*) in *Bible*, Genesis 1:2.

[268] *Bible*, Genesis 1:6.

[269] *Cf.* Hesiod, *Theogony* 947. Bronze Minotaur by Sophie Ryder 1996.

[270] In French, the word is a feminine substantive.

[271] *Cf.* Chevalier, *dictionnaire des symboles*, III p. 353.

[272] Ramana Maharshi, *The Spiritual Teaching...*, pp. 3 and 4 (2 and 4), 4 (8), (16) and 10 (21), underlining is ours.

[273] Andrews, *Animal...*, pp. 199-1. The turkey was introduced in Europe in the XVI century by the English navigator William Strickland. He depicted the animal on his family coat of arms. The turkey was so popularly American that Franklin proposed to substitute the eagle with this bird as a US national emblem. and

[274] Chevalier, *dictionnaire...*, III, p. 307.

[275] *W.* p. 1286a. Sāyaṇācārya (?-1387) was a Vedic commentator.

[276] *Bible,* Mark 1:10. *Cf.* John 1:32.

[277] Rocci, p. 1485.

[278] Budge, *Egyptian Book of the Dead*, 15, pp. 124-5.

[279] Chevalier, *dictionnaire...*, III, p. 307.

[280] Chevalier, *dictionnaire...*, III, p. 245.

[281] *Cf.* Kaplan, *Sefer Yetzirah*, pp. 5, 23, 32, 117, 140.

[282] Chun Siong Soon, *Unconscious determinants...*, p. 543 and № "n.1: Libet, B. et al. *Behav. Brain Sci.* 8, 529–566 (1985). n.2: Wegner, D.M., *Trends Cogn. Sci.* 7, 65–69 (2003). n.3: Haggard, P. *Trends Cogn. Sci.* 9, 290–295 (2005)."

[283] *UB* IV.3.30. *na* (not) *vijānāti* (does know) *vijānan* (knowing) *vai* (verily) *tan* (that) *na* (not) *vijānāti* (does know) *na* (not) *hi* (verily) *vijñātur* (the knower) *vijñāter* (knower) *viparilopo* (separation) *vidyate* (there is) *avināśitvāt* (imperishable) *na* (not) *tu* (however) *tad* (that) *dvitīyam* (second) *asti* (is) *tato'* (therefore) *nyad* (opposit) *vibhaktam* (divided) *yad* (that) *vijānīyāt* (he may know).

[284] *Cf. B.U.* IV.3.32.

[285] *UMaitrī* VI.17. *evaisha* (so this) *kṛtsna-* (after all) *kshaya* (remains) *eko* (alone) *jāgartīti* (awake thus) *etasmād* (from this) *ākāśād* (vacuity) *esha* (this) *khalv* (truly) *idaṃ* (this) *cetāmātram* (of pure awareness consisting) *bodhayati* (awakes) *anenaiva* (by this verily) *cedam* (and this) *dhyāyate* (meditating) *asmin* (in that) *ca* (and) *pratyastam* (disappearance) *yāti* (disappears)

[286] *UMaitrī* IV.3.15-16-17 *punaḥ* (again) *pratinyāyam* (in inverted order) *pratiyony* (to source or origin) *ādravati* (hasten towards)

[287] <<Simonelli, *Beyond Immortality*, p. 72.>>

[288] Chevalier, *dictionnaire...*, IV, p. 211.

[289] Gray, *Net of Being*, p. 151. "*The Center*," oil on canvas.

[290] *W.* p. 301ab.

[291] As when we say the word *tri-angle*, it implies an *ideal* geometrical figure with necessarily three-angles, without which, it would not be a triangle.

[292] Thoreau, *A Year...*, July 16, 1851.

[293] In French, the word is a feminine substantive.

[294] *Bible*, Exodus 20:11.

[295] *Bible*, Genesis 2:7.

[296] *Bible*, Genesis 2:10.

[297] *Bible*, Genesis 1:9 to 12; 16; 20 to 22; 24-25.

[298] *UB* I.4.5. *sṛshṭāṃ* (creation) *hāsyaitasyām* (indeed of this one in this) *bhavati* (becomes) *ya* (who) *evaṃ* (thus) *veda* (knows).

[299] Carbonara, *Introduzione alla filosofia*, p. 75.

[300] *Cf.* Chevalier, *dictionnaire...*, I, p. 236 & IV, pp. 270 fol.

[301] *Bible*, Genesis 34: 28.

[302] Sanskrit *ajo* "A driver, mover, ... leader; N. of Indra, ... of Agni, of the sun, of Brahmā, ... a he-goat, ram" (*W.* 9b); *cf. sārathiṃ* charioteer, *UK.* III.3 & *UŚ* IV.5.

[303] *UB.* V.8.1. *vācam* (the word) *dhenum* (as the milk cow) *upāsīta* (let be honored) . . . *tasyāḥ* (her) *pāṇa* (the vital spirit) *ṛshabhaḥ* (bull) *mano* (the mind) *vatsaḥ* (the calf).

[304] *Cf.* Chevalier, *dictionnaire...*, II, pp. 249 fol.; IV, pp. 313 fol. & 388 fol.

[305] *UB* I.2.4. "*kālam* (space of time) ... *yāvān* (as long as) *saṃvatsaraḥ* (year);" *cf. also* I.2.7; *UMaitrī* VI. 15. & *VṚ* I. X. 190. 2. etc.

[306] *Bible*, Genesis 1:5,8,13,19,23,31.

[307] *Cf. UB* I. 2. 2 & 6 & *Bible*, Genesis 2:2.

[308] *UB* III.4.2. *na* (not) *dṛshṭer* (see) *drashṭāram* (the seer) *paśyeḥ* (of seeing) / *na* (not) *śruter* (hear) *śrotāraṃ* (the hearer) *śṛṇuyāḥ* (of hearing)/ *na* (not) *mater* (think) *mantāraṃ* (the thinker) *manvīthāḥ* (of thinking) / *na* (not) *vijñāter* (understand) *vijñātāraṃ* (the understander) *vijānīūyāḥ* (of understanding)/ *esha* (this) *ta āītmā* (your Self) *arvāntaraḥ* (in everything).

[309] *UĪśa* 4 *anejad* (motionless) *ekam* (one) *manaso* (than the mind) *javīyo* (faster) *nainad* (not this) *devā* (the faculties of the senses) *āpnuvan* (could reach) *pūrvamarshat* (ahead moving quick) *tad* (it) *dhāvato'* (running) *nyān-* (other objects) *atyeti* (surpasses) *tishṭhat* (being still) *tasminn* (in it) *apo* (all the activity) *mātariśvā* (the fire and air) *dadhāti* (sustains).

[310] *UB* III. 3.1 (*lokānām*) (the worlds') *antān* (*ends*), 2. *dvātriṁśatam* (thirty-two times) *vai* (indeed) *deva-* (of the god's) *ratha-* (chariot) *ahnyāny* (the daily course) *ayaṁ* (this) *lokaḥ* (location) *taṁ* (that) *samantaṁ* (all around) *pṛthivī* (the earth) *dvis* (twice) *tāvat* (as much) *paryeti* (surrounds it) *tāṁ* (that) *samantam* (all around) *pṛthivīm* (the earth) *dvis* (twice) *tāvat* (as much) *samudraḥ* (the ocean) *paryeti* (surrounds it).

[311] *UB* IV. 1. 5.

[312] *UB* I. I. 2.

---

[313] *Bible,* Genesis 1:2 & 7.
[314] *VṚ* X. 129. 1 "*ámbhaḥ* (Celestial Waters) ... *gahanaṁ* (depth) *gabhīráṁ* (of inscrutable)."
[315] XXV. 246.
[316] *UK* I. 3. 5.
[317] *UC* VIII. 3. 3 "*sa vā esha ātmā hṛdi ... hṛdayam.*"
[318] IV. 3. 35.
[319] *BU* III. 3. 2),
[320] Kant, I, II, §9, p. 29-30.
[321] *Bible,* Job 9:8.
[322] *Bible,* Job 11.
[323] *UĪśa* 5 *tad* (that) *ejati* (moves) *tan* (that) *na* (not) e*ijati* (moves) *tad* (that) *dūre* (far) *tad* (tat) *vad* (also) *antike* (near) *tad* (that) *antarasya* (within this) *sarvasya* (of all) *tad* (that) *u* (again) *sarvasyāsya* (of all this) *bāhyataḥ* (outside).
[324] <<Simonelli, *Beyond Immortality,* p. 95.>>
[325] *Cf. VṚ* I. 164. 20 *fol.* (African Two Heads Janus Bronze - Benin, Nigeria, 1950).
[326] *Bible,* Revelation 1:15 & *cf.* Hebrew 12:19.
[327] Nikhilānanda, *Śaṅkara's Commentary of Gauḍapāda's Kārikā* p. 25.
[328] *UB* IV. 3. 18 & 19
[329] *VṚ* VI.9.6. *jyotir* (the light) *hṛdaya* (in the heart).
[330] *UB* I, IV.3.7. *katama* (which one) *ātmeti* (the self then) *yo* (who) *yaṃ* (this) *vijñānamayaḥ* (composed of knowledge) *prāṇeshu* (among the vital senses) *hṛdy* (heart) *antarjyotiḥ* (the light within) *purushaḥ* (person) *sa* (he) *samānaḥ* (serenely centered in itself) *sann* (being) *ubhau* (both) *lokāv* (worlds) *anusañcarati* (penetrates) *dhyāyatīva* (thinking as if) *lelāyatīva* (moving to and fro as if) *sa* (he) *hi* (upon) *svapno* (dream state) *bhūtvā* – (becoming) *imaṃ* (this) *lokam* (dimension) *atikrāmati* (beyond goes) *mṛtyo* (death) *rūpāṇi* (the forms).
[331] Chevalier, *dictionnaire...,* I, p. 178 (2).
[332] Singular סְפִירָה of the plural Sephiroth.
[333] *Bible,* Deuteronomy 32:2.
[334] *Cf.* Evola, *La Tradizione Ermetica,* p. 125.
[335] *Cf.* Patañjali, *Yoga-Sūtra,* VII.22-23.
[336] By Vyasa, *Mahā-bhārata = The Great War of the Descendants of the Bearer of Oblation,*" 9th c. BC.
[337] *Cf.* Simonelli, *Awareness,* p. 107.
[338] *BG.* II.48 *yogasthaḥ* (in a state of union) *kurū* (perform) *karmāṇī* (actions) *saṃgaṃ* (attachment) *tyaktvā* (having rejected *siddhayasiddhayoḥ* (in success in non success) *samo* (same) *bhūtvā* (be).
[339] *Bible,* Matthew 8:22.
[340] *BG* II.19 *ya* (he) *enaṃ* (this) *vetti* (views) *hantāraṃ* (killer) *yaś* (he) *cainaṃ* (and this) *manyate* (considers) *hatam* (killed) / *ubhau* (the two) *tau* (those) *na* (not) *vijānīto* (know) *nāyaṃ* (not this) *haṃti* (kills) *na* (not) *hanyate* (is killed) //
[341] *Bible,* I Corinthians 7, 30.
[342] *B.G.* 14.(22) *prakāśaṃ* (illumination) *ca* (and) *pravṛttiṃ* (accomplishment) *ca* (and) *moham* (delusion) *eva* (even) *ca* (and)... / *ta* (not) *dveṣṭi* (does hate) *saṃpravṛttāni* (taking place) *na* (not) *nivṛttāni* (vanished) *kāṅkṣati* (desires)
(23) *udāsīnavad* (neutral like) *āsīno* (seated) *guṇair* (by *virtues and/or passions*) *yo* (who) *na* (not) *vicālyate* (disturbed)/ *guṇā* (*virtues and/or passions*) *vartanta* (remains) *ity* (thus) *eva* (even) *yo-* (who) *vatiṣṭhati* (stays) *neṅgate* (unmoved)
(24) *sama-*(equal) *duḥkha-* (in pain) *sukhaḥ* (in pleasure) *svasthaḥ* (staying) *sama-* (equally) *loṣṭā-* (a lump of earth) *nśma-* (stone) *kāñcanaḥ* (gold)/ *tulya-* (equally) *priy-*(loved) *āpriyo* (unloved) *dhīras* (firm) *tulya-* (equally) *nindāt* (in insult) *masaṃstutiḥ* (praise)
(25) *mānā-* (in honor) *pamānayos* (dishonor) *tulyas* (equally) *tulyo* (equally) *mitr-* (friend) āri- (enemy) pakṣayoḥ (in sides)/ *sarv-* (all) *ārambha-* (endeavor) *parityāgī* (renouncer) *guṇ-* (*virtues and/or passions*) *ātītaḥ* (to have transcended) *sa* (he) *ucyate* (is said).

[343] Governor from 6 AD, was born in 46 BC and committed suicide in 9 AD after losing *legiones* XVII, XVIII & XIX.

[344] At Kalkriese Hill in Lower Saxony, near modern Osnabrück, Germany.

[345] 18 BC – AD 21, he was chieftain of the Germanic Cherusci Roman auxiliary forces and a traitor, since he was also a Roman citizen.

[346] Suetonius, *De Vita XII Caesarum, Divus Augustus* 23.1. "*Adeo denique consternatum ferunt, ut per continuos menses barba capilloque summisso caput interdum foribus illideret vociferans: "Quintili Vare, legiones redde!" diemque cladis quotannis maestum habuerit ac lugubrem.*"

[347] *La Divina Commedia*, Purgatorio, XXXI, 102, "*ove convenne ch'io l'acqua inghiottissi,*" and XXVIII, 128, *"che toglie altrui memoria del Peccato."* Gustave Doré, illustration of the river Lethe in Purgatory.

[348] *Cf*, Chevalier, *dictionnaire des symboles*, II, pp. 65-72.

[349] *Bible*, Genesis 28:18, 22.

[350] *Bible*, Numbers 12:5.

[351] *Cf.* Chevalier, *dictionnaire des symboles*, II, p. 306.

[352] The original 1677 Plate 5 has only round Doric columns, which does not change the general symbolism.

[353] *Cf.* Kant, C*ritique of pure reason*, § 17 Introduction.

[354] *Cf. Māṇḍūkya* (frog-like cyclical composition) *Upanishad* 3. *Cf.* "the image (צלם *tselem* - εἰκών *eikÓn* – *imago*) of God" (*Bible*, Genesis, 1:26).

[355] Has the same meaning as "'*Viśvānara*'... 'he who is all and man' (i.e. the individual soul), or 'he to whom souls belong' (in so far as he is their maker and ruler)" (*Vedānta-Sūtras*, I.2.28; vol. I. p. 150).

[356] "If we adopt the etymology *agni* = *agraṇi*, i.e. he who leads in front" (*Vedānta-Sūtras*, I. 2. 28; vol. I. p. 150).

[357] *UB* V.9.1. *agnir* (the Divine-flame) *vaiśvānaro* (Digestive-fire) *yo* (who) *yam* (this) *antaḥ* (within) *purushe* (a person) *yenedam* (by whom this) *annam* (food) *pacyate* (is cooked) *yad* (which) *idam* (this) *adyate* (is eaten).

[358] *UB* I.4.6. *etāvad* (thus much) *vā* (indeed) *idaṃ* (this here) *sarvam* (all) *annaṃ* (food) *caivānnādaś* (and eater of food) *ca* (and) *soma* (ambrosia) *evā-* (verily) *nnam* (food) *agnir* (fire) *annā-* (food) *daḥ* (eater).

[359] *Cf. Bhagavad-Gītā*, XV. 14.

[360] *Vedānta-Sūtras* (string of aphorisms of the Vedas's end), III. 1. 7; vol. II p. 111.

[361] *Śiva Sūtra Vārttika* (explanation of the Auspicious-one's string of aphorisms), II. 9. *jñānam-* (knowledge) *annam* (food).

[362] *Ideas*, § 43, p.140. Cf. the fish in Plate 3.

[363] This distinction is not present in the 1677 first edition. However, the column in general indicates a distinction and delimitation of separates rooms.

[364] *Cf.* Chevalier, *dictionnaire des symboles*, II, p. 306.

[365] *Cf.* Chevalier, *dictionnaire des symboles*, II, p. 306.

[366] *Cf.* Chevalier, *dictionnaire des symboles*, III, p. 287.

[367] Narmadā River stone *liṅga*. *Abadir* (= the unknown God? Or *Ob-Adur* = Orus the god serpent?) *cf.* Drummond, *Origines: Phoenicia. Arabia*, p. 435.

[368] Hesiod, *Theogony*, 455-85. Kronos (Κρόνος) = Roman Saturn = Khronos-Time (Χρόνος), *Cf.* Kronos (Κρόνος) = Khronos (Χρόνος) in the Cretan *Leges Gortinae* (Rocci, p. 1092a).

[369] *Cf.* Khunrath, *Anfiteatro...*, Tavola 9. Pietra filosofale – III, detail.

[370] *W.* p. 1074ab (brass, Nepal 1980).

[371] Chevalier, *dictionnaire des symboles*, III, p. 155. *Cf. UG* 6 "the sun of knowledge (*sūryas*)... the moon of reflection (*candramās*)." *Cf. W.* "*prati-√mā...* f. an image, likeness... reflection (in comp. after a word meaning "moon")... shadow." (p. 669a) "*Ma...* 4th note... moon... mā mother... light... knowledge... measure... death (771b). "indriyá... organs of perception ... each being presided over by its own ruler ... manas by the Moon." (167b).

372 *UB* I.2.1. *na-* (no) *iv-* (verily) *eha* (here) *kiṃcan-* (nothing at all?) *āgra* (in the beginning) *āsīt* (was) *mṛtyuna-* (by death) *iv-* (verily) *edam* (this) *āvṛtam* (concealed) *āsīt* (was) *aśanāyayā* (by hunger) *aśanāyā* (hunger) *hi* (because) *mṛtyuh* (death) *tan* (this) *mano* (the mind) *kuruta* (he projected) *ātmanvī* (a being for-myself) *syām* (let me be) *iti* (thus). *Cf.* Damasio, *Self Comes to Mind.* See the Café in the Crypt, St.Martin in the Fields, London, UK, where Death, hunger is combined with food.

373 *Cf. UB* I.2.2 & <<Simonelli, *Beyond Immortality*, p. 46.>>

374 √*pat cf. W.* p. 580c "to fall down or off,... down to hell;... (in a moral sense), lose... position to drive away... to... ruin, ... to ... inflict (punishment) to seduce to... [*Cf.*.. Gk. πέτομαι... Lat. *peto.*]" *Cf.* Genesis 1:27 "*Et creávit Deus hóminem ad imáginem suam;... másculum et féminam...* [28] *et ait: Créscite et multiplicámini...* [2:24] *et erunt duo in carne una.* [3:12] *Múlier...* [13] *respóndit: Serpens decépit me...* [23] *Et emísit eum Dóminus Deus de paradíso voluptátis...* [16] *Mulíeri quoque dixit:... sub viri potestáte eris et ipse dominábitur tui...*[24] *Eiecítque Adam.*"

375 *UB.* I.4.3. *sa* (he) *dvitīyam* (a second) *aicchat* (desired) *sa* (he) *haitāvān āsa* (extended) *yathā* (as) *strī-*(woman) *pumāṃsau* (man) *samparishvaktau* (in a loving embrace) *sa* (he) *imam* (this) *evātmānaṃ* (self) *dvedhā-* (in two parts) *pātayat* (divided) *tataḥ* (from that) *patiś* (the ruler, husband) *ca* (and) *patnī* (the possessor, wife) *cābhavatām* (and they became)... *tato* (thus) *manushyā* (humanity) *ajāyanta* (was generated).

376 *UB* I.2.4. "*so* (he) *kāmayata* (desired) *dvitīyo* (a second) *ma* (from me) *ātmā* (self) *jāyeteti* (let be born) *sa* (he) *manasā* (with the Mind) *vācam* (Mother Word) *mithunaṃ* (pairing) *samabhavad* (united) *aśanāyā* (Hunger) *mṛtyuḥ* (Death) *tad* (that) *yad* (which) *reta* (the flow of semen) *āsīt* (was) *sa* (that) *saṃvatsaro* (the year) *'bhavat* (became) *na* (not) *ha* (indeed) *purā* (in the beginning) *tataḥ* (then) *saṃvatsara* (the year) *āsa* (was) *tam* (him) *etāvantaṃ* (so far) *kālam* (space of time) *abhibhaḥ* (parented) *yāvān* (as long as) *saṃvatsaraḥ* (year) *tam* (him) *etāvataḥ* (thus) *kālasya* (time) *parastād* (afterwards) *asṛjata* (he projected) *taṃ* (him) *jātam* (generated) *abhivyādadāt* (opened his mouth to swallow) *sa* (he) *bhāṇ* (aaahhh) *akarot* (made) *sa-* (that) *iva* (indeed) *vāg* (speech) *abhavat* (became)." *Cf. W.* 752b *bhāṇ* (aaahhh) from √*bhaṇ* = to speak, "onomat. imitation of the noise of breathing."

377 *BU* I.2.5. "*sa* (he) *aikshata* (thought) *yadivāimam* (verily him) *abhimaṃsye* (if I will kill) *kanīyo'* (very small) *nnaṃ* (food) *karishya* (I will accomplish) *iti* (thus)." It must be said that Mṛtyu in Sanskrit means death. Therefore, the act of eating would have corresponded to inflicting death on the child.

378 *UB* III.4.2. *na* (not) *mater* (think) *mantāraṃ* (the thinker) *manvīthāḥ* (of thinking) / *na* (not) *vijñāter* (understand) *vijñātāraṃ* (the understander) *vijānīūyāḥ* (of understanding).

379 *Cf. UB* I.5.1 *fol.*

380 *Cf.* Simonelli, *Beyond Immortality*, p. 48.

381 Francisco Goya (1819 – 1823, Museum of the Prado, Madrid, Spain) poster.

382 *Cf.* Simonelli, *Beyond Immortality*, p. 72.

383 *Cf.* Zaorski, *Open heart surgery.*

384 The brain corresponds to the waking state, the breathing to dream (REM) and the heart to the dreamless sleep (NREM) state.

385 Carbonara, *Introduzione alla filosofia*, p. 75, "*non deve pensar di pensare ... perchè ... é presente a se stesso, senza bisogno di mediarsi, cioè di vedersi dinanzi a sè medesimo come oggetto del proprio conoscere.*" *Cf. Vedānta-Sūtras,* II. 3. 7; vol. II, p. 14; II. 2. 28; vol. I, pp. 423 *fol.*

386 *UB* IV.3.30. *na* (not) *vijānāti* (does know) *vijānan* (knowing) *vai* (verily) *tan* (that) *na* (not) *vijānāti* (does know) *na* (not) *hi* (verily) *vijñātur* (the knower) *vijñāter* (knower) *viparilopo* (separation) *vidyate* (there is) *avināśitvāt* (imperishable) *na* (not) *tu* (however) *tad* (that) *dvitīyam* (second) *asti* (is) *tato'* (therefore) *nyad* (opposit) *vibhaktam* (divided) *yad* (that) *vijānīyāt* (he may know).

387 *UB* IV.3.32 *salila* (like water) *eko* (one) *drashṭādvaito* (seer without a second) *bhavati* (becomes).

388 *UMaitrī* VI. 8. *agnir* (fire) *iv-* (verily) *āgninā* (by fire) *pihitaḥ* (concealed).

389 Ramana Maharshi, *Spiritual teachings*, p. 44 and 46.

390 *Cf. UŚ* IV. 6 *fol.*

---

391 *Cf.* תרדמה *tardemah* deep sleep, *Torah*: - Genesis, 2, 1.

392 *UM.* 5 *yatra* (where) *supto* (one asleep) *na* (not) *kaṃcana* (any) *kāmaṃ* (desire) *kāmayate* (does desire) *na* (not) *kaṃcana* (any) *svapnaṃ* (dream) *paśyati* (does see) *tat* (that) *sushuptam* (deep unconscious sleep) *sushupta* (deep unconscious sleep) *sthāna* (state) *ekī -bhūtaḥ* (one-become) *prajñāna-ghana* (knowledge-compact) *evānanda-mayo* (alone-bliss-made) *hyānanda-bhuk* (verily-bliss-enjoyer) *ceto-mukhaḥ* (consciousness-mouth) *prājñas-* (the knower) *tṛtīyaḥ* (third) *pādaḥ* (quadrant).

393 *Cf.* Sleep

394 Dement, *Some Must Watch* ..., p. 24 and 27.

395 Harrison, *General anesthesia research: aroused from a deep sleep?*

396 Anch, *Sleep: A Scientific Perspective*, p. 141.

397 *Psyche and Symbol*, p. 79.

398 <<Simonelli, *Beyond Immortality*, p. 69.>>

399 *UKa*. III. 3. *Yatraitat* when thus) *purushaḥ* (a person) *suptaḥ* (sleeping) *svapnaṃ* (dream) *na* (no) *kañcana* (whatsoever) *paśyaty* (he sees) *athāsmin* (that self) *prāṇa* (breathing) *evaikadhā* (verily one) *bhavati* (becomes) *tad* (that) *enam* (him) *vāk* (speech) *sarvaiḥ* (with all) *nāmabhiḥ* (names) *sahāpyeti* (together goes to it) *cakshuḥ* (the eye) *sarvaiḥ* (with all) *rūpaiḥ* (forms) *sahāpyeti* (together goes) *śrotraṃ* (the ear) *sarvaiḥ* (with all) *śabdaiḥ* (sounds) *sahāpyeti* (together goes) *manaḥ* (the mind) *sarvaiḥ* (with all) *dhyānaiḥ* (thoughts) *sahāpyeti* (together goes) *sa* (he) *yadā* (when) *pratibudhyate* (he awakens) *yathāgner* (as from a fire s) *jvalataḥ* (blazing) *sarvā* (in, all) *diśo* (regions) *visphuliṅgā* (sparks) *vipratishṭherann* (spread out) *evam* (thus) *evaitasmād* (so this therefore) *ātmanaḥ* (from the self) *prāṇā* (the vital breaths) *yathāyatanaṃ* (each in its own place) *vipratishṭhante* (spread out) *prāṇebhyo* (from the vital breaths) *devāḥ* (the resplendent senses) *devebhyo* (from the resplendent senses) *lokāḥ* (the worlds)

400 *Cf. W. supta* from "√*svap* ... to sleep" (1280b); 1) "*supta* [*cf. UKa*. III. 3] ... asleep... paralyzed, numbed, insensible ... closed ... resting, inactive, dull, latent" (1230a); 2) "*sushupta* ... fast

asleep ... *sushupti*...(in phil. 'complete unconsciousness')" (1237c). In the West, oneiric studies started a century ago, while Indian texts go back two millennia.

401 Electroencephalogram: *Electro* = electrical - *Encephalo* = brain's activity - *Gram* = graphic recording.

402 Dement, *Some Must Watch* ..., p. 26. *Cf. UM.* 5.

403 Anch, *Sleep: ...,* "paroxysmal wave form of high amplitude standing out from a low-amplitude background in the EEG" p. 125.

404 Dement, *Some Must Watch* ..., p. 28, wth examples of Polygraph records of NREM sleep; *cf.* slow delta-wave sleep (SWS) in stage 3.

405 *UM.* 6 *esha* (this) *sarveśvara* (all Lord) *esha* (this) *sarvajña* (omniscient) *esho'ntaryāmy* (this internal regulator) *esha* (this) *yoniḥ* (female source) *sarvasya* (of all) *prabhavāpyayau* (the cause and vanishing) *hi* (verily) *bhūtānām* (of beings).

406 *Cf. B.U.* IV.3.32.

407 *UMaitrī* VI.17. *evaisha* (so this) *kṛtsna-* (after all) *kshaya* (remains) *eko* (alone) *jāgartīti* (awake thus) *etasmād* (from this) *ākāśād* (vacuity) *esha* (this) *khalv* (truly) *idaṃ* (this) *cetāmātram* (of pure awareness consisting) *bodhayati* (awakes) *anenaiva* (by this verily) *cedam* (and this) *dhyāyate* (meditating) *asmin* (in that) *ca* (and) *pratyastam* (disappearance) *yāti* (disappears).

408 *UMaitrī* IV.3.15-16-17 *punaḥ* (again) *pratinyāyam* (in inverted order) *pratiyony* (to source or origin) *ādravati* (hasten towards).

409 *Bible*, Genesis 28:11 & 12.

410 Campbell, *The Power of Myth*, p. 49.

411 *Bible*, Exodus 3:14 אֶהְיֶה אֲשֶׁר אֶהְיֶה (היה *hayah* to be אֲשֶׁר *'ashér* that).

412 *Bible*, John 12:46, (our translation) ἐγὼ φῶς εἰς τὸν κόσμον ἐλήλυθα ἵνα πᾶς ὁ πιστεύων εἰς ἐμὲ ἐν τῇ σκοτίᾳ μὴ μείνῃ, (πιστεύων *pisteúōn*, credit)*ego lux in mundum veni ut omnis qui credit in me in tenebris non maneat.*

413 *Cf.* Chevalier, *dictionnaire des symboles*, IV pp.70-77 and 417.

[414] *UM.* 12 *amātraś-* (without metrical letters) *caturtho'* (the fourth) *vyavahāryaḥ prapañcopaśamaḥ* (uncorrelated of the manifestation the cessation) *śivo'* (the final emancipation) *dvaita* (one without a second) *evam-* (thus) *oṅkāra* (the sacred mystical syllable AUM) *ātmaiva* (Self verily) *saṁiśaty-* (merges into) *ātmanātmānaṃ* (with the Self the Self) *ya* (who) *evaṃ* (thus) *veda* (knows) *ya* (who) *evaṃ* (thus) *veda* (knows).

[415] Macdonell, *Sanskrit*, p. 5.

[416] *UKai.* 18.

[417] *Bible*, Mark 1:15.

[418] <<Simonelli, *Beyond Immortality*, p. 84.>>

[419] *Bible*, John, 14:20 and 30.

[420] *Bible*, John 17:21 and 11, 22, 23 [world (κόσμος *kosmos*) = world affairs].

[421] Spadaro, *Intervista a Papa Francesco*, pp. 468-469 "*Dio in tutte le cose... Dio è nella vita di ogni persona... Anche se ... è stata un disastro... lo si deve cercare in ogni vita umana. Anche se ... è un terreno pieno di spine ed erbacce.*"

[422] Ramana Maharshi, *Spiritual teaching*, Jung's *Foreword*, p. ix.

[423] *Cf.* Jung, *Psychology and Alchemy*.

[424] Descartes, René (1596-1650), *Discourse on Method*, pp. 1 (I), 15 (II), 34-35 (IV), underlining is ours.

[425] Kant (1724 –1804), *The Critique of Pure Reason*, § 12, p. 49. *Cf.* also *Prolegomena...*

[426] *Cf.* Nikhilānanda, *Māṇḍūkyopanishad ...*, I. 6 (2).

[427] Ramana Maharshi, *Spiritual teaching*, p. 36.

[428] The Sphinx (Σφίγξ *sphígx* = dissolute strangler), according to Hesiod (*Theogony*, 319-326 ff.), was the daughter of Chimera (goat), the fire breathing monster with three natures (goat, lion, serpent) and her brother Orthros (dawn), the two-three headed dog of hell (brother of the three headed Cerberus, another dog from hell) and owned by Geryon (the Titan with three bodies) for guarding his heard of read cattle.

[429] μίαν [*mían*, one = μίᾰ (*miá*), Sanskrit *éka*] ἔχον (*échon*, has) φωνὴν [*phōnhèn*, sound; φωνή (*phōnéh*) Sanskrit *kāra* (*UM* 1)].

[430] Apollodorus, *The library*, III.V.8. Tί ἐστιν ὃ μίαν ἔχον φωνὴν. "The rendering φωνή is supported by" the great majority of ancient sources. "On the other hand the reading μορφή [*morphé*, shape] is supported [only] by some MSS." (346 n. 2).] τετρά-πουν [four-footed; τετρά-πούς (*tetrá-poús*) Sanskrit *catush-pada* (*UM* 2)] καὶ δί-πουν [two-footed; δί-πούς (*dí-poús*) Sanskrit *dví-pada* (*UM* 3-4)] καὶ τρί-πουν [three-footed; τρί-πούς (*trí-poús*) Sanskrit *trí-pada* (*UM* 1)] γίνεται [becomes; γίνομαι = γίγνομαι (*gínomai* = *gígnomai*) Sanskrit *jan*]... Σφίγξ ἀπὸ τῆς ἀχροπόλεως ἑαυτὴν ἔρριψεν "The Sphinx [Sanskrit Man-beast *purusha-mṛga*] threw herself from the citadel."

[431] Wilford, *Asiatic Researches* (300).

[432] πούς *poús*, also means sound, Rocci, 1548a, "4)... d) *suono*."

[433] *UB* IV.3.9 *tasya* (of that) *vā* (verily) *etasya* (of this) *purushasya* (person) *dve* (two) *eva* (only) *sthāne* (conditions) *bhavataḥ* (are) *idaṃ* (this) *ca* (and) *para-* (beyond) *loka-* (world) *sthānaṃ* (condition) *ca* (and).

[434] Grimal, The dictionary of classical mythology, p. 324a.

[435] *UB* IV.3.9 *sandhyaṃ* (in between) *tṛtīyaṃ* (third) *svapna-* (dream) *sthānam* (condition).

[436] *Pausanias, Description of Greece, Boeotia IX.XXVI.4,* (ὀνείρατος - *oneíratos* – in a dream).

[437] <<Simonelli, *Beyond Immortality*, pp. 183-4.>>

[438] Campbell, *The Power of Myth*, p. 152.

[439] Sphinx seated right, as it appears on the reverse of a Greek coin [AE12, 309 BC, from Kaunos (Καῦνος) in present Anatolia, Turkey].

[440] *SATOR AREPO TENET OPERA ROTAS*:

[→*SATOR* (sower) *ROTAS*← (wheels)]; [→*TENET*← (holds)]; {→*OPERA* (production) *AREPO*← [field (Celtic *àrepos* from *arpennis* = fields, land)]}.

The oldest example of this inscription dates before 79 AD and was found in the house of Publius Paquius Proculus in Pompeii (*NSc*).

[441] Saying of the Roman censor Appius Claudius Caecus (4th-3rd cent. BC), "*fabrum esse suae quemque fortunae*" (Sallust, *Ad Caesarem Senem* I) & Wheels of Dharma, design on a Tibetan religious silk shawl (detail).

[442] *UŚ* V.7. *phala*-(recompense) *karma*-(action producing) *kartā* (maker) *kṛtasya* (of fortune) *tasyai*- (his) *va* (verily) *sa* (he) *c*- (and) *opabhoktā* (the one who enjoys).

[443] *Bible*, Luke 9:62.

[444] <<Simonelli, *Beyond Immortality*, p. 74.>>

[445] *UB*. I. 4. 6. *atisṛshṭtyāṃ* (in higher creation) *hāsyaitasyāṃ* (indeed this in this) *bhavati* (becomes) *ya* (who) *evaṃ* (verily) *veda* (knows).

[446] *UC* VIII. 2. 10. *yaṃ* (whathever) *kāmaṃ* (desire) *kāmayate* (desires) *so'* (he) *sya* (of this) saṃ*kalpād* (conceptual determination) *eva* (verily) *samuttishṭhati* (it appears).

[447] *Bible*, Song of Songs 5:2.

[448] Anonymous Pilgrim, *The Way of a Pilgrim*, pp. 5 and 178-9.

[449] *Yoga-Sūtra* VII.22-23.

[450] <<Simonelli, *Beyond Immortality*, p. 179.>>

[451] *UB* I.4.5. *so'* (he) *vet* (knew) *ahaṃ* (I) *vāva* (indeed) *sṛshṭir* (creation) *asmi* (am) *ahaṃ* (I) *hīdaṃ* (this) *sarvam* (all) *asṛkshīti* (produced) *tataḥ* (he) *sṛshṭir* (creation) *abhavat* (became) *sṛshṭāṃ* (creation) *āsyaitasyām* (indeed of this one in this) *bhavati* (becomes) *ya* (who) *evaṃ* (thus) *veda* (knows).

[452] *Cf.* Chevalier, *dictionnaire des symboles*, II pp. 328 fol.

[453] *UY* 10.6 in Varenne, *Yoga..*, p. 221.

[454] *UKai* [*Kaivalya* (epistemic detached beatific loneliness) *Upanishad* belonging to the *VA*] 19, "*mayy* (in me) *eva* (verily) *sakalaṃ* (everything) *jātam* (born) *mayi* (in me) *sarvam* (all) *pratishṭhitam* (founded) *mayi* (in me) *sarvaṃ* (all) *layam* (dissolution) *yāti* (reaches) *tad* (that) *brahm-ā-dvayam* (Supreme-Spirit without a second) *asmy* (am) *aham* (I)."

[455] *Bible*, John 10:9.

[456] *UMu* II.2.4 *praṇavo* (mystical syllable Om) *dhanuḥ* (bow) *śaro* (arrow) *hy* (indeed) *ātmā* (self).

[457] *Bible*, Leviticus 2:9, 13 & 16.

[458] *Bible*, Matthew 5:13.

[459] Chevalier, *dictionnaire...*, IV, pp. 168-9.

[460] *VṚ* X.129.4. *sató* (being) *bándhum* (connection) *ásati* (in being) *nír* (non) *avindan* (found) *hṛdí* (in the heart) *pratíshyā* (searching) *kaváyo* (the seers) *manīshā* (with reflection) //

[461] *UB* I.2.1.

[462] *VṚ* X.129.4. *kāmas* (desire) *tád* (consequently) *ágre* (in the beginning) *sám avartatādhi* (sprung about) *mánaso* (of the mind) *rétaḥ* (flowing seed) *prathamáṃ* (the original) *yád* (that) *āsīt* (was) /

[463] *UB* I.2.2 *Tad* (that) *yad* (which) *apāṁ* (of the water) *śara* (spume) *āsīt* (was) *tat* (that) *samahanyata* (became solid) *sā* (that) *pṛthivy* (the earth) *abhavat* (became) *tasyām* (on it) *aśrāmyat* (he rested) *tasya* (from him) *śrāntasya* (rested) *taptasya* (heated by Awareness = *tapas*) *tejo* (light) *raso* (fluid essence) *niravartatā*-(came forth) *gniḥ* (fire).

[464] Chevalier, *dictionnaire des symboles*, III, p. 287.

[465] *Cf.* Lazar, *Functional brain*.

[466] *UB* V.9.1. *agnir* (the Divine-flame) *vaiśvānaro* (Digestive-fire) *yo* (who) *yam* (this) *antaḥ* (within) *purushe* (a person) *yenedam* (by whom this) *annam* (food) *pacyate* (is cooked) *yad* (which) *idam* (this) *adyate* (is eaten). *Cf.* *Maitrī* (friendship) *Upanishad*. II.6.

[467] Mahadevan, *Ramana Maharshi*, It. tr., p. 39.

[468] Tolle, *The Power of Now*, p. 93.

[469] *rétas* (flowing seed) *W.* p. 887c "flow of semen;" *raśmí* (measuring beam of light) *W.* p. 869b "a measuring cord, ... a ray of light, beam."

[470] <<Simonelli, *Beyond Immortality*, p. 47.>>

[471] *BU* I.2.4. *so* (he) *kāmayata* (desired) *dvitīyo* (a second) *ma* (from me) *ātmā* (self) *jāyeteti* (let be

born) *sa* (he) *manasā* (with the Mind) *vācam* (Mother Word) *mithunaṃ* (pairing) *samabhavad* (united) *aśanāyā* (Hunger) *mṛtyuḥ* (Father Death) *tad* (that) *yad* (which) *reta* (the flow of semen) *āsīt* (was) *sa* (that) *saṃvatsaro* (the year) *'bhavat* (became) *na* (not) *ha* (indeed) *purā* (in the beginning) *tataḥ* (then) *saṃvatsara* (the year) *āsa* (was) *tam* (him) *etāvantaṃ* (so far) *kālam* (space of time) *abhibhaḥ* (parented) *yāvān* (as long as) *saṃvatsaraḥ* (year) *tam* (him).

472 *Cf. VṚ* I. 164. 48 & X. 190. 2. *Cf. W.* p. 1114a "*saṃ-vatsará ... (Cfr. Pari-v°).*"

473 *kalā Cf. W.* p. 261a "*Kal ...* one-sixteenth of the moon's diameter."

474 *VṚ* I.164.48. *dvā̆daśa* (twelve) *pradháyaś* (fellies) *cakrám* (wheel-year) *ékaṃ* (one) ... *tásmin* (in that) *sākáṃ* (joined together) *triśatā̆* (three hundred) ... *śaṅkávo'* (spokes) *rpitā̆h* (inserted) *shashṭir* (sixty) X. 190. 2. *samudrā̆d* (Ocean) *arṇavad* (foaming) *ádhi* (from) *saṃvatsaro'* (year) *ajāyata* (was projected).
A wheel of the Sun Temple. One of the wheels (Rs 4^{00}) of the Sun Temple at Konark (Orissa, India. 2001 India postage). Compare to the *svastika* wheel, a Greek cross spun at its center ⊕: the "*svastika...* auspicious object... solar symbol... the wheel of the... course of the Sun... auspicious words *su* [well] *astí* [being] [*svasti* [well-being]]... amongst *jainas* it is... auspicious ... the crossing of the arms or hands on the breast... formed like a triangle (... to symbolize the *liṅga*)... mode of sitting practised by *yogins* (... toes are placed in the inner hollow of the knees)" (*W.* p. 1283a). Also see the Tibetan Prayer Wheels.

475 *UB* I. 5. 14. *sa* (he) *esha* (this) *saṃvatsaraḥ* (year) *prajā-* (of creatures) *-patiḥ* (father).

476 *Cf. Voynich Manuscript* p. 71-129.

477 London, Soane Museum: head inside border of the coffin of Seti I (1318 - 1304 BC, XIX Dynasty), son of Ramses I, father of Ramses II the Great. This sarcophagus, the most beautiful one in the Kings' Valley (West of Thebes – Egypt), was discovered in 1817 by Giovanni Belzoni (*Cf.* Budge, *Mummy*, p. 418- 9). *Cf.* the word sarcophagus with its Greek etymology σαρκο-φᾰγέω (*sarko-fagéō*) meat-eater.

478 Budge, *The Egyptian Book...*, p. civ.

479 *Coffin Text* 714; Rundle-Clark, *Myth and Religion*, p. 74.

480 *Cf. Bible*, Genesis 1:5, 8, 13, 14, 16, 18, 19, 23, 31 and 2:2, 3, יום *yowm* day, also with the meaning of year.

481 *Cf.* "the day and night of God" in *BG* VII. 17. *ahaḥ* (day) ... *brahmṇaḥ* (of God) ... *rātriṃ* (night).

482 *Cf. UMaitrī* VI.1.

483 *Bible*, 2 Peter 3:8.

484 *Bible*, Genesis 1:31 and 2:2.

485 *Bible*, John 17:5 and "thou lovedst me *before* the foundation of the world" 24 (Italic is ours).

486 To the family of the deceased Italian-Swiss physicist Besso (Dyson, *Disturbing the Universe*, Ch. 17, Science and the Search for God).

487 Budge, *The Book of the Dead - Papyrus of Nebseni* (British Museum 4, N. 9900, Sheet 23-24), LXIV Chapter of the Coming Forth by Day, pp. 112-113.

488 *Bible*, John 8:58.

489 Bahá'u'lláh, *The Kitáb-i-Íqán*, 52.

490 Welsh, *Myrddhin*, Old Celtic *Mori-dunon* "sea-hill"? By assonance, *Merlin*: *Mṛ-liṅ* = *Mṛ-tyu-liṅ-ga* "death's procreative power mark?" *Liṅga*, as a natural stone from the Narmadā "pleasure-giver" river in central India. Merlin, artistic rendering.

491 Malory, XIV, II and VIII, 1. Underlining is ours.

492 <<Simonelli, *Beyond Immortality*, p. 49 fol.>>

493 A serpent, also after decapitation, may bite its own tail (*Cf.* CorriereTv, *Il serpente decapitato*). Slow metabolism and motor neurons' electrical signals allow a severed serpent to have still nerve and muscle twitches and spasms.

494 Budge, *The Gods of the Egyptians*, II, p. 202.

495 Chevalier, *dictionnaire des symboles*, II, p. 270-1.

496 √*pat cf. W.* p. 580c "to fall down or off,... down to hell;... (in a moral sense), lose... position to drive

away... to... ruin, ... to ... inflict (punishment) to seduce to... [*Cf*... Gk. πέτομαι... Lat. *peto.*]" *Cf.* Genesis 1:27 "*Et creávit Deus hóminem ad imáginem suam;... másculum et féminam...* [28] *et ait: Créscite et multiplicámini...* [2:24] *et erunt duo in carne una.* [3:12] *Múlier...* [13] *respóndit: Serpens decépit me...* [23] *Et emísit eum Dóminus Deus de paradíso voluptátis...* [16] *Mulíeri quoque dixit:... sub viri potestáte eris et ipse dominábitur tui...*[24] *Eiecítque Adam.*"

497 *UB.* I.4.3. *sa* (he) *dvitīyam* (a second) *aicchat* (desired) *sa* (he) *haitāvān āsa* (extended) *yathā* (as) *strī-*(woman) *pumāṃsau* (man) *samparishvaktau* (in a loving embrace).

498 *BU* I.2.4. *etāvantaṃ* (so far) *kālam* (space of time) *abhibhaḥ* (parented) *yāvān* (as long as) *saṃvatsaraḥ* (year) *tam* (him) *etāvataḥ* (thus) *kālasya* (time) *parastād* (afterwards) *asṛjata* (he projected) *taṃ* (him) *jātam* (generated) *abhivyādadāt* (opened his mouth to swallow) *sa* (he) *bhāṇ* (aaahhh) *akarot* (made) *sa-* (that) *iva* (indeed) *vāg* (speech) *abhavat* (became). *Cf. W.* 752b *bhāṇ* (aaahhh) from √*bhaṇ* = to speak, "onomat. imitation of the noise of breathing."

499 *BU* I.2.5. "*sa* (he) *aikshata* (thought) *yadivāimam* (verily him) *abhimaṃsye* (if I will kill) *kanīyo'* (very small) *nnaṃ* (food) *karishya* (I will accomplish) *iti* (thus)."

500 *Bible*, Revelation, 12:4.

501 *Cf.* Chevalier, *dictionnaire des symboles*, III, p. 286-7.

502 Budge, *The Gods of the Egyptians*, II, p. 215.

503 *UK* IV.7 (II.I.7) *guhāṃ* (in the secret of the heart) *praviśya* (having entered the shade) *tishṭhantī* (standing firmly).

504 *UK* IV.8 (II.I.8) *araṇyor-* (within both fire-sticks) *nihito* (placed) *jāta-* (all) *vedā* (knower) *garbha* (foetus) *iva* (like) *subhṛto* (well borne) *garbhiṇībhiḥ* (by pregnant women) / *dive* (day) *diva* (after day) *īḍyo* (to be praised) *jāgṛvadbhir-* (by the awakened) *havishmadbhir-* (offering oblations) *manushyebhir-* (by men) *agniḥ* (fire of knowledge) / *etad* (this) *vai* (verily) *tat* (that) / Same verse in *VṚ* III.29.2. (*sudhitogarbhiṇīshu*); *cf. VS* I.II.3.7.

505 *Cf. W.* p. 417c "all-possessor ... knowing [or known by] all created beings ... N. of *agni* ... fire."

506 *Cf. W.* p. 349bc *gárbha* "√*grabh* = *grah*, 'to conceive' ... the inside, middle ...'having in the interior , containing , filled with'... fetus or embryo, child... fire... joining, union"; *cf.* Rocci, p. 367. *Cf. UB* I.2.6-7.

507 *W.* p. 1299c.

508 <<Simonelli, *Beyond Immortality*, p. 184.>>

509 *Bible*, Matthew 1:23.

510 *Bible*, Luke 2:7,15-16. Bethlehem לחםבית *Beyth Lechem*; brought forth ἔτεκε *éteke*; firstborn πρωτότοκος *protótokos*; swaddling clothes ἐσπαργάνωσεν *espargánōsen*; manger φάτνῃ *phatne* (7); men ἄνθρωποι anthrōpoi (15); babe βρέφος *bréphos*; lying, sitting κείμενον *keimenos*; in ἐν *en*; manger φάτνῃ *phatne* (a section of a room used to store hay and other food for animals) (16). Latin *praesaepe* from πατέομαι (*pateomai*) to eat √*pat*, (Latin *pasco, pastor, panis*). See: βοῦς (*bus*) ἐπὶ (*epi*) φάτνῃ (*phatne*) "ox in the manger" - *i.e.* well fed - (Homer, *The Odyssey*, 4, 535 & 11, 411) used by the Greek sophist Philostratus (170-244/9 AD) as a metaphor (828) for "man in opulence" (*cf.* Rocci p. 1944-5). The third-century BC Greek poet Aratos (*Phénoménes*) named a "little mist" of stars (cluster M44) "the Manger" and two connected stars, that seem to be eating from it, are called the Northern Ass (Asellus Borealis, Gamma Cancri) and the Southern Ass (Asellus Australis, Delta Cancri.

511 Bernini's (1666) Holy Spirit as a dove, alabaster window, main altar (Saint Peter's Basilica, Vatican City).

512 *Cf.* Smith, *The Cambridge companion...*, p. 55.

513 Hebrew סְפִירוֹת *Səphîrôṯ* means emanations or enumeration.

514 *Cf.* Riccius, *Portae Lucis.*

515 Chemical symbol S.

516 Chevalier, *dictionnaire des symboles*, IV, p. 230.

517 Sal ammoniac, inorganic mineral composed of ammonium chloride NH_4Cl.

518 Paracelsus, *Paracelsus...*, pp. 529 fol.

519 *Cf. VṚ* X.121 *hiraṇyagarbha.*

---

[520] *Cf.* Chevalier, *dictionnaire des symboles*, III, p. 205.
[521] p. 52-162.
[522] *Bible*, Genesis, 2:21. תרדמה *tardemah* deep sleep.
[523] P. 114.
[524] *Cf.* Warren, *Buddhism in translations...*, p. 81. *Cf. Jātaka* I.74.[25] Tibetan votive Tsa Tsa clay tablet, Chinese Yuan Dynasty (1271-1368).
[525] *Bible*, Matthew 16:18-19.
[526] *Bible*, John 2:6.
[527] *Cf. W.* 783c.
[528] *UP* IV.2 *yathā* (as) ... *maricayor* (rays) *arkasyāstaṃ* (of the sun) *gacchataḥ* (the setting) *sarvā* (all) *etasmiṃs* (in this) *tejo-* (of light) *maṇḍala* (circle) *ekī-*(united) *bhavanti* (become) *tāḥ* (those) *punaḥ* (again) *punar* (again) *udayataḥ* (the rising) *pracaranti* (radiate) *evam* (so) *ha* (indeed) *vai* (verily) *tat* (that) *sarvam* (all) *pare* (higher) *deve* (in the shining entity) *manasy* (in I-think) *ekī-* (one) *bhavati* (becomes) *tena* (thus) *tarhy* (then) *esha* (this) *purusho* (person) *na* (not) *śṛṇoti* (hears) *na* (not) *paśyati* (sees) *na* (not) *jighrati* (smells) *na* (not) *rasayate* (tastes) *na* (not) *spṛśate* (feels) *nābhivadate* (not speaks) *nādatte* (not takes) *nānandayate* (not enjoys) *na* (not) *visṛjate* (evacuates) *neyāyate* (not moves) *svapitīty* (sleeps) *ācaksate* (says).
[529] *Cf.* Homer, *Odyssey*.
[530] Echoed in Plato's *Phaedrus.*, XXV. 246.
[531] *UK* III. 5-7 (I.3.5-7) *yas-* (who) *tv-* (thus) ... *bhavaty-* (is) *ayuktena* (un-concentrated) *manasā* (with the faculty of the mind) *sadā* (always) / *tasyendriyāṇy-* (his faculties) *avaśyāni* (un-submissive) *dushṭāśvā* (vicious horses) *iva* (like) *sāratheḥ* (for the driver)/
yas- (who) *tu* (however) *vijñānavān-* (with intuition) *bhavaty-* (is) *yuktena* (yoked in concentration) *manasā* (with the faculty of the mind) *sadā* (always) / *tasyendriyāṇy-* (his faculties) *vaśyāni* (submissive) *sadaśvā* (good horses) *iva* (like) *sāratheḥ* (for the driver) /
yas- (who) *tv-* (also) *avijñānavān-* (without intuition) *bhavaty* (is) *amanaskaḥ* (without intellect) *sadāśuciḥ* (always impure) / *na* (not) *sa* (he) *tat-* (that) *padam-* (goal) *āpnoti* (does attain) *saṃāraṃ* (the flow of worldly illusions) *cādhigacchati* (falls into) /
[532] *UŚ* II.9 *dushṭāśva-* (restive horses) *yuktam* (yoked) *iva* (verily) *vāham* (the chariot) *enaṃ* (this) *vidvān* (the knower) *mano* (the mind) *dhārayetā* (should control) *pramattaḥ* (vigilant).
[533] In the Latin sense of *un-animus* (of one mind) = *unus* (one) *animus* (mind, spirit).
[534] *Bible*, Matthew 5:8.
[535] *Cf.* Nikhilānanda, *Māṇḍūkyopanishad*,I, 5.
[536] *UK* III.3-6. *yuktena manasā sadā.*
[537] *W*, p. 515a.
[538] *Cf.* XXX, Budge, *The Egyptian Book of the Dead*, pp. 255.
[539] *Cf. ibid*, XXX, Budge, *The Egyptian Book of the Dead*, pp. 256-258 (Scale, water color on papyrus, Egypt 1986).
[540] *Bible*, Revelation 6:5.
[541] *Bible*, Daniel 5:27.
[542] *Cf. ŚB.* I.9.3. and Dasgupta, *A history of Indian philosophy*, p. 25.
[543] *Cf.* Budge, *The Mummy*, pp. 228 and 311.
[544] Ramana Maharshi, *The Spiritual Teaching* ..., p. 23 (9), 91 and 103. *Hṛt*, in composition for *hṛd*.
[545] *Bible*, Matthew 6:22.
[546] Eliade, *Images and Symbols*, p. 87.
[547] Scene from the Rāmāyaṇa, Rāma discharging an arrow (etching on rice paper, Thailand).
[548] *UMu* II.2.4 *śaro* (arrow) *hy* (indeed) *ātmā* (self) *brahma* (Supreme Spirit) *tal* (that) *lakshyam* (the target) *ucyate* (is said) / *apramattena* (without any distraction) *veddhavyam* (one should hit) *śaravat* (as an arrow) *tanmayo* (with that united) *bhavet* (one must become).
[549] Plutarch, *Moralia, Isis and Osiris*, ch. IX.
[550] Novalis, *The Novices of Sais*, p. 17. Sais is Osiris grave location (Herodotus, II, 171).

551 *Cf.* Chevalier, *dictionnaire des symboles*, IV p.404.
552 As depicted in the first 1677 edition.
553 *Cf.* Chevalier, *dictionnaire des symboles*, II p. 201-2.
554 *Bible*, Matthew 6:6.
555 *Bible*, Matthew 19:6.
556 *Cf.* תרדמה *tardemah* deep sleep, *Torah*: - Genesis, 2, 1.
557 *UM.* 5 *sushupta* (deep unconscious sleep) *sthāna* (state) *ekī -bhūtaḥ* (one-become) *prajñāna-ghana* (knowledge-compact) *evānanda-mayo* (alone-bliss-made).
558 Gruppo di Ur, *Introduzione alla Magia*, I, Leo, *Oltre Le Soglie Del Sonno*, pp. 141, 166-8. "*Il primo passo della pratica iniziatica è conoscere quel silenzio e quella concentrazione di cui si è trattato... il secondo passo consiste nel portare il senso di sè dalla testa al cuore, cioè da una coscienza riflessa ad una coscienza organica centrale... Allora si apre la possibilità di prender contatto col corpo sottile... Come lo vive il tipo umano comune, il sonno è un annullamento della coscienza, una specie di morte appena illuminata dal miraggio dei sogni... Ma quando si è conseguita una maggiore introversione, quando la vita interiore, fortificata, diviene preponderantee il mondo esterno cessa di essere sentito come l'unico centro d'interesse – si ha vagamente il senso che la vita del sonno sia una continuazione invece di una pausa, una integrazione della vita di veglia invece di una interruzione brusca, periodica ed incomprensibile... La notte, invece, è un risveglio cosmico, un affiorare, un palpitare e un risuonare di forze spirituali che la luce fisica solare sopraffà con la sua violenza. È un sole spirituale che sorge e che il nostro corpo sottile va a cercare orientandosi verso di esso. Bisogna coltivare un senso di aspettazione per una forma di vita incommensurabilmente più libera ed estesa della vita ordinaria di veglia... Da uno stato di coscienza all'altro, nell'addormentarsi, vi è un momento di oscuramento e di discontinuità che bisogna superare... Bisogna apprendere l'arte dell'addormentarsi* (1)*... (1)Ad essa fa da controparte l'are del morire – ars moriendi- non meno trascurata e andata perduta della prima. [N. d. U.]*
Leo, viz. pseudonym of Giovanni Colazza (1877-1953), a member of the *Group* and, like the pharmacist Isaac Baulot (Altus?), a man of science and a prominent Roman physician.
The *Gruppo di Ur* (*Group of Ur*) was an Italian occultist-traditionalist movement, founded around 1927. According to Julius Evola, one of the directors, the *Group* had the purpose to help its members to operate magically and to influence the political forces of the time.
Evola (1898), *lost in the meanders of traditional-romantic Arthurian courts,* passed away in 1974 calling out for his friend Massimo (Scaligero, anthroposophist, viz. Antonio Massimo Sgabelloni, 1906-1980).
559 Different from Plate 2, where there was only one. Not present in the 1677 first edition.
560 Dante, *La divina commedia*, Paradiso XXXIII, 82-87, 91-92, 145. "*Oh abbondante grazia ond' io presunsi/ ficcar lo viso per la luce etterna,/ tanto che la veduta vi consunsi!/Nel suo profondo vidi che s'interna / legato con amore in un volume, / ciò che per l'universo si squaderna... / La forma universal di questo nodo/credo ch'i' vidi.../ L'amor che move il sole e l'altre stelle.*" & Knot, design on a Tibetan religious silk shawl (detail).
561 Paul Gustave Doré (1832 –1883), Dante Alighieri, *La divina commedia*, p. 613 (Paradise XXI 40-42).
562 *UMu* III.2.7. *devāś-* (senses) *ca* (and) *sarve* (all) *prati-* (in corresponding) *devatāsu* (deities) *karmāṇi* (the deeds) *vijñānamayaś-* (intellectual) *ca* (and) *ātmā* (self) *pare'* (the Supreme) *vyaye* (Imperishable One) *sarva* (all) *ekī-* (one) *bhavanti* (they become).
563 *Cf. UB* III. 2.13 the self in space, bodily fluids in water and atmosphere and in all the other gods like, the two Aśvins, Pracetas, Indra, Vishṇu, Mitra, Prajāpati, Brahman, Śiva, and Vishṇu as Acyuta.
564 Gruppo di Ur, *Introduzione alla Magia*, I, Leo, p. 141.
565 *UK* VI.17 (II.3.17) *aṅgushṭha-* (of a thumb) *mātraḥ* (size) *purusho'* (the Person) *ntar-* (the inner) *ātmā* (self) *sadā* (always) *janānāṃ* (of the creature) *hṛdaye* (in the heart) *sannivishṭaḥ* (seated)/ *taṃ* (him) *svāc-* (one's own) *charīrāt* (from body) *pravṛhen-* (should draw out) *muñjād-* (from the reed) *iv-* (like) *eshīkāṃ* (the stalk) *dhairyeṇa* (with firmness)/ *taṃ* (him) *vidyāc-* (should realize)

chukram- (pure) *amṛtaṃ* (immortal) *taṃ* (him) *vidyāc-* (should realize) *chukram-* (pure) *amṛtam-* (immortal) *iti* (indeed)/

566 *UC* III.14.3. *esha* (this *esha* [*vai prathamaḥ*] this [before mentioned]) *ma* (my) *ātmā-* (Self) *-ntar* (within) *hṛdaye'* (the heart) *ṇīyān* (smaller than) *vrīher* (a grain of rice) *vā* (or) *yavād* (a barley-corn) *vā* (or) *sarshapād* (a mustard seed) *vā* (or) *śyāmākād* (a grain of millet) *vā* (or) *śyāmāka-* (of a grain of millet) *-taṇḍulād* (a kernel) *vā* (or) *esha* (this) *ma* (my) *ātmā-* (Self) *-ntar* (within) *hṛdaye* (the heart) *jyāyān* (greater than) *pṛthivyāḥ* (the earth) *jyāyān* (greater than) *antarikshāj* (the sky) *jyāyān* (greater than) *divaḥ* (heaven) *jyāyān* (greater than) *ebhyo* (these) *lokebhyaḥ* (universes).

567 Jung, *Psyche and Symbol*, pp. 80 and 120.

568 *Bible*, Mark 9:37, Luke 18:17.

569 A letter to his spiritual father Agostino da San Marco in Lamis, in April 18, 1912, Sicari, *Il secondo grande libro...*, p. 791."*Il cuore di Gesù ed il mio, permettetemi l'espressione, si fusero. Non erano più due i cuori che battevano, ma uno solo. Il mio cuore era scomparso, come una goccia d'acqua che si smarrisce in un mare.*"

570 Dante, *La Divina Commedia, Paradiso* 1.70-1, "*Trasumanar significar per verba / non si poria; però l'essemplo basti.*"

571 Ramana Maharshi, *The Spiritual Teaching ...*, p. 23 (9) and 91.

572 *UMu.* III.2.7. *devāś-* (senses) *ca* (and) *sarve* (all) *prati-* (in corresponding) *devatāsu* (deities) *karmāṇi* (the deeds) *vijñānamayaś-* (intellectual) *ca* (and) *ātmā* (self) *pare'* (the Supreme) *vyaye* (Imperishable One) *sarva* (all) *ekī-* (one) *bhavanti* (they become).

573 *UC.* III.13.1. *tasya*(of this) *ha vā-*(verily) *etasya* (here) *hṛdayasya* (heart) *pañca* (five) *deva-*(gods) *sushayaḥ* (channels).

574 Latin *ignis*. *Cf.* Dowson, *A Classical Dictionary of Hindu Mythology*, p. 6 *fol.*; Aurobindo, *Hymns to the Mystic Fire*.

575 *VṚ* I.12.3. *agne* (o Divine-flame) *devāṅ* (the gods) *ihā* (here) *vaha* (bring).

576 *Vedānta-Sūtras*, I. 2. 25; vol. I. p. 145.

577 *Cf. ŚB.* X.6.1.11. *sa* (he) *esho'* (this) *gnirvaiśvānaro* (digestive fire common to all humans) *yat-* (in other words) *purushaḥ* (the Cosmic-being) ... *purushe*(in the human being) *ntaḥ* (within) *pratishṭhitaṃ* (rooted).

578 Chevalier, *dictionnaire des symboles*, I p. 298.

579 Chevalier, *dictionnaire des symboles*, III p. 218-9.

580 Chevalier, *dictionnaire des symboles*, II p. 202-3.

581 Giordano Bruno (1548 –1600), born as Filippo, in Nola, Naples, Italy (his statue in Nola). We present, in note format, a biography of this philosopher to highlight the feeling that a persecuted truth-seeker like Isaac Baulot must have felt in exile.

Bruno came to life the year after the viceroy of Naples, Don Pedro de Toledo, "*with the pretext of wanting to preserve Religion,*"(*Spaccio*, I, 3) attempted to introduce the Inquisition. Opposition to the Spanish regime continued under the next viceroy, Fernando Álvarez de Toledo the bloody duke of Alva (1556-58), and the papal dogmatic authority of Pius IV. Hence, Bruno felt that, in order to restore the peaceful "*ancient Way of Living,*" his Neapolitan compatriots would have preferred an international intervention of "*the maritime power of the Turk*" and the "*Gallic fury.*"(*Spaccio*, II, 3). At twelve, Bruno went to Naples to study "*humanity, logic and dialectics.*"(Thayer, p. 259) Ominously, in 1564 in that city, Gianfrancesco Alois and Giovan Bernardino Gargano, accused of heresy, had been burned at the stake. Filippo studied at the Convent of San Domenico Maggiore and joined the Dominican order (1572) with the monastic name of Giordano. Nevertheless, the confining dogmatic walls of the cloister could not hold him for long. Schopenhauer recognized that he did not belong to this "*part of the globe...* [His tragic] *death in this Western world...* [is] *like that of a tropical plant in Europe. The banks of the sacred Ganges were* [his] *true spiritual home; ...* [there, he] *would have led a peaceful and honored life among men of like mind...* [like in the interfaith theological discussions sponsored by Emperor Akbar (1556-1605). Giordano's tragic mission in the West was for] *the welfare of all mankind... for universal, important truths, and for the eradication of great errors...* [In the West, when Nations were confirming their sovereignty through dogmas and religious wars, his cosmopolitan view was alien. He] *stands by himself and alone,*"(Schopenhauer, *The world as will ...*, I, 375) not belonging to his age. Giordano remained in the convent eleven years.(*Candelaio, Introduzione e note di* Guerrini Angrisani, pp. 25-6) There, he felt that his "*wings had been cut off, that he may not fly to unveil the clouds*"(*La cena*, I) of ignorance. Thus, he "*put off the gown*"(Thayer, p. 261) and left the order. His journeys, however, more than for fear of persecution, were led "*solely out of love for* [his] *beloved mother, philosophy, and zeal for her affronted majesty.*"(*De la causa*, I). After traveling throughout Italy, he left his country in 1578. From Chambéry in France, he went to Geneva, where he intended "*to live in liberty.*"(Thayer, p. 262) However, this was not possible among a Calvinist community. Thus, in 1579 Giordano was back on French soil, in Toulouse. The Nolan praised "*antiquity for its ways, when the philosophers were such that from their ranks were promoted the legislators, counselors, and kings... and from this station they were exalted priesthood. But in these times* [c. 1584], *most of the priests are so degenerate that they are despised and, through them, the divine laws are also despised. Also most, of all those philosophers that we see, are the same way.*"(*De la causa*, I) After receiving his doctoral degree at the University of Toulouse, "*on account of the Civil Wars*"(Thayer, p. 263) between Catholics and Huguenots, he went to Paris. King Henry III granted him the post of "*lecturer extraordinary.*"(Thayer, p. 264). Grateful, Giordano dedicated his *De umbris idearum* (1582) to the sovereign. In his mind, "*this most Christian King*" came from the stock of the ancient philosophers, he was "*holy, religious and pure*"(*Spaccio*, III, 3) and loved peace. However, the religious and doctrinal frenzies of the narrow minded dogmatists had made, "*across the spine of Europe, the Tiber run angry, the Po menacing, the Rhone violent , the Seine bloody, the Garonne muddy, the Ebro raging, the Tagus furious, the Meuse grieved, the Danube unquiet.*"(*De la causa*, end of I). In 1583, the Nolan, "*on account of the tumults*" in France, "*with letters from the king himself,*"(Thayer, p. 264) followed to England his new protector, the French Ambassador Michael de Castelnau, the "*defender of the unjust outrages that I endure.*"(*De la causa*, Prefatory Epistole) In England, Queen Elizabeth appeared to him "*divine... epithet, which the ancient used also to bestow on princes...* [and he] "*often went with the ambassador to court.*"(Thayer, p. 283. *Cf. De la causa*, I) The "*regal splendor*" of the Queen's castles, "*with the light of their great civility,*"(*La cena*, II) seemed to Giordano as sanctuaries of tolerance. Nevertheless, the royal British majesty contrasted considerably with the everyday squalor of the cities and the myopic misery of the academic world.(*La cena*, II) He despised those English academicians, describing them as "*a constellation of very obstinate pedantic ignorance and presumption, mixed with rustic incivility that would thwart Job's patience.*"(*La cena*, IV) Nevertheless, the Nolan, with a truly cosmopolitan view, was quick to affirm that he was in no way denigrating a foreign country. On the contrary, "*If I said that similar and yet more criminal customs are to be found in Italy, in Naples, in Nola? Would I perhaps belittle this region, blessed by heaven and set at the same time at the head and at the right hand of the globe, governor and ruler of all the other nations?*"(*De la causa*, I) In 1585, Bruno returned to Paris, where, renewed religious rioting and an unfavorable ecclesiastic authority forced him to escape, in 1586, to Wittenberg, Germany. There, Giordano did not find the academic institution he had hoped. However, he found the friendship of Alberigo Gentile who introduced him to international law. Bruno envisioned a universal Natural Law, stemming, as the daughter of Wisdom or Truth, directly from the Divine Providence. Kings and Queens should reign according of this Natural Law. Bruno further explained his vision of the *ius gentium* in his *Oratio consolatoria*(*Opera Latine*, I, 1, pp. 27 ff.) to commemorate the death of the Duke of Brunswik. In that work, Giordano restated his vision of the ruler's role as an ancient sage and seer. This one should guarantee, against any sectarian or Papal intrusion, the free expression of learning and philosophy, thus, becoming, as expression of the Divine Providence, three times great, Trismegistus. In 1589, his former protector, King Henry III of France was assassinated. Bruno returned to Italy, this time in Venice (1591). There, in 1593, the gray eminence condemned him of heresy. On February 17, *Anno Domini* 1600 "*in Roma, al Campo di Flora,*"(*La cena*, II) Giordano told to that gray power that was setting fire to his pyre, that they had "*greater fear than*"(Thayer, p. 301) him who was being burned alive. None of those executioners was immortalized in the sky. Whereas, on the Far Side of the Moon, mapped and photographed (9/6-5/5, 1994) by the Clementine spacecraft's Lunar Mapping Mission, "*the brightest crater larger than 20 km diameter is Giordano Bruno, which is probably less than 50 million years old.*"(Leung, *Clementine*) Nostradamus (in 1555–1558) seems to describe him well: "*He will come to reach in the far side of the Moon, /He will be captured and put in a strange land: / The unripe fruits will be of great scandal, / Great blame, together with great praise.*" (*Dedans le coing de Luna viendra rendre, / Où sera prins & en terre estrange, / Les fruicts immeurs seront à grand esclandre, / Grand vitupere, à l'vn grande loüange*).(Century IX, 65)

582 *Eroici furori*, II, 4, Minutolo.
583 *Spaccio*, I, 1, Sophia.
584 *Cf.* Carbonara, *La filosofia di Plotino*, p. 134.
585 *De la causa*, II & V, Dicson & Teofilo.
586 *De la causa*, I, Filoteo-Bruno.
587 *Eroici furori*, pt. I, IV, Cicada.
588 Bruno, *Opere italiane*, *Eroici furori*, II, 4, Minutolo.
589 I, 3, Mercury reporting to Sophia.
590 I, 3, Sophia.
591 Locality east of Nola presently between Via Nazionale and Via Casavisciano. Gentile's correction of the old reading of "*stanza*" in "*Starza*" Opere *italiane*, p. 74, n. 1.
592 A XII century fortress on the homonymous hill northeast of Nola (*cf.* Simonelli, *Hyria-Nola*).
593 Presently Livardi, "that stands" northeast, "on the other side of""*Che sta da là del monte de Cicala*" (*Candelaio*, Marta, Act I, scene XIII).[18] Cicala's slopes, on the road to Marzano (Av).
594 *Spaccio*, I, 3, Sophia.
595 *Cf. De la causa*, II, Teofilo.
596 *Spaccio*, II, 1.
597 *Cf.Opere italiane*, II, 75-7, n. 5.
598 Thayer, p. 301.
599 *Cf.* *La cena*, III, Teofilo.
600 *De Immenso*, IV, 3.
601 *Cf. De umbris idearum*, 234, N173 ff.
602 See Yates, *Giordano Bruno and the Hermetic tradition*; in *Articuli adversus mathematicos* (the design is reproduced).
603 *De la causa*, I, Teofilo.
604 *La cena*, II, Teofilo.
605 "*Cittadino e domestico del mondo, figlio del padre Sole e de la Terra madre*" (*Spaccio, Explanatory Epistle*).
606 "*Al vero filosofo ogni terreno è patria*" (*De la causa*, I, Filoteo).
607 *Spaccio*, I, 1, Saulino.
608 *Cf.* vol. I, cap. 1.
609 *De la causa*, V, Teofilo.
610 *De la causa*, I, Elitropio.
611 *Spaccio*, I, 1, Sophia. *Cf.* *Spaccio*, I, 2, Jupiter's speech & III, 3, Saulino and Sophia..
612 *De l'infinito*, I.
613 Wilford, J. N., *At Long Last*.
614 Bruno: minutes of the Inquisition of Venice (Thayer, p. 269).
615 *UY* 10.6 in Varenne, *Yoga..*, p. 221.
616 *Cf.* Hesiod, *Theogony*, 211-7. In Latin *nona* means ninth, *decima* means tenth and *morta* means dead. Flemish tapestry, Victoria and Albert Museum, London. Wikipedia public domain http://en.wikipedia.org/wiki/File: The_Triumph_of_Death,_or_The_Three_Fates.jpg.

---

617 *Bible*, Matthew 27:45 & Mark 15:33 & Luke 23:44.

618 *Bible*, Exodus 34:21; *cf.* Luke 13:14.

619 Schimmel, *The Mystery of Numbers*, p. 123. *Bible*, Genesis 1:1, *in the beginning* (רֵאשִׁית *re'shith*), *He created Six* (בָּרָא שֵׁשׁ *bara' shesh*).

620 *Cf.* Chevalier, *dictionnaire des symboles*, IV pp. 211-13.

621 *Bible*, Revelation 13:18.

622 *UK* V.3 (II.2.3) *madhye* (in the middle) *vāmanam-* (the dwarf) *āsīnaṃ* (seated).

623 *UŚ* III.13. *angushṭha-* (of a thumb) *mātraḥ* (size) *purusho'* (the person) *ntarātmā* (the inner self) *sadā* (always) *janānāṃ* (of creatures) *hṛdaye* (in the heart) *sannivishṭaḥ* (dwells) / *hṛdā* (by the heart) *manvīśo* (wisdom) *manasābhikḷpto* (with the mind in accordance).

624 *UK* I.5 & IV.12 *aṅgushṭha-mātraḥ.*

625 *Psyche and Symbol*, p. 78.

626 *BU* I.2.4.

627 *BU* I.2.5.

628 *Psyche and Symbol*, pp. 119, 128, 138.

629 *Cf.* Chevalier, *dictionnaire der symboles*, II pp. 188-91.

630 *līlā* in Sanskrit.

631 *Cf.* Lao tzu, Tao te Ching, 42, 陰 *yīn* dark feminine and 陽 *yáng* light masculine constitute the *Taijitu*, the Diagram of the Supreme Ultimate.

632 Kant, *The Critique of Pure Reason*, part 17.

633 *VṚ* VIII.1 a woolen strainer, *pavitra* "straining-cloth &c (made of thread or hair or straw, for clarifying fruits, esp. the soma" (*W.* p. 611a).

634 *UM.* 5.

635 *UB* IV.3.30.

636 *Cf.* Chevalier, *dictionnaire des symboles*, II pp. 201-2.

637 Schimmel, *The Mystery of Numbers*, p. 180.

638 del-Vasto, *Return to the Source*, p. 218.

639 Hesiod, *Theogony,* 517-21 and 274. Lee Oscar Lawrie (1877-1963), Atlas 1936 (New York City, 630 Rockefeller Center, 5th Ave & 51-50 Street).

640 *Cf.* Simonelli, *Beyond Immortality*, pp. 31 and 207.

641 *UB.* III.4.2; *cf.* 4.4.18 and *UKe* I.2.

642 *UK* V.2 (II.2.2) *haṃsaḥ* (I am that Supreme Swan Spirit) *śucishat* (dwelling in the light clear waters) *vasur-* (the beneficent) *antarikshasat* (dwelling in the intermediate region) *hotā* (the sacrificer) *vedishat-*(on wheel-shaped-altar-of-knowledge sitting) *atithir-*(the guest) *duroṇasat* (residing in the house)/ *nṛshat* (dwelling in the human being) *varasat-* (sitting in the circle) *ṛtasat* (dwelling in the order of truth) *vyomasat-* (dwelling in the air) *abjā* (born in water) *gojā* (born in the earth's-milky-rays-of-knowledge) *ṛtajā* (born in truth's order) *adrijā* (the soul produced from the friction of stones) *ṛtaṃ*(the truth) *bṛhat* (the wide)/
Verse from *VṚ* IV.40.5 *śucishad. antarikshasad. dhotā. vedishad. duroṇasad. nṛshad. varasad. ṛtasad. vyomasad.* (*bṛhat* missing).

643 *VṚ* XXVIII 1,3,5; Griffith, *The Hymns of the Ṛgveda*, I p. 36.

644 *Cf.* Chevalier, *dictionnaire des symboles*, II pp. 87-8.

645 *Cf.* Chevalier, *dictionnaire des symboles*, III p. 169.

646 Prinke, *Hermetic Heraldry*, p. 62.

647 *Cf.* Ouroboros in Haven, Dr. Marc, *Le Traité symbolique de la Pierre philosophale par Jean-Conrad BARCHUSEN*, Plate 14, ns. 54 & 55.

648 Paramahansa Ramakrishna (1836-1886) in ecstasy (*samādhi*). Photograph 9/21/1879 (Calcutta), scan from Gupta, *The Gospel of Sri Ramakrishna*. Work is in the public domain, File:Ramakrishna trance 1879.jpg, http://en.wikipedia.org/wiki/File:Ramakrishna_trance_1879.jpg.

649 Al-Ghazali, *Inner Dimensions of Islamic Worship*, § 1, Prayer Prostrating *Sujūd.*

650 Arabic جهاد *ǧihād* = struggle "*striving hard in God's cause,*" *Koran*, The Cow, 2:218.

651 *Cf. UK* IV.12, *UT* I.6.1 and *UŚ* III. 13.

[652] Dante, *La Vita Nova*, chapter XXIV "*Io mi senti' svegliar dentro a lo core | un spirito amoroso che dormia: | e poi vidi venir da lungi Amore,*" underlining is ours.

[653] *Cf.* Jung (1875 - 1961) *Psyche and Symbol.*

[654] Koran, 5:35, يَا أَيُّهَا الَّذِينَ آمَنُوا اتَّقُوا اللَّهَ وَابْتَغُوا إِلَيْهِ الْوَسِيلَةَ وَجَاهِدُوا فِي سَبِيلِهِ لَعَلَّكُمْ تُفْلِحُونَ

[655] Evola, *Rivolta contro il mondo moderno*, p.153; *cf.* also Armstrong, *Muhammed...*

[656] *Cf.* Gandhi (1869 - 1948), *An Autobiography...*

[657] *ājñā cakra*, see Tefillin, *Bible*, Deuteronomy 6:8 and Exodus 13:16, "*as frontlets between thine eyes* (עין` *ayin*)."

[658] Dante, *La Divina Commedia, Paradiso*, XVIII. 4. "*Quella donna ch'a Dio mi menava,*" and *La Vita Nova*, chapter XXVI, "*Tanto gentile ...*" *una cosa venuta /*7 *di cielo in terra a miracol mostrare. /*8 *Mostrasi sì piacente a chi la mira, |*9 *che dà per gli occhi una dolcezza al core, /*10 *che intender non la può chi non la prova*" **/**11.

[659] *Cf.* Teresa of Avila, *The Interior Castle.*

[660] *UK* VI.16 (II.3.16) *śataṃ* (hundred) *ca-* (and) *ikā* (one) *ca* (and) *hṛdayasya* (of the heart) *nāḍyas-* (vein-channels) *tāsāṃ* (of them) *mūrdhānam-* (crown of the head) *abhi-*(towards) *niḥsṛta-* (gone out) *ikā* (one)/ *tay-* (through that) *ordhvam-* (up) *āyann-* (going) *amṛtatvam-* (immortality) *eti* (achieves) *vishvaṅṅ-* (different) *anyā* (others) *utkramaṇe* (for going astray) *bhavanti* (are)/Same verse in *UC* VIII.6.6; *cf. UB* IV.2.3 and *UKa* IV.19 and .

[661] *W.* 544b and *ni-sṛta* unsheathed 564a.

[662] Malory, *Le Morte DĀrthur*, Book I, Chapter V.

[663] *Cf.* Ratti, *Secrets of the Samurai*, p. 275.

[664] *Cf. Bible*, Matthew 13:30.

[665] << Simonelli, *Beyond Immortality*, pp. 152, 213, 228 fol.>>

[666] *UK* VI.17 (II.3.17) *aṅgushtha-* (of a thumb) *mātraḥ* (size) *purusho'* (the Person) *ntar-*(the inner) *ātmā* (self) *sadā* (always) *janānāṃ* (of the creature) *hṛdaye* (in the heart) *sannivishṭaḥ* (seated)/ *taṃ* (him) *svāc-* (one's own) *charīrāt* (from body) *pravṛhen-* (should draw out) *muñjād-* (from the reed) *iv-* (like) *eshīkāṃ* (the stalk) *dhairyeṇa* (with firmness)/ *taṃ* (him) *vidyāc-* (should realize) *chukram-* (pure) *amṛtaṃ* (immortal) *taṃ* (him) *vidyāc-* (should realize) *chukram-* (pure) *amṛtam-* (immortal) *iti* (indeed)/

[667] World War II naval Japanese samurai Katana (curved) sword with scabbards.

[668] *UB* IV.4.8 *aṇuḥ* (narrow) *panthā* (moves) *vitataḥ* (far reaching) *purāṇaḥ* (ancient) *māṃ* (by me) *spṛshtó* (has been traveled) *nuvitto* (has been realized) *mayaiva* (by me verily) *tena* (by it) *dhīrā* (the sages) *api* (also) *yanti* (go to) *brahmavidaḥ* (knowers of the Supreme Reality) *svargaṃ* (heavenly) *lokam* (world) *iti* (therefore) *ūrdhvaṃ* (having reached up) *vimuktāḥ* (liberated).

[669] *UK* VI.15 (II.3.15) *yadā* (when) *sarve* (all) *prabhidyante* (are cut) *hṛdayasy-* (of the heart) *eha* (here) *granthayaḥ* (the knots)/ *atha* (then) *martyo'* (the mortal) *mṛto* (immortal) *bhavaty-* (becomes).

[670] *Cf.* Ouroboros in Haven, Dr. Marc, *Le Traité symbolique de la Pierre philosophale par Jean-Conrad BARCHUSEN*, Plate 17, n. 67.

[671] *Cf. Śūraṅgama Sūtra* 4:237 and 5:1 fol. Statues from Thailand.

[672] *Bible*, John 12:35-36, be certain (πιστεύετε *pisteuete*).

[673] Hercules is Latin; Heracles is the Greek version (Ἡρακλῆς *Hēraclēs*).

[674] *Cf.* DeCaro, *Il Museo Archeologico Nazionale di Napoli*, p. 333, Ercole Farnese, n. 6001, from Rome, *Terme di Caracalla.*

[675] *Cf.* Hesiod *Theology* , ll. 507-543.

[676] *Bible,* Genesis 2:17. *Cf.* Plaut, *The Torah*, p. 30 n. 17: "*good and bad ...*'everything'."טוב *towb* good and רצ *ra* 'evil.

[677] The goddess Kālī on Śiva (Painted brass, devotional art, India 1988).

[678] Kant, *The Critique of Pure Reason*, part 17.

[679] <<Simonelli, *Beyond immortality*, p. 150>>. Union taking place on a skull. (Peruvian carved wood incense burner, Cuzco 2001).

[680] *Cf. UMaitrī* I.3.

[681] The Gospel of Thomas, 56.

682 Ramana Maharshi, *Spiritual teaching*, pp. 3 (2), 42.

683 Ramana Maharshi, *The Spiritual Teaching...*, pp. 3 and 4 (2 and 4), 4 (8), (16) and 10 (21), underlining is ours.

684 *VṚ* X.129.4-5. *sató* (being) *bándhum* (connection) *ásati* (in being) *nír* (non) *avindan* (found) *hṛdí* (in the heart) *pratíshyā* (searching) *kaváyo* (the seers) *manīshā* (with reflection) *//... tiraścīno* (across) *vítato* (spread) *raśmír* (measuring cord - beam of light) *eshām* (their) *adháḥ* (below) *svid* (indeed) *āsīd* (was) *upári* (above) *svid* (indeed) *āsīt* (was) */ Cf. The Tabula Smaragdina.*

685 *Bible*, Luke 9:60.

686 Ramana Maharshi, *The Spiritual Teaching...*, pp. 3 and 4 (2 and 4), 4 (8), (16) and 10 (21), underlining is ours.

687 *Bible* Mark 14:38.

688 Experimentation πειρασμός *peirasmos* (commonly translated as temptation).

689 *Bible*, Matthew 26:41 and Mark 14:38, pay attention γρηγορέω *grēgoreō*, from ἐγείρω *egeirō* to arouse from the sleep of death; experience πειρασμός *peirasmos*, from πειράζω *peirazō* to experiment.

690 *Bible*, Luke 18:1.

691 *Oculatus abis* is an anagram (with *a* left out) of both Iacobus Saulat and Isaacus Baulot.

692 *Cf.* The Eye of Awareness that "consents =*annuit cœptis* = the endeavors" (Charles Thomson, 1782, USA Great Seal also on the one-dollar bill inspired by Virgil, *Aeneis*, IX, 625 and the eye in the Masonic symbols deriving from the Hermetic Tradition).

693 *Cf.* Budge, *The Gods of the Egyptians*, II, pp. 372-3. Two Egyptian papyruses.

694 Budge, *The Gods of the Egyptians*, I, pp. 363, 457 & 467.

695 Akshapāda Gautama (II century BC) was the author of the *Nyāya Sūtras*, a treatise on *Nyāya*, one of the six Indian philosophical perspectives (*darśana*). *Cf. W.* pp. 3c & 617ab. Feet with eyes, design on an Indian religious silk shawl (detail).

696 *Bible*, Revelation 11:12.

697 Falconar, *Sufi Literature ...*, p. 106.

698 *Bible*, John 14:20,30; 17:21 and 11, 22, 23 [world (κόσμος *kosmos*) = world affairs].

699 Ramana Maharshi, *Spiritual teaching*, p. 55 and 105.

700 Ramana Maharshi, *Spiritual teaching*, Jung's *Foreword*, p. ix.

701 del-Vasto, *Return to the Source*, p. 94.

702 Natarajan, *Timeless in Time...*, p. 67.

703 Khan, *Sufi Teachings...*, p. 55.

704 <<Simonelli, *Beyond Immortality*, p. 85.>>

705 *The Sage of Arunacala Ramana Maharshi* (1.03.37-45).

706 *Cf. VṚ* X.129.1.

707 *Bible*, Luke 12:33-34 (παλαιόω). Haven, Trésor Hermétique. *Le Traité symbolique de la Pierre philosophale, par Jean-Conrad BARCHUSEN*, Plate 19, n. 78.

708 *UB* I.2.1.

709 *Cf.* NASA/CXC/SAO, *Proxima Centauri*. Light travels at the speed of 299,792,458 $m \cdot s^{-1}$ (meters x second),
about 186,282.4 miles x sec.

710 *Bible*, Genesis 2:17.

711 Khunrath, *Anfiteatro ...*, 11. *Laboratorio Oratorio*. – IV.

712 Corbett, *Art & Alchemy*, §10, p. 250.

713 Arcère, *Histoire de la ville de La Rochelle*, p. 384.

714 Physician and alchemist (1560–1605) from Dresden (Saxony, Germany). *Cf. Anfiteatro ..., Chiave... Prologo.* He was a man of science, like Altus and Colazza.

715 Benvenuti (1924-1990), *La scienza dello Spirito*, "*La Scienza dello Spirito non è una teoria, ma una*

pratica... A coloro che... ci rivolgono critiche e appunti, dobbiamo grande gratitudine, perché sono in quel momento i nostri maestri... Da noi, dipendono molte cose di valore collettivo, umano... non... dalle comunità mondiali" L'Archetipo, La posta dei lettori, p. 27.

[716] Khunrath, *Anfiteatro ...*, 4. *Prologo, che è una introduzione.*

[717] Khunrath, *Anfiteatro ...*, 5. *Cristo in croce* – I.

[718] Mahadevan, *Ramana Maharshi*, It. tr., p. 39.

[719] *UY* 4.51.

[720] Cytowic, *The Man Who Tasted Shapes*, p. 56, as described by Kandinsky, *Concerning the Spiritual in Art.*

[721] Farinata degli Uberti (1212 - 1264) Italian heretic military leader, Dante Alighieri, *La divina commedia, Inferno* X, 32-63 "*Farinata che s'è dritto... com'avesse l'inferno a gran dispitto.*" Gustave Doré, illustration of Farinata degli Uberti.

[722] <<Simonelli, *Beyond Immortality*, pp. 229-30.>>

[723] Gustavo Doré's illustration of Dante Alighieri, *La divina commedia, Inferno* VIII 29-30.

[724] *Bible*, Psalm 46:10.

[725] *Bible*, 1 Crorinthias, 15:58.

[726] *Histories*, 6. 129.4 "*οὐ φροντίς* (*ou phrontis*) no worry."

[727] Dante Alighieri, *La divina commedia, Purgatory* 5, 14 "*sta come torre fermo, che non crolla/ Giammai la cima per soffiar de' venti.*"

[728] Dante Alighieri, *La divina commedia, Inferno* 3, 51 "*non ragioniam di lor, ma guarda e passa.*"

[729] *Bible*, I Corinthians 7, 30.

[730] *Bible* Matthew 6:25 & 33.

[731] *Bible*, Matthew 26:41 & Mark 14:38.

[732] <<Simonelli, *Beyond Immortality*, pp. 229-30.>>

[733] <<Simonelli, *Beyond Immortality*, pp. 229-30.>>

[734] *Bible*, Matthew, 13:44.

[735] *Bible*, John 19:28.

[736] Ramana Maharshi, *The Spiritual Teaching...*, p. 61. *Cf.* p. 35 (5).

[737] Matthew 25:29.

[738] *Bible*, Matthew 10:39; *cf.* also 16:25, Marc 8:35 and Luke 9:24.

[739] <<Simonelli, *Beyond Immortality*, pp. 229-30.>>

[740] *VṚ* V.3.1. *tve* (in you) *viśve* (all) *sahasas* (of Power) *putra* (son) *devās* (gods).

[741] *UC.* III.14.4. *sarva-* (all) *-karmā* (actions) *sarva-* (all) *-kāmaḥ* (desires) *sarva-* (all) *-gandhaḥ* (scents) *sarva-* (all) *-rasaḥ* (flavors) *sarvam* (all) *idam* (this) *abhyātto'* (encompassing) *vāky* (not speaking) *anādaraḥ* (indifferent) *esha* (this) *ma* (my) *ātmā-* (Self) *-ntar* (within) *hṛdaye* (the heart) *etad* (this) *brahma* (the Supreme Transcendent Spirit) *etam* (This One) *itaḥ* (thus) *pretyā-* (upon dying) – *bhisambhavitāsm-*(I shall reach) *-īti* (thus) *yasya* (for whom) *syāt* (should tend towards) *addhā* (certainly) *na* (no) *vicikitsā-* (doubt) *-stī-* (is) *-ti* (thus) *ha* (verily) *smāha* (used to say) *śāṇḍilyaḥ* (Śāṇḍilya) *śāṇḍilyaḥ* (Śāṇḍilya) [*vidyā* (knowledge)].
Śāṇḍilya derived from *ilya* (?) mythical tree in the other world.

[742] *Cf.* Ouroboros in Haven, Dr. Marc, *Le Traité symbolique de la Pierre philosophale par Jean-Conrad BARCHUSEN*, Plate 17, n. 67.

[743] Ramana Maharshi, *The Spiritual Teaching...*, p. 31 (4).

[744] *Bible*, Mark 14:38, watch (*Greek Text*: γρηγορεῖτε *grēgoreîte*, *Vulgate*: vigilate), pray (*Greek Text*: προσεύχεσθε *proseúchesthe*, *Vulgate*: orate), temptation (πειρασμόν *peirasmón*).

[745] *Bible*, Luke 12:33-34 (παλαιόω *palaióo*).

[746] <<Simonelli, *Beyond Immortality*, pp. 231-33.>>

[747] Rumi, in Star, *A Garden Beyond Paradise...*, ode 442.

[748] Oil on canvas and actual photograph of the sun at 3:00 pm, as seen from the church-square in Medjugorje (Bosnia-Herzegovina) on 6/24/1981.

SELECTED and QUOTED BIBLIOGRAPHY & FILMOGRAPHY

preceded, in boldface, by bibliographies of the original plates

~ I EDITION ~ 1677 ~

***Altus. (1677). *Mutus Liber.* Rupellae: Petrum Savouret.**

~

Altus. (1979). *Mutus Liber, reproduction des 15 planches en couleur d'un manuscrit di XVIII siècle. Introduction et commentaire par Jean Laplace.* (J. Laplace, Ed.) Milano: Arché.

Altus, Baulot, Isaac. (2013). *Mutus liber La Rochelle's Edition Rupellae: apud Petrum Savouret, 1677.* Retrieved September 2, 2013, from Alchemy, Magic and Kabbalah, Foundation of the Works of C.G.Jung (Stiftung der Werke von C.G.Jung, Zürich) http://www.e-rara.ch/: http://www.e-rara.ch/doi/10.3931/e-rara-4322

Canseliet, Eugene, ed. (1967). *L'alchimie et son livre muet (Mutus liber).* Paris: Jean-Jacques Pauvert.

Marra, Massimo. (2012, 05 26). *Altus (Isaac Baulot) - Mutus Liber (1677) - Con una nota bio-bibliografica introduttiva di Massimo Marra* . Retrieved 9 25, 2013, from massimo marra web archive: http://www.massimomarra.net/1089/Altus-Isaac-Baulot-Mutus-Liber-1677-Con-una-nota-biobibliografica-introduttiva-di-Massimo-Marra

~ II EDITION ~ 1702 ~

****Mangeti, J. J. (1702). *Bibliotheca Chemica Curiosa, Seu Rerum ad Alchemiam pertinentium Thesaurus Instructissimus quo non tantum artis auriferæ, ac scriptorum in ea nobiliorum historia traditur: lapidis veritas argumentis & experimentis innumeris, immo; & juris consultorum...* (Vol. Tomus Secundus). Geneva: De Tournes.**

~

Haven, Dr. Marc. (1914). *Collection D'Albums Ésotériques. Trésor Hermétique comprenant Le Livre d'Images sans paroles (Mutus Liber)... par le Docteur Marc HAVEN et Le Traité symbolique de la Pierre philosophale par Jean-Conrad BARCHUSEN... Paul SERVANT* (Nouvelle ed.). Lyon: Paul Derain.

Hellesøe, K. Trans. (1996). *MUTUS LIBER. wherein all operations of Hermetic Philosophy are described and represented PRECEDED BY AN EXPLICATIVE HYPOTYPOSE OF MAGOPHON.* Retrieved 5 10, 2013, from The Hermetic Library at Hermetic.com: http://hermetic.com/caduceus/articles/1/3/mutus-liber.html#text1

McLean, A. (1991). *A Commentary on the Mutus Liber.* Grand Rapids, MI: Phanes Press.

McLean, A. (2011). *Alchemical Sequences (colorized Mutus Liber).* Glasgow, UK: Alchemy Web Site.

~ III EDITION ~ 1725 (?)~

***Laplace, J. (Ed.). (1979). *Altus, Mutus Liber, reproduction des 15 planches en couleur d'un manuscrit di XVIII siècle. Introduction et commentaire par Jean Laplace.* Milano: Arché.**

Adler, Ada. (1928-1938). *Lexicographi graeci recogniti et apparatu critico instructi* (Vol. 5). Leipzig: Teubner.

Adler, Alfred. (1956). *The Individual Psychology of Alfred Adler.* (Ansbacher&Ansbacher, Ed.) New York: Harper Torchbooks.

Al-Ghazali. (1983). *Inner Dimensions of Islamic Worship.* (M. Holland, Trans.) Leicestershire, UK: The Islamic Foundation.

Allan, J. (1864). *A catalogue of the books, autographs, engravings, and miscellaneous articles.* New York: C.A. Alvord.

Anch A. M., Browman C. P., Mitler M. M. , Walsh J. K. (1988). *Sleep: A Scientific Perspective.* Englewood Cliffs, New Jersey: Prentice Hall.

Andrews, T. (2012). *Animal Speak. The Piritual & Magical Powers of Creatures Great & Small.* Woodbury, Minnesota: Llewellyn Publications.

Angel, H. (2009). *Snow Monkeys: The Gentle Giants of the Forest (Wildlife Monographs).* London: Evans Mitchell Books, Csi.

Angelini, G. (1959). *Nuovo dizionario Latino-Italiano.* Milano, Roma, Napoli, Città di Castello: Socioetà Editrice Dante Alighieri p.a.

Anonimo. (2012, 05 25). *Anonimo - Recensione al Mutus Liber (dal Journal des Savans del 16 agosto 1677). Traduzione di Massimo Marra* . Retrieved 9 25, 2013, from massimo marra web archive: http://www.massimomarra.net/dettaglio.php?id=1090&prev=1

Anonymous Pilgrim. (1993). *The Way of a Pilgrim and The Pilgrim Continues His Way.* (R. French, Trans.) Pasadena, CA: Hope Publishing House.

Apollodorus, of Athens. (1961). *Apollodorus : The library (Vol. 1)* (Vol. I). (J. Frazer, Trans.) Cambridge, Mass: Harvard University Press, Loeb classical library.

Arcère, L.-É. (1756-1757). *Histoire de la ville de La Rochelle et du pays d'Aulnis* (Vol. 2). La Rochelle: R.-J. Desbordes.

Aristotle. (2001). *The Basic Works of Aristotle, De Generatione et Corruptione (On Generation and Corruption).* New York: Random House, Inc.

Armstrong, K. (1993). *Muhammed: A biography of the Prophet.* San Francisco: Harper.

Austin, J. H. (2000). *Zen and the Brain.* Cambridge, Massachusetts, London, England: The MIT Press.

Bahá'u'lláh. (1989). *The Kitáb-i-Íqán.* Wilmette, Il.: US Bahá'í Publishing Trust.

Barbault, A. (1975). *Gold of a Thousand Mornings.* London: Spearman.

Bastian, A. (1895). *Ethnische Elementargedanken in der Lehre vom Menschen.* Berlin: Weidmansche Buchhandlung.

Benvenuti, M. (Anno X, 2005, Agosto). La scienza dello Spirito non è una teoria, ma una pratica. (DiLieto, Ed.) *L'Archetipo, mensile di ispirazione antroposofica, numero 8 -- http://www.cazzanti.net/archivi/letture/L'archetipo%20-*

%20Mensile%20di%20ispirazione%20antroposofica/2005/ago2005.pdf (www.larchetipo.com Tribunale di Roma N. 104/89 del 4.3.1989, p. 27.

BG. (1926). *Bhagavad-Gītā Text* (Vol. Besant). Adyar, Madras, India: Theosophical Publishing House.

Bible. (1958). *The Holy Bible* (King James ed.). Philadelphia, PA : The National Bible Press.

Boas, F. (1911). *The Mind of Primitive Men.* New York: The Macmillan Company.

Borbély, A. (1986). *Secrets of Sleep.* (Schneider, Trans.) New York: Basic Books, Inc.

Bruno, G. (1879-91). *Opera Latine conscripta, publicis sumptibus edita* (Vol. 3). (Fiorentino-Tocco-Vitelli-Imbriani-Tallarigo, Ed.) Neapolis, Florentiae: Morano, Le Monnier.

Bruno, G. (1925-7). *Opere italiane. (Vols. I, DIALOGHI METAFISICI, II, DIALOGHI MORALI, III, COMMEDIA)* (Vol. III). (Gentile-Spampanato, Ed.) Bari: Laterza.

Bruno, G. (1925-7). *Opere italiane, Vol. I - DIALOGHI METAFISICI: De la causa, principio e uno; De l'infinito, universo et mondi; La cena de le ceneri* (Vol. 3). (G.Gentile, Ed.) Bari: Laterza.

Bruno, G. (1925-7). *Opere italiane Vol. II, DIALOGHI MORALI: Asino cillenico; Cabala del cavallo Pegaseo; De gli eroici furori; Lo spaccio de la bestia trionfante* (Vol. 3). (G.Gentile, Ed.) Bari: Laterza.

Bruno, G. (1925-7). *Opere italiane Vol. III COMMEDIA: Candelaio* (Vol. 3). (V.Spampanato, Ed.) Bari : Laterza.

Bruno, G. (1976). *Introduzione e note di Guerrini Angrisani.* Milano: Biblioteca Universale Rizzoli.

Budge, E. A. Wallis. (1967). *The Egyptian Book of the Dead, (The Papyrus of Ani) Egyptian Text Translitteration and Translation.* New York: Dover Publications, Inc.

Budge, E. A. Wallis. (1969). *The Gods of the Egyptians* (Vols. I-II). New York: Dover Publications, Inc.

Budge, E. A. Wallis. (1978). *An Egyptian Hieroglyphic Dictionary* (Vol. I & II). New York: Dover Publications, Inc.

Budge, E. A. Wallis. (1989). *The Mummy. A Handbook of Egyptian Funerary Archeology.* New York: Dover Publications.

Cabrera, L. (1970). *ANAGÓ Vocabulario Lucumi (El Yoruba que se habla en Cuba).* Miami, Florida: Cabrera y Rojas, Coleccion del Chihereкú.

Campbell, J., Free, B. (Producers), & Walter, R. (Director). (2007). *Mythos I: The Shaping of Our Mythic Tradition, "On Being Human" (DVD)* [Motion Picture].

Campbell, J. (1988). *The Power of Myth, with Bill Moyers.* New York: Doubleday.

Carbonara, C. (1967). *Introduzione alla filosofia.* Napoli: L.S.E.

Carbonara, C. (1964). *La filosofia di Plotino.* Napoli: LSE.

Carrington Bolton, H. (1882, January 6). Chemical Literature. (E.J.Davey.Pub., & W. Crookes, Eds.) *The Chemical News and Journal of Physical Science, XLV*(1154), 146-148.

Chevalier, Jean, & Gheerbrant, Alain. (1974). *dictionnaire des symboles.* Paris: Seghers.

Chögyam Trungpa. (2002). *Cutting Through Spiritual Materialism.* Boston & London: Shambhala.
Chrysogonus Polydorus. (1541). *De Alchimia.* Nuremberg: Chrysogonus Polydorus.
Chun Siong Soon, et al. (2008). Unconscious determinants of free decisions in the human brain. *Nature Neuroscience 11 (5)*, 543-545.
Coffin texts. (1935-61). *The Egyptian coffin texts* (Vol. 7). (A. deBuck, Ed.) Chicago: University of Chicago Press.
Copenhaver, B. P. (1992). *Hermetica: The Greek Corpus Hermeticum and the Latin Asclepius in a new English translation, with notes and introduction* (I ed.). Cambridge: Cambridge University Press .
Corbett J. R. (2006). *Art & Alchemy.* (J. Wamberg, Ed.) Copenhagen S, DK: Museum Tusculanum Press.
CorriereTv. (2013, agosto 15). *Il serpente decapitato che si mangia da solo.* Retrieved August 15, 2013, from CORRIERE DELLA SERA.IT Scienze, Animali http://www.corriere.it/: http://video.corriere.it/serpente-decapitato-che-si-mangia-solo/8cf25a58-05c0-11e3-95f7-ac31e2b74e2c#.Ug0Wapz0As4.gmail
Cytowic, R. E. (2003). *The Man Who Tasted Shapes.* Cambridge, MA: MIT Press.
Cytowic, R. E. (2003). *The Man Who Tasted Shapes.* Cambridge, MA: MIT Press.
Damasio, A. (2010). *Self Comes to Mind: Constructing the Conscious Brain.* New York: Pantheon Books.
Dante Alighieri. (1930). *La divina commedia illustrata da Gustavo Doré .* Milano: Casa Editrice Sonzogno.
Dante Alighieri. (1999). *La Vita Nova.* Milano: Arnoldo Mondadori.
Dasgupta, S. (1922). *A history of Indian philosophy* (Vol. 1). Cambridge: Cambridge University Press.
Davies, B. (1993). *The Thought of Thomas Aquinas.* Oxford: Clarendon Press, Oxford University Press.
DeCaro, S. (Ed.). (1994). *Il Museo Archeologico Nazionale di Napoli.* Napoli: Soprintendenza Archeologica di Napoli e Caserta, Guide Artistiche Electa.
del-Vasto, L. (1972). *Return to the Source.* (J.Sidgwick, Trans.) New York: Schocken Books.
Dement, W. (1976). *Some Must Watch While Some Must Sleep.* San Francisco: San Francisco Book Co.
Descartes, R. (1952). *Rules for the direction of the mind; Discourse on the method; Meditations on first philosophy: Objections against the meditations and replies; The geometry.* (Founders', Ed., & Latham/Smith, Trans.) Chicago: Encyclopaedia Britannica.
Drummond W. (1826). *Origines: Phoenicia. Arabia* (Vol. III). London: A.J. Valpy & Badwin and Co.
Dylan, T. (1934). *18 Poems.* London: The Sunday Referee and the Parton Bookshop.
Dyson, F. (1979). *Disturbing the Universe.* New York: Harper & Row.
Eliade, M. (1991). *Images and Symbols. Studies in Religious Symbolism.* Princeton, NJ: Princeton University Press.

Euripides. (1990). *The Bacchae of Euripides : a new version.* (C. Williams, Trans.) New York: Noonday Press.

Evola, J. (1996). *La Tradizione Ermetica.* Roma: Edizioni Mediterranee.

Evola, J. (1969). *Rivolta contro il mondo moderno.* Roma: Edizioni Mediterranee.

Evola, J. (1941). *Sintesi di dottrina della razza.* Milano: Hoepli.

Faivre, A. (1995). *Eternal Hermes: From Greek God to Alchemical Magus.* (J. Godwin, Trans.) Grand Rapids, MI: Phanes Press.

Falconar, A. E. (1991). *Sufi Literature and the Journey to Immortality.* New Delhi: Motilal Banarsidass Publ.

Flouret, J. (1976, April-June). À propos de l'auteur du Mutus Liber. *Revue française d'histoire du livre, n° 11 – N.S, 11,* 206-211.

Freud, S. (1962-1974, 1953-c1962). *The standard edition of the complete psychological works of Sigmund Freud* (Vol. 24). (A. Richards, Ed., & J. Strachey, Trans.) London: Hogarth Press and the Institute of Psycho-Analysis.

Gandhi, M. (1993). *An Autobiography: The Story of My Experiments with Truth.* (M.H.Desai, Trans.) Boston, MA: Beacon Press.

Gilgamesh. (1986). *The Epic of Gilgamesh.* (N. Sandars, Trans.) England, Canada, Australia, NY USA: Penguin Books.

González-Wippler, M. (1974). *Santeria. African Magic in Latin America.* NY: Doubleday.

Gray A. & A. (2012). *Net of Being.* Rochester,Vermont – Toronto, Canada: InnerTraditions.

Griffith. (1963). *The Hymns of the Ṛgveda* (Vols. I-II). (T. V. Griffith (1963). The Hymns of the Ṛgveda (Vol. 2). (R. T. Griffith, Trans.) Varanasi, India: The Chowkhamba Sanskrit Series Office.

Grimal, P. (1985). *The dictionary of classical mythology.* Oxford, England ; New York, NY: Blackwell.

Gruppo di Ur. (1971). *Introduzione alla Magia* (Vols. I-II-III). (Gruppo-di-Ur, Ed.) Roma: Edizioni Mediterranee.

Gupta, M. (1942). *The Gospel of Sri Ramakrishna.* (Nikhilananda, Trans.) New York: Ramakrishna-Vivekananda Center.

Halberg F., Peterson R. E., Silber R. H. (1959). Phase relations of 24-hour periodicities in blood corticosterone, mitoses in cortical adrenal parenchyma and total body activity. *Endocrinology 64. [109],* 222-230.

Harrison, N. L. (2002). General anesthesia research: aroused from a deep sleep. *Nature Neuroscience 5, doi:10.1038/nn1002-928,* 928 - 929.

Herodotus. (1960-1963). *Herodotus, with an English translation* (Vol. 4). (A.Godley, Trans.) Cambridge, Mass: Harvard University Press, Series Loeb classical library.

Hesiod. (1914). *Theogony, Text.* (H. G. Evelyn-White, Trans.) Cambridge, MA., London: Harvard University Press: Harvard University Press; William Heinemann Ltd.

Historia Deorum Fatidicorum. (1680). *Historia Deorum Fatidicorum, Vatum Sybillarum Phoebadum Apud Priscos Illustrium: cum corum Iconibus est Disertatio De Divinatione & Oraculis.* Francofurti: Ludovicj Bourgeat.

Homer. (1995). *Odyssey. English & Greek.* (A. Murray, Trans.) Cambridge, Mass: Harvard University Press, The Loeb classical library; L104-Ll05.

Husserl, E. (1958). *Ideas. General Introduction to Pure Phenomenology.* (W. B. Gibson, Trans.) London, New York: G. Allen & Unwin, The Macmillan Co.

Jagadguru-Śaṅkaracāryā-Śrī-Bhāratī-Kṛshṇa-Tīrtha-Mahārāja. (1975). *Vedic Mathematics or 'Sixteen simple Mathrmatical Formulae from the Vedas.* (V. Agrawala, Ed.) Delhi, Patna, Varanasi: Motilal Banarsidass.

Jātaka. (1969). *The Jātaka.* London: Published for the Pali Text Society by Luzac & Co.

Jourdan, L. (1869). Les émigrés de La Rochelle – Relation de la fuite de Baudouin de la Bruchardière et de sa famille. *Bulletin Historique et Littéraire de la Société de l'Histoire du protestantisme Français, Tome XVIII*(deuxième série, quatrième année), pp. 424-428.

Jung, C. G. (1958). *Psyche and Symbol. A selection from the Writings of C. G. Jung Archetype, The Phenomenology of the Spirit in Fairy Tales, The Psychology of the Child.* (V. S. Laszlo, Ed.) Garden Ciyy, NY: Doubleday Anchor Books.

Jung, C. G. (1980). *Psychology and Alchemy (Collected Works Vol. 12).* London: Routledge.

Kandinsky, W. (2001). *Concerning the Spiritual in Art.* (A. Glew, Ed., & M. T. Sadler, Trans.) New York and London: MFA Publications and Tate Publishing.

Kant, I. (1952). *The Critique of Pure Reason (All three Critiques and Metaphysics of Morals)* (Vol. XLII of the Great Books of the Western World series). (M. D. Meiklejohn, Trans.) Chicago, London, Toronto, Geneva, Sydney, Tokyo: Encyclopaedia Britannica.

Kant, I. (1953). *Prolegomena to any future metaphysics that will be able to present itself as a science.* Manchester: Manchester University Press.

Kaplan, A. (1977). *Sefer Yetzirah: The Book of Creation.* York Beach, ME: Red Wheel/Weiser, LLC.

Khan, H. I. (1994). *Sufi Teachings: Lectures from Lake O'Hara.* Victoria: Ekstasis Editions Canada Ltd.

Khunrath, H. (1609). *Amphiteatrum Sapientiæ Æternæ Solius Veræ, Christiano-Kabalisticum, Diuino-Magicum, nec non Physico-Chymicum, Tertriunum, Catholicon.* Hannover: Wilhelm Anton.

Kleitman, N. (1952 [187]). Sleep. *Scientific American*, 34-38.

Koran. (1977). *The Holy Qur'an, Arabic text.* (T. M. Association, Ed., & A. Y. Ali, Trans.) USA: American Trust Publications.

Lao Tzu. (1990). *Tao Te Ching, The Classic Book of Integrity and the Way. Based on the Ma-Wang-Tui manuscripts.* (V.Mair, Trans.) N.Y., Toronto, London, Sydney, Auckland: Bantam Books.

Lazar, Sara W.; Bush, George; Gollub, Randy L.; Fricchione, Gregory L.; Khalsa, Gurucharan; Benson, Herbert. (2000). Functional brain mapping of the relaxation response and meditation. *Neuroreport. 11(7), May 15,* 1581-1585.

Leung, K. (1999, July 5). *Clementine's Lunar Mapping Mission: An Overview of Science Results.* (leung@lpi.jsc.nasa.gov) Retrieved 2003, from 8NASA funded Lunar and

Planetary Institute, Houston, Texas: http://cass.jsc.nasa.gov/newsletters/lpib/lpib72/clem.html
Locke J. (1953). *Locke's travels in France, 1675-1679 : as related in his journals, correspondence and other papers.* (J. Lough, Ed.) Cambridge: Cambridge University Press.
Macdonell, A. (1927, Reprint 1955). *A Sanskrit Grammar for Students.* London: Oxford University Press.
Mahadevan, T. (1977 -- Italian traslation: 1980). *Ramana Maharshi. The Sage of Arunacala.* London (Italian traslation: Roma): Unwin (Italian traslation: Mediterranee ed.).
Malory, T. (1961). *Le Morte Dārthur, The Book of King Arthur and his Knights of the Round Table* (Vol. 2). New York: University Book.
Margulis, E. H. (2007, June). Silences in Music Are Musical Not Silent: An Exploratory Study of Context Effects on the Experience of Musical Pauses. *Music Perception .*
Martyn, W. C. (1866). *A History of the Huguenots.* New York City: The American Tract Society.
NASA/CXC/SAO. (2004, 11 9). *Proxima Centauri: The Nearest Star to the Sun.* Retrieved October 5, 2013, from The Internet Archive: http://archive.org/details/CHAN-1239
Natarajan, A. R. (2006). *Timeless in Time Sri Ramana Maharshi.* Bloomington, Indiana: Printed in China by World Wisdom.
Newton, Isaac. (2005, 11 15). *Decoding Newton 's Notebooks [1675?]. NOVA. Yale University, Beinecke Library, Mellon catalogue MS. 79.* Retrieved 5 8, 2013, from Bill Newman, Newton's Alchemy. A Guide to the Alchemical Manuscript: http://www.pbs.org/wgbh/nova/physics/newton-alchemy.html
Nikhilānanda, Swamị. (1936 - ed. 1968). *The Māṇḍūkyopanishad, with Gauḍapāda's Kārikā and Śaṅkara's commentary (V ed.).* Mysore: Sri Ramakrishna Ashrama.
Nostradamus, Edgar Leoni. (2000). *Nostradamus and His Prophecies.* Mineola, New York: Dover Publications, Inc.
Novalis. (2005). *The Novices of Sais: With illustrations by Paul Klee.* (R. Manheim, Trans.) Brooklyn, NY: Archipelago Books.
NSc. (1929). *Notizie degli scavi di antichità, VI serie 5, no. 112,* 449.
Overbye, D. (2002, March 12). Peering Through the Gates of Time. *The New York Times (Science Time),* p. F 1.
Ovid. (1960). *Metamorphoses.* (Miller, Trans.) Cambridge Mass., London: The Loeb Classical Library, Harvard University Press, William Heinemann Ltd.
Paracelsus. (2008). *Paracelsus. Theophrastus Bombastus Von Hohenheim, 1493-1541. Essential Theoretical Writings.* Leiden, The Netherlands: Brill.
Patañjali. (1955). *Yoga Sutras of Patanjali.* (Ballantyne&Sastri-Deva, Trans.) Calcutta: Susil Gupta.
Pausanias. (1961). *Pausanias Description of Greece, with an English translation (Vol. 4)* (Vol. 4). (W. H. Jones, Trans.) Cambridge, Mass.; London: Harvard University Press; W. Heinemann; The Loeb classical library.

Pierce, P. (2009). *The Intuitive Way. The Definitive Guide to Increasing Your Awareness.* New York, NY & Hillsboro, Oregon: Atria Paperback, A Division of Simon & Shuster Inc. and Beyond Words.

Plato. (1955-63). *Text and English translations in Plato* (Vol. 10). (Loeb-classical-library, Ed.) Cambridge, London: Harvard University Press, W. Heinemann.

Plutarch. (1936). *Moralia, Isis and Osiris.* (Loeb-Classical-LibraryNo.306, Ed., & F. C. Babbitt, Trans.) Cambridge, MA: Harvard University Press.

Prinke, R. T. (1989). Hermetic Heraldry. *The Hermetic Journal*, 62-78.

Ramana Maharshi & Devaraja Mudaliar, A. (2000). *Gems From Bhagavan - A Necklace of Sayings by Ramana Maharshi on various vital subjects strung together by A. Devaraja Mudaliar.* (A. D. Mudaliar, Ed.) Tiruvannamalai: Sri Ramanasramam.

Ramana Maharshi. (1988). *Who am I? The Spiritual Teaching of Ramana Maharshi.* Boston & London: Shambhala.

Ramana Maharshi. (2005, 5 3). *The Collected Works of Sri Ramana Maharshi.* Retrieved 11 16, 2010, from HolyBooks.com – download free ebooks http://www.holybooks.com: http://holybooks.com/wp-content/uploads/2010/05/The-Collected-Works-ofSri-Ramana-Maharshi-by-Ramana-Maharshi-zipped-PDF-at-sriramanamaharshi.org_.pdf

Ratti, O. & Westbrook, A. (1973). *Secrets of the Samurai.* Rutland, Vermont; Tokyo, Japan: Charles E. Tuttle Company.

Read, J. (1936). *A Prelude to Chemistry.* London: G. Bell and sons.

Reuven Sivan, Levenston Edward. (1986). *The New Bantam-Megiddo Hebrew & English Dictionary.* Toronto - NY - London - Sydney, Auckland: Bantam Books.

Riccius, Paulus. (1516). *Portae lucis : haec est porta Tetragrammaton, iusti intrabunt per eam.* Augsburg: Miller.

Rivière, P. (2006). *Fulcanelli: His True Identity Revealed.* Grande Prairie, Canada: Red Pill Press.

Rocci, L. (1952). *Vocabolario Greco - Italiano (VII ed.). Roma, Napoli, Citta' di Castello: Dante Alighieri & S. Lapi Coeditori.* (VII ed.). Roma, Napoli, Citta' di Castello: Dante Alighieri & S. Lapi Coeditori.

Rundle-Clark, R. T. (1978). *Myth and Religion in Ancient Egypt.* New York: Thames and Hudson.

Salaman, van Oyen, Wharton, Mahe. (2000). *The Way of Hermes: New Translations of The Corpus Hermeticum and The Definitions of Hermes Trismegistus to Asclepius.* (Salaman-vanOyen-Wharton-Mahe, Trans.) Rochester, Vermont: Inner Traditions International.

Sallustius Crispus, Gaius. (1970). *Epistulae ad Caesarem senem de re publica* (Vol. I). (A. Kurfeß, Ed.) Leipzig: Teubner, Bibliotheca scriptorum Graecorum et Romanorum Teubneriana Appendix Sallustiana ed.

Santos, F. (2013, May 24). Mistrial Set in Penalty for a Killer in Arizona. *The New York Times.*

Schimmel, A. (1993). *The Mystery of Numbers.* New York, Oxford: Oxford University Press.

Schopenhauer, A. (1958). *The world as will and representation* (Vol. 2). (Payne, Trans.) Indian Hills, Col: Falcon's Wing Press.
Shaikh Abd al-Qadir al Jilan. (2000). *The Book of the Secret of Secrets and the Manifestation of Lights.* (M. Holland, Trans.) Oakland Park, FL US: Al-Baz Publishing Inc.
Sicari, A. (2006). *Il secondo grande libro dei ritratti di santi.* Milano: Jaca book.
Simonelli, P. (2013). *Awareness. The Book of Ethic, Morals and Behavior.* West Long Branch, NJ: Sacer Equestris Aureus Ordo Inc.
Simonelli, P. J. (2012). *Beyond Immortality. The Electron Frog-Jump Past the Edge of Death's Abyss.* Charleston, SC: Sacer Equestris Aureus Ordo ISBN-13: 978-0615637068 ISBN-10: 061563706X.
Skinner, B. F. (1991). *The Behavior of Organisms .* Acton, MA: Copley Publishing Group .
Smith, R. (1995). *"Logic". In J. Barnes (ed) The Cambridge companion to Aristotle.* (J. Barnes, Ed.) Cambridge: Cambridge University Press.
Spadaro, A. (2013, Settembre 19). Intervista a Papa Francesco. *La Civiltà Cattolica*, pp. 449-477.
Star, J. and Shiva, S. (1992). *A Garden Beyond Paradise: The Mystical Poetry of Rumi.* New York: Bantam Books.
Stanley Redgrove H. (1920). *Bygone Beliefs Being a Series of Excursions in the Byways of Thought.* London: William Rider & Son, LTD.
Stein, G. (2003). *The Language That Rises: 1923-1934.* Evanston, Illinois: Northwestern University Press.
Suda. (1705). *Suidae Lexicon, Graece & Latine.* Cantabrigiae: Berolinensi.
Suetonius, C. Tranquillus. (1913). *De Vita XII Caesarum.* (Loeb-Classical-Library, Ed., & J. Rolfe, Trans.) London and Cambridge, Mass: Harvard University Press.
Śūraṅgama Sūtra. (2003). *The Śūraṅgama Sūtra With Commentary.* (H. Hua, Trans.) Ukiah, CA: Buddhist Text Translation Society.
Tagore, R. (1916). *Gitanjali: Song Offerings* (Bolpur ed.). (W. Butler-Yeats, Trans.) New York: The Macmillan Co.
Taittirîya-Saṃhitâ. (1871-1872). *Die Taittirîya-Saṃhitâ.* (A.Weber, Ed.) Leipzig: Brockhaus (Indische Studien, 11-12).
Teresa of Avila. (2007). *The Interior Castle. (B.Zimmerman-Intro.).* (Benedictines-of-Stanbrook, Trans.) New York: Cosimo Classics.
Thayer, W. R. (1899). *Throne makers.* Boston, New York: Houghton, Mifflin and company.
The Gospel of Thomas. (n.d.). *The Gospel of Thomas.* (T.O.Lambdin, Trans.) Vols. Nag Hammadi Library II, 2, pp. 118 fol.
The Nag Hammadi Library. (1977 - 1990, 1990 revised ed.). *The Nag Hammadi Library.* (J.M.Robinson, Ed., & C.G.Christianity, Trans.) N.Y: Harper & Row Pub.
The Sage of Arunacala Ramana Maharshi (1992). [Motion Picture]. New York: Arunacala Ashrama.

Thoreau, H. D. (19993). *A Year in Thoreau's Journal: 1851.* New York: Penguin Books USA Inc.

Tolle, E. (2003). *Stillness Speaks.* Novato, California & Vancouver, Canada: New World Library & Namaste Publishing.

Tolle, E. (2006). *Eckhart Tolle A New Earth: Awakening to Your Life's Purpose.* New York: A Plume Book.

Torah. (1981). *The Torah. A modern commentary.* (W. G. Plaut, Ed.) New York: Union of American Hebrew Congregation.

UA. (1850). *Aitareya Upanishad, in Tāittirīya, Āitareya and Śvetāśvatara Upanishads.* (E. Röer, Ed.) Calcutta: Bibliotheca Indica.

UAb. (2005). *Amritabindu Upanishad in Krishna-Yajurvediya . In The Scriptural Commentaries of Yogiraj Sri Sri Shyama Charan Lahiri Mahasaya* (Vols. 1, pp. 209, Ch. 4). (Y. Niketan, Trans.) New York, Lincoln, Shanghai: iUnivese, Inc.

UB. (1889). *Bṛhadāraṇyaka Upanishad, in der Mādhyadina Recension.* St. Petersburg (and Leipzig): Herausgegeben und übersetzt von O. Böhtlingk.

UC. (1889). *Chāndogya Upanishad.* Leipzig: Kritisch herausgegeben und übersetzt von Otto Böhtlingk.

U-Deussen-Paul. (1980). *Sixty Upanishads of the Veda.* (Bedekar&Palsule-from-German, Trans.) New Delhi: Motilal Banarsidass.

UG. (1965). *Gaṇapati Upanishad, text* (Vol. XVIII). (L. Renou, Ed., & J. Varenne, Trans.) Paris: Libraire d'Amérique et d'Orient Adrien-Maisonneuve.

U-Hume. (1962). *The thirteen principal Upanishads.* Madras: Oxford University Press.

UĪśa. (1850). *Īśa Upanishad.* (E. Röer, Ed.) Calcutta: Bibliotheca Indica.

UK. (1850). *Kaṭha Upanishad.* (E. Röer, Ed.) Calcutta: Bibliotheca Indica.

UKaBr. (1861). *Kaushītaki Brāhmaṇa Upanishad.* (E. Cowell, Ed.) Calcutta: Bibliotheca Indica.

UKai. (1898). *Amritabindu and Kaivalya Upanishad with commentaries.* (A. Mahadeva-Sastri, Trans.) Madras: Thompson and Co. Minerva Press. .

Ukai. (1952). *Kaivalyopaniṣad Texte et traduction.* (L. Renou, Ed., & Tubini, Trans.) Paris (VI): Librairie D'Amerique et d'Orient Adrien-Maisonneuve.

UKena. (1850). *Kena Upanishad.* (E. Röer, Ed.) Calcutta: Bibliotheca Indica.

UM. (1850). *Māṇḍūkya Upanishad.* (E. Röer, Ed.) Calcutta: Bibliotheca Indica.

UMaitrī. (1870). *Maitrī Upanishad.* (E. B. Cowell, Ed.) Calcutta, London: Bibliotheca Indica.

UMu. (1850). *Muṇdaka Upanishad.* (E. Röer, Ed.) Calcutta: Bibliotheca Indica.

U-Muller. (1962). *The Upanisads.* ((. Muller, Trans.) New York: Dover Publications.

U-Nikhilananda. (1949-1952-1956-1959). *The Upanishads (Vols. I-II-III-IV).* (Vols. I-II-III-IV). (Nikhilananda, Trans.) New York: Bonanza Books, Harper & Brothers.

UNr. (1871). *Nṛsiṃhottaratāpanī Upanishad Bhasya.* (R. Tarkaratna, Ed.) Calcutta: Bibliotheca Indica 70.

U-Oupnek'hat. (1801-2). *Oupnek'hat, Latin translation from a Persian rendering* (Vol. 2). (Anquetil-du-Perron, Trans.) Strassburg: Levrault.

UP. (1850). *Praśna Upanishad.* (E. Röer, Ed.) Calcutta: Bibliotheca Indica.

U-Renou. (1954-65). *Les Upanishad, texte.* (Renou, Ed.) Paris: Librairie d'Amérique et d'Orient Adrien-Maisonneuve.

UŚ. (1850). *Śvetāśvatara Upanishad, in Tāittirīya, Āitareya and Śvetāśvatara Upanishads.* (E. Röer, Ed.) Calcutta: Bibliotheca Indica.

U-Sankaracharya. (1951). *The Upanishads: Katha, Isa, Kena, and Mundaka with the commentary of Sri Sankaracharya.* London: Phoenix House.

UT. (1850). *Taittirīya Upanishad, in Tāittirīya, Āitareya and Śvetāśvatara Upanishads.* (E. Röer, Ed.) Calcutta: Bibliotheca Indica.

U-The Principal Upanishads. (1953). *U. The Principal Upanishads edited with Introduction, Text, Translitteration and Notes.* (S. Radhakrishnan, Ed., & T. T. U-The Principal Upanishads. (1953). U. The Principal Upanishads edited with Introduction, Trans.) London: George Allen & Unwin Ltd.

UV. (n.d.). *Vajrasūcika Upanishad, Text in The Principal Upanishad .*

UY. (n.d.). *Yoga Darshana Upanishad. Translation in Varenne, Yoga...*

VA. (1966). *Atharva Veda Sanhita text.* (Roth/Whitney, Ed.) Hannover, Hamburg, München: Ferd. Dümmlers Verlang, Bonn.

VA. (1980). *The Atharva Veda. Sanskrit text with English translation.* (D. Chand, Trans.) New Delhi: Munshiram Manoharlal Publisher Pvt. Ltd.

Vamana Purana. (2005). *Vamana Purana : Sanskrit Text and English Translation with an Exhaustive Introduction, Notes and Index of Verses.* (Bimali-Joshi, Ed., & Bimali-Joshi, Trans.) Delhi: Parimal Pub.

Varenne, J. (1976). *Yoga And the Hindu Tradition.* (D. Coltman, Trans.) Chicago and London: The University of Chicago Press.

Vedānta-Sūtras. (1904 - 1968). *The Vedānta-Sūtras, with the commentary by Śaṅkarācārya* (Delhi 1968 ed., Vol. I & II). ((. Muller, Ed., & G. Thibaut, Trans.) Oxford, Delhi, Varanasi, Patna: The Sacred Books of the East, Motilal Banarsidass.

Venci, A. (1955). *La Canzone Napolitana nel tempo, nella letteratura, nell'arte.* Napoli: Alfredo Guida.

Virgil P. (1910). *Vergili Maronis Aeneis in usum scholarum iterum recognovit Otto Ribbeck.* Lipsiae: in aedibus B. G. Teubneri.

Voynich Manuscript. (2001, March 10). *The Voynich Manuscript, Voynich_Manuscript_ text.pdf-Expert PDF Reader.* (YALE UNIVERSITY LIBRARY) Retrieved October 7, 2013, from Internet Archive's Terms of Use, Privacy Policy, and Copyright Policy: http://archive.org/details/TheVoynichManuscript

VṚ. (1968). *Die Hymnen des Ṛigveda* (Vols. I-II). (T. Aufrecht, Ed.) Wiesbaden: Otto Harrassowitz.

VS. (2004). *Hymns Of The Samaveda.* (R. Griffith, Trans.) Whitefish, MT: Kessinger Publishing Company.

W. Monier Williams. (1899 - Reprint 1974). *Monier-Williams, A Sanskrit-English Dictionary.* London: Oxford University Press.

Warren, H. C. (1922). *Buddhism in translations: passages selected from the Buddhist sacred book* (Vols. Three, Eighth-Issue). (Harvard-Oriental-Series, Ed.) Cambridge, Massachusetts: Harvard University Press.

Wheeler, J. A. (1982). Bohr, Einstein, and the Strange Lesson of the Quantum. (R. Q. Elvee, Ed.) *Mind in nature / Nobel Conference XVII Gustavus Adolphus College, St. Peter, Minnesota with contributions by John Archibald Wheeler ... [et al.]*, 1-30. San Francisco: Harper & Row.

Wilford, C. (1798). *Asiatic Researches V.*

Wilford J. N. (1999, April 16 & 20). At Long Last, a New Sun With a Family of Planets & Plethora Of Planets, New Fields Of Science. *The New York Times & Science Times*, p. A1 & F 1.

Yates, F. A. (1969). *Giordano Bruno e la tradizione ermetica.* (Pecchioli, Trans.) Bari: Edizioni Laterza.

Zaorski, J. R., Hallman, G. L., Cooley, D. A. (1972, February). Open heart surgery for acquired heart disease in Jehovah's Witnesses: A report of 42 operations. *The American Journal of Cardiology, From the Texas Heart Institute of St. Luke's-Texas Children's Hospitals , 29*(2), 186–189.

OCULATUS
ॐ
A WONDROUS AM
" The cup that I drink of"
(Mark 10:39; Psalm 116:13)
ELA